Remote Sensing with IDRISI® Taiga
A Beginner's Guide

Timothy A. Warner

David J. Campagna

ISBN 978-962-8226-27-6

Published by

Geocarto International Centre
G.P.O. Box 4122, Hong Kong
Tel: (852) 2546-4262   Fax: (852) 2559-3419
E-mail: geocarto@geocarto.com
Website: http://www.geocarto.com

Copyright

Reproduction

A note about errors

We deeply regret any problems you may have in using this manual. The authors have made every effort to double check the text. Nevertheless, in a book of this size, it is inevitable that there will be occasional errors. If you run into problems, please check for corrections at:

http://idrisimanual.blogspot.com/

If you find any errors that are not listed at the site, we would be most grateful if you could post a clear description of the problem through the website. Thank you very much for your help.

Trademarks

Contents

About the authors

Timothy A. Warner is Professor of Geology and Geography at West Virginia University, in Morgantown, West Virginia, USA. He has a BSc (Hons) in Geology from the University of Cape Town, and a PhD in geobotanical remote sensing from Purdue University. His research specialties include the spatial properties of images, high resolution remote sensing, and lidar. He has served as a founding board member and Secretary of AmericaView, and as Chair of the Remote Sensing Specialty Group (RSSG) of the Association of American Geographers (AAG). He received the 2006 *RSSG Outstanding Contributions Award*, and the 2006 *Boeing Award for Best Paper in Image Analysis and Interpretation* from the American Society of Photogrammetry and Remote Sensing. He is the co-editor of the Letters section of the *International Journal of Remote Sensing*, and also serves on the editorial board of *Geographical Compass*. He is a co-editor of the book, *The SAGE Handbook of Remote Sensing.*

David J. Campagna is a remote sensing geologist with over 20 years of non-profit, industry and academic experience. He consults for environmental groups using imagery to aid historical changes that document the impact of human activity on the landscape. In this role he also advises SkyTruth, Inc, where he was a founding board member for this non-profit remote sensing group and serves in the capacity of their Chief Science Officer. He consults for numerous energy firms worldwide in the investigations of unconventional natural gas reservoirs. He also serves as Adjunct faculty in the Department of Geology and Geography at West Virginia University mentoring Ph.D. remote sensing students in their research. Dr. Campagna holds a Ph.D. in structural geology and remote sensing from Purdue University, MS in geology from University of Kentucky and a BA from Knox College.

Acknowledgments

The authors would like to acknowledge the patient support of Mr. K. N. Au and Geocarto International Center through the long process of the writing and production of this manual.

We would like to thank Lucy Kammer, Paula Hunt, and Ann Stock for testing this manual and helping to improve the contents. Special thanks to Laurie Canavan and James Toledano of Clark Labs for assistance with this project.

The authors would also like to acknowledge the support of West Virginia View in completing this project.

Chapter 1   Introduction

1.1 Guide to Using the Manual

1.1.1 Objectives

The objectives of this manual are twofold. The first objective is to introduce the reader to the display and basic processing procedures for enhancement, analysis and classification of satellite imagery. The second objective is to train the user in how to accomplish these tasks within the IDRISI environment. IDRISI is an excellent software suite for illustrating image processing in that the program has a wide array of basic programs, which the user combines in order to undertake an analysis. This ensures that each operation within the overall analysis is transparent and ultimately understandable.

You will be exposed to a wide variety of image analysis approaches and techniques through this manual. However, no single manual could ever be a comprehensive guide to either remote sensing or IDRISI. Nevertheless, at the end of this manual you should have the confidence and experience to continue exploring the wide range of functionality in IDRISI, and learning new approaches to image analysis. Indeed, probably the most important skill you will learn from this manual is not how to use IDRISI, but rather how to approach remote sensing problems.

1.1.2 Organization

This training manual is primarily designed to be a stand-alone self-study guide. The skills you need before starting this training manual are only those of basic familiarity with the personal computer environment. Specifically, you need understanding of files and directory structures, and the ability to maneuver around in the Windows environment. Basic knowledge of image processing concepts is useful, but not essential. However, access to a general remote sensing text (Table 1.1.2.a) is strongly recommended as a supplement to the coverage of topics introduced in this manual. More advanced texts may also be a useful supplement (Table 1.1.2.b).

The format of this manual was chosen to help the reader perform the included topical exercises. A section covering a specific image analysis topic begins with a brief general introduction to the subject matter, and then is followed by detailed instructions associated with example exercises.

- The **exercise instructions** are generally contained within a textbox with blue-colored text (Figure 1.1.2.a). These textboxes give step-by-step instructions in performing tasks in IDRISI. The first line of the text box, printed with a blue background, provides a summary of the activity. The second line, also with a blue background, gives the **menu location** of the IDRISI module described.

- **Icons** that provide shortcuts to Modules, or commands within modules, are printed in the left banner, next to the appropriate text (Figure 1.1.2a).

- **Program names**, such as DISPLAY LAUNCHER, are given in capitals.

Table 1.1.2.a   Example introductory remote sensing texts.

Campbell, J. 2007. *Introduction to Remote Sensing.* Guilford Press, New York, NY, 626p.

Jensen J R 2005. *Introductory Digital Image Processing: A Remote sensing perspective.* Prentice Hall Inc., Upper Saddle River, NJ, 526p.

Jensen, J. R. 2007, *Remote Sensing of the Environment: An Earth Resources Perspective.* Prentice Hall Inc., Upper Saddle River, NJ, 592p.

Lillesand, T. M., R. W. Kiefer, and J. W. Chipman, 2008. Remote Sensing and Image Interpretation. Wiley, New York, 756p.

Richards, J. A., and X. Jia, 2006. *Remote Sensing Digital Image Analysis: An Introduction.* Springer, Berlin, 439p.

Vincent, R. K., 1997. *Fundamentals of Geological and Environmental Remote Sensing.* Prentice Hall Inc., Upper Saddle River, NJ, 366p.

Table 1.1.2.a   Example advanced remote sensing texts.

ASPRS Manual of Remote Sensing, 3rd Edition

Henderson, F. M., and Anthony J. Lewis (eds), 1998. *Principles & Applications of Imaging Radar.* Volume 2. John Wiley & Sons, NY, 866p.

Rencz, A. (ed), 1999. *Remote Sensing for the Earth Sciences.* Volume 3. John Wiley & Sons, NY, 707p.

Ustin, S. (ed), 2004. *Remote Sensing for Natural Resource Management and Environmental Monitoring.* Volume 4. John Wiley & Sons, NY, 736p.

Ridd, M. K., and J. D. Hipple (eds), 2006. *Remote Sensing of Human Settlements.* Volume 5. ASPRS, Bethesda, MD, 752p.

Grower, J. F. R. (ed), 2006. *Remote Sensing of the Marine Environment.* Volume 6. ASPRS, Bethesda, MD, 338 p.

Other advanced texts

Maune, D. F. (ed), 2007. *Digital Elevation Model Technologies & Applications*, 2nd Edition. ASPRS, Bethesda, MD., 620pp.

Liang, S., 2004. *Quantitative Remote Sensing of Land Surfaces.* John Wiley & Sons, NY, 534p.

Warner, T. A., M. D. Nellis and G. Foody (eds), 2009. *The SAGE Handbook of Remote Sensing.* SAGE, London UK, 490pp.

Displaying an image
Menu Location: **Display – DISPLAY LAUNCHER**
1. Start the DISPLAY LAUNCHER. 2. Within the *DISPLAY LAUNCHER* window, select a file by clicking on the browse button (…) and then click on the ***etm_pan*** raster file in the pick list window. 3. Select *GreyScale* in the *Palette File* section in the lower left corner of the DISPLAY LAUNCHER window. 4. Click on *OK* to display the image

Figure 1.1.2.a   Example of instructions for the DISPLAY LAUNCHER program. Note that the first line is a general explanation of the task. The second line gives the menu location, as well as the IDRISI menu icon, if available.

- The **names of dialog boxes and windows** are printed in italics, e.g. *DISPLAY LAUNCHER* window.

- **Text within the IDRISI program windows and dialog boxes** is also printed in italics. For example, the name of an input text box might be *Input file name*.

- **Names of files** that already exist are printed in bold italics (e.g. ***etm_pan***).

- Text that you, the reader, should enter in a program (e.g. through a text box) is given in bold, including the names for new files you will generate. For example the text may specify: Enter the file name **pca_123** in the text box.

- Terms that we wish to highlight are also shown in bold, for example **ground control point**.

- Finally, the sequence of menu options you should select to start programs is also highlighted in bold: e.g. **Display - DISPLAY LAUNCHER**.

1.1.3 Sample Data

This manual comes with sample data covering a number of different locations around the globe (Table 1.1.3.a). The locations were chosen to cover a variety of natural and human-modified environments.

The first data set, used in Chapters 1 through 4, comprises Landsat Thematic Mapper (TM) imagery of the coastal region of Hong Kong, China and part of the Pearl River estuary. We will be using these data to illustrate the importing, displaying, merging and creating maps. In addition, combination of imagery and elevation data will be used to create 3D displays and fly-throughs. The elevation data were acquired through the Shuttle Radar Topography Mission (SRTM), in which the Spaceborne Imaging Radar-C (SIR-C) was flown aboard the NASA Space Shuttle Endeavour during 11-22 February, 2000. The SRTM mission generated a near-global digital elevation model (DEM) of the Earth using overlapping radar images, through a process called radar interferometry (Maune, 2001).

Table 1.1.3.a   Image data and directory location on the CD.

Directory Name	Geographic Area	Data
Chap1-4	Hong Kong, China	Landsat TM ETM+ (Multispectral & Pan), SIR-C SRTM Digital Elevation
Chap1-4/Raw images	Hong Kong, China	Landsat TM ETM+ (Tiff format)
Chap5/Chap5_3	African continent	Advanced Very High Resolution Radiometer (AVHRR)
Chap5/Chap5_4	Washington State, USA	Landsat TM
Chap5/Chap5_5	Atacama, Bolivia/Chile	Landsat TM
Chap6/Chap6_3	Hawaii	Thermal Infrared Multispectral Scanner (TIMS)
Chap6/Chap6_4	Hong Kong, China	Landsat TM (resampled to 90 meter pixels)
Chap6/Chap6_4alt	Hong Kong, China	Landsat TM (full resolution – 30 meter pixels)
Chap7	West Virginia, USA	Landsat TM (Summer)
Chap8/Chap8_3	West Virginia, USA	Mosaicked Digital Orthophotos (& results from Chapter 7 classification
Chap8/Chap8_4	West Virginia, USA	Landsat TM (Autumn)
Chap9	Las Vegas, Nevada, USA	Landsat MSS (1972 & 1992)

Chapter 4 is followed by two chapters on image enhancement. Chapter 5 explores image ratios. In this chapter we first use coarse-resolution Advanced Very High Resolution (AVHRR) imagery of Africa to generate a continental scale vegetation map. We will then use Landsat data of Washington State to develop an index to discriminate snow from clouds. Finally, we will use TM imagery from the Andes of the Atacama region along the Chile-Bolivia border, where we will examine how image ratios can be used for geologic mapping.

Chapter 6 is the second chapter on image enhancement. In the first half of this chapter, we will use Thermal Infrared Multispectral Scanner (TIMS) imagery of lava flows from Hawaii to investigate a range of enhancement methods for highly correlated data. The second half of the chapter draws on the Hong Kong TM data set, already used in Chapters 1-4, to investigate segmentation and non-standard false color composites.

For the classification in Chapter 7 we will use TM imagery of Morgantown, West Virginia, and the neighboring areas in the Appalachian Plateau of West Virginia, USA. The area is marked by deciduous forest and some farming activity.

Chapter 8 also has two major sections. First, the procedures for an accuracy assessment will be discussed using a classification from the previous chapter and a digital orthophotography mosaic. The latter half of the chapter is a linear pixel unmixing, and uses an autumn Landsat TM image.

The final data set comprises two multi-temporal Multispectral Scanner (MSS) images of Las Vegas, Nevada, USA, which is used in Chapter 9. The arid city of Las Vegas and its surrounding valley will be used to demonstrate the mapping of change, in this case urban growth around the city of Las Vegas over two decades.

1.1.4 Working with the Manual

This manual is written assuming that you will work progressively through the material. Thus, instructions are more detailed in the beginning chapters, especially Chapters 1-4. The instructions are generally slightly briefer the second and subsequent times any program is described. If you should find that the instructions for any program are too brief, you may wish to return to the earlier sections, to review the particular program or procedures described, and also draw on the extensive Help in IDRISI, as described below.

Some readers may prefer to sample the manual selectively. This should be fine, but do note that many chapters draw on images prepared earlier in the chapter, or skills developed in prior sections. If this is a barrier to your completing the exercise, you will need to do the earlier work first.

1.2 IDRISI Software

1.2.1 What's in a Name?

The IDRISI software is named after the cartographer and botanist, Abu Abd Allah Mohammed al-Idrisi (1100-1165 or 1166 A.D.) (Wikipedia 2005, Eastman 2009). Al-Idrisi was one of the most important medieval scholars, producing maps for the Norman King, Roger II of Sicily that would serve as a primary reference for the next 500 years. In addition, he made a major contribution in cataloging medicinal and other plants, which had not previously been recorded.

1.2.2 History and Overview of IDRISI

First released in 1987, IDRISI provides raster-based GIS and image processing modules in a single integrated package (Warner and Campagna 2004). The latest version of IDRISI, IDRISI Taiga, is a 32-bit version designed for Windows, and is the sixteenth release.

IDRISI specializes in analytical functionality covering the full spectrum of GIS and remote sensing analysis from database query, to spatial modeling, to image enhancement and classification. Although IDRISI is primarily oriented towards the use of raster data, vector data can also be displayed and used in some of the programs.

IDRISI includes routines for environmental modeling and natural resource management, including change and time series analysis, land change prediction, multi-criteria and multi-objective decision support, uncertainty analysis and simulation modeling. Spatial operations include interpolation, Kriging and conditional simulation. For image processing, a suite of tools for image restoration, enhancement and spectral transformation are available. IDRISI has a particularly sophisticated range of classification algorithms, including traditional "hard" classifiers, in which each pixel is assigned to a single class, as well as "soft" classifiers, in which multiple classes are potentially associated with each pixel. In addition, IDRISI offers hyperspectral image classification procedures, designed for use with images with hundreds of spectral bands (a *band* is an image layer associated with a specific wavelength region of the electromagnetic spectrum). IDRISI Taiga is specifically designed to allow programmers and modelers to incorporate IDRISI routines into their own applications. Despite the highly sophisticated nature of these capabilities, the system is still easy to use.

The nearly 300 modules which make up IDRISI are organized in menus in seven major groups, with most of the analytical functionality concentrated in the *GIS Analysis* and *Image Processing* Menus. Because IDRISI tends to generate many individual files, a program for file management is an important component of the File menu.

A particularly effective IDRISI program module is the graphical MACRO MODELER, which allows users to develop and link a sequence of IDRISI modules. This program is useful for designing an image analysis in a conceptual manner, for speeding up implementation of a complex sequence of tasks, for building a macro for repeating an analysis sequence on different data sets, and for documenting analysis procedures.

IDRISI tends to be highly modular in design. This modular design tends to make an analysis in IDRISI more complex because of the many steps involved. However, this approach makes IDRISI a superb teaching tool, because the user is forced to understand every step in each procedure.

1.3 Starting IDRISI and the IDRISI Workspace

1.3.1 Copying the Data from the CD

Before starting the IDRISI program, we will need to create and organize file folders for our project data.

We will begin by creating a folder called **ID Man** (short for IDRISI Manual), in which we will store our data. Depending on your preferences, you may wish to create this new folder on your desktop, the root directory (C:\) or elsewhere. We find that there is some advantage in keeping the paths (directory names) short, and so for this manual the examples we give will be based on creating this directory in the root directory. The choice of where to place the data, however, is up to you.

There are a number of ways to create a folder on your desktop, and one way is described below.

IDRISI folder creation
1. Click on the Windows *Start* button and select *My Computer*.
2. Double click on the *C:* drive. (Note if you want to create your new folder in a location other than *C:*, then you should now navigate to that location.)
3. Right-click in the folders panel.
4. Select *New*, then select *Folder* and name the folder **ID Man**.

We are now ready to copy some of the data provided with this project to your computer.

Data transfer
1. Put in the data CD to your CD drive.
2. If the file explorer window does not open automatically, double click on *My Computer*.
3. Double click on the CD drive.

4. Right-click on the CD folder labeled *Chap1-4*, and select *Copy* from the pop-up menu.

5. Move up the directory tree to *My Computer* and select the *C:* drive. (Note if you created the *ID Man* folder in a location other than *C:*, then you should now navigate to that location.)

6. Double click on *ID Man* folder.

7. Move cursor to the main folders pane, right click, and select *Paste* from the pop-up menu.

At the start of each section you will be prompted for the appropriate data for that section, so you do not need to transfer the remaining data from the CD now.

A very important final step in preparing your data each time you copy data from the CD is to set the appropriate folder properties. The data on the CD is marked as *Read-only*, which means the files cannot be changed. Therefore we must modify the *Read-only* attribute, as described below.

Remove *Read-Only* attribute from the data folder

1. Use the *Windows Explorer* or *My Computer* (as described in the previous instruction box) to display the contents of the *ID Man* folder (Figure 1.3.1.a).

2. Right click on the *Chap1-4* folder. (Note: Instead of selecting the *Chap1-4 folder*, you can alternatively select the parent *ID Man* folder if you need to apply the *Read-only* attribute change to more than one folder in the *ID Man* directory.

3. Select the *Properties* option from the pop-up menu (Figure 1.3.1.a).

4. The Properties window will now open for that folder. Uncheck the *Read-only* attribute check box (Figure 1.3.1.b).

5. A *Confirm Attribute Changes* Window will open. Ensure that the radio button for the default option of *Apply changes to this folder, subfolder and files* has been selected automatically. (Figure 1.3.1.c).

6. Click on *OK*.

7. The check box in the *Properties* window will now be blank.

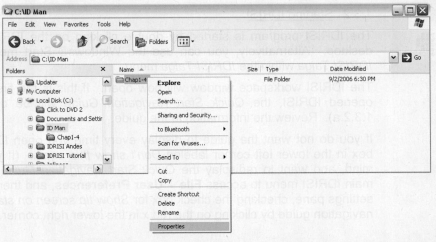

Figure 1.3.1.a   Right click on the folder name to access a pop-up menu that includes the option to set the folder properties.

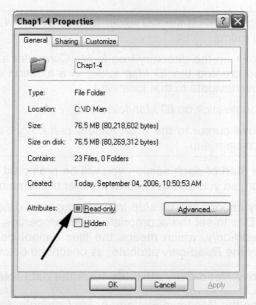

Figure 1.3.1.b   Uncheck the *Read-only* attribute for the folder.

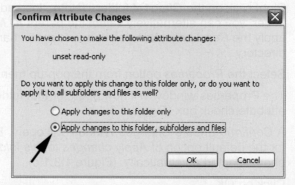

Figure 1.3.1.c   Ensure the default option to apply changes to the folder, subfolders and files, has been selected.

1.3.2 Starting IDRISI

The IDRISI program is started by double clicking on the IDRISI icon on your desktop. Alternatively, you can use the Windows® Start menu, by selecting *IDRISI Taiga* within the *IDRISI Taiga* menu.

The IDRISI workspace window will now open. If this is the first time you have opened IDRISI, the *Quick Start Navigation Guide* will be displayed (Figure 1.3.2.a). Review the information in the guide.

If you do not want the guide to display every time you open IDRISI, check the box in the lower left corner labeled *Don't show this again.* (If you change your mind, and want to redisplay the *Quick Start Navigation Guide,* simply use the main IDRISI menu to access **File – User Preferences**, and then, on the System settings pane, checking the check box for *Show tip screen on start up.*) Close the navigation guide by clicking on the red *x* in the lower right corner.

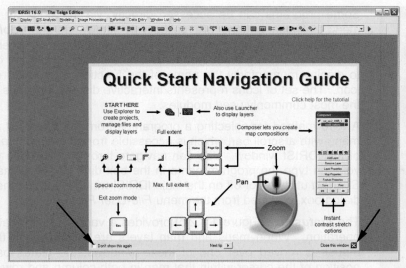

Figure 1.3.2.a   The IDRISI workspace with the *Quick Start Navigtaion Guide*, which may be displayed when IDRISI first starts.

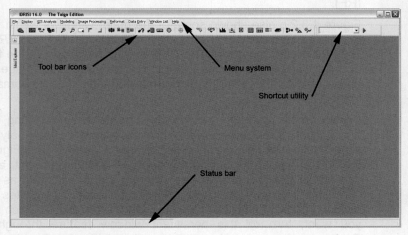

Figure 1.3.2.b   The IDRISI workspace.

The IDRISI workspace includes the **toolbar**, the **menu system**, the **shortcut utility**, and the **status bar** (Figure 1.3.2.b). There are many ways to start an individual program.   One of the simplest ways is through the **menu system**, which is at the top of the application window (Figure 1.3.2.b).

You can activate the menus by clicking on the menu with the mouse. If you select a menu option that includes a right-pointing arrow, a submenu will appear. You can navigate through the submenus using the arrows on the keyboard (on the number pad) or using the *Enter* key. Clicking on a menu option without a right-pointing arrow will cause a dialog box for that module to appear.

Alternatively, you can navigate through the menus with the keyboard, by depressing the ALT key and a particular letter. When you first press ALT, an initial letter of each menu is underlined, to help you identify the appropriate key. This will open the menu, which can then be navigated by pressing the key associated with first letter of the submenu or program. If you wish to access a submenu that starts with the same letter as an earlier submenu, press the key for the letter twice. You will then need to press the ENTER key to start the program.

Some programs can be accessed directly, via the icons, or buttons, below the menu. These buttons are collectively known as the **tool bar.** Each icon represents either a program module or an interactive operation that can be selected by clicking on that button with the mouse. Hold the cursor over an icon to display momentarily the name of the function or module represented by that icon. The set of icons represents interactive display functions as well as some of the most commonly used modules.

A third method for selecting a program is from the **shortcut utility**, a pull-down menu with a scroll bar, which is accessible from the *status bar*, along the bottom of the IDRISI window. You can navigate through this menu with the mouse, or you can type the program name in the box directly. Note that you can turn the *Shortcut* utility on or off on the main IDRISI window through the User Preferences dialog box, obtained from the menu *File-User Preferences*.

The **status bar** (Figure 1.3.2.c) provides a variety of information about program operation. When maps and map layers are displayed on the screen and the mouse is moved over one of these windows, the status bar will indicate the position of the cursor within that map in both column and row image coordinates and X and Y map reference system coordinate. In addition, the *Status Bar* indicates the scale of the screen representation as a Representative Fraction (RF).

Figure 1.3.2.c also shows some of the major windows within IDRISI that we will be using extensively. On the left is the *IDRISI EXPLORER* window, which is used for organizing data. The *Display* window, shown in the figure in the center of the IDRISI window, is the major tool for visualizing images. The *Composer* dialog box, on the far right, allows one to manipulate how images are displayed in the *Display* window.

If one or more program modules are currently still processing, the **status bar** will also indicate the progress of the most recently launched analytical operation with a percent done measure, and sometimes a graphic bar (Figure 1.3.2.d). Note that in the figure, the program dialog box remains present, even though it was that dialog box that created the program that is indicated as still running. This "persistent window" approach is useful because it facilitates running programs multiple times without having to reopen the dialog box each time. (You can, if you want, turn off this persistent window feature through the *File - User Preferences* menu, and unchecking the option for *Enable persistent dialogs*.) Despite the benefit of persistent windows, users should exercise caution in exploiting this capability because you should not try to open a file that is still being processed by another program.

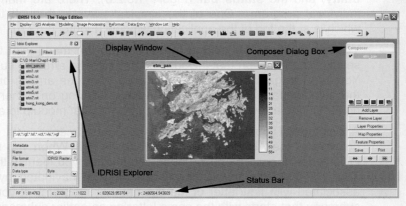

Figure 1.3.2.c   The IDRISI status bar, and related main windows.

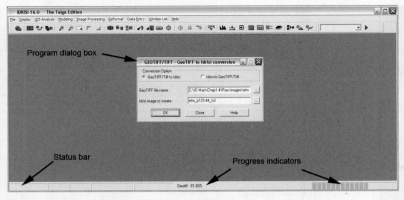

Figure 1.3.2.d   Progress indicator within the status bar.

Since IDRISI has been designed to permit multi-tasking of operations, it is possible that more than one operation may be working simultaneously. To check active processes and their status, simply double click on the bottom right hand part of the *status bar* panel. A *Progress of modules* window will open, listing the current programs running. Modules may also be terminated from this window.

Figure 1.3.2.d also shows a typical program dialog box. Dialog boxes are used to provide information to the IDRISI programs regarding input and output data, as well as important processing parameters.

1.3.3 IDRISI On-Line Help

IDRISI has excellent on-line documentation and help. In our own use of IDRISI, and in developing this manual, we have drawn extensively on the IDRISI help material, and we encourage all users of this manual to take advantage of this outstanding resource.

You can access the IDRISI help from the main IDRISI menu bar: **Help – Contents.**

Another way to access the on-line help is through the button labeled *Help*, found in the dialog box that controls each program (Figure 1.3.3.a). This button automatically opens the help material for the particular program from which the help was called. The help material is very useful for understanding the general nature of each program, as well as the limitations, such as the type of data that can be used. The on-line help also provides a comprehensive **glossary** and an **index**, which can be found through the *Glossary* and *Index* tabs on the left hand

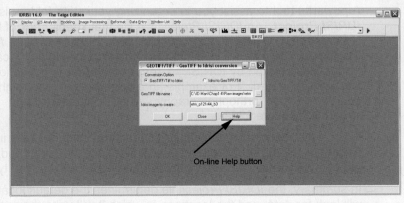

Figure 1.3.3.a   Typical dialog box showing button for on-line help.

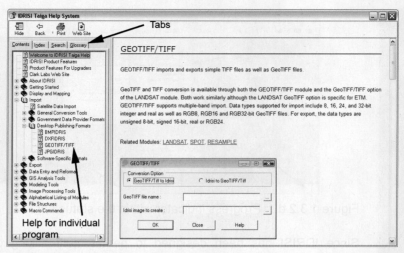

Figure 1.3.3.b   The IDRISI on-line Help.

side of the Help window (Figure 1.3.3.b). The glossary is helpful for clarifying the meaning of remote sensing terminology in general, and IDRISI terms in particular.   The index provides a tool for rapid searches through the main sections of the Help system. You can also identify the specific subsections within the Help, by clicking on the *Contents* Tab, and navigating through the hierarchical structure, as shown in Figure 1.3.3.b.

In addition, a very good PDF-format tutorial document can be accessed from the main IDRISI menu: **Help – IDRISI Tutorial.**

1.3.4   Managing IDRISI Project Files with the IDRISI EXPLORER

In a typical image analysis activity you will produce many files. It is therefore essential to have an effective method to organize your files. Firstly, you should specify meaningful file names for files you generate with IDRISI. Do not simply use the IDRISI default names. Instead use names that have meaning within your analysis, perhaps referring to the program used, or crucial parameters used in the processing. In addition, you should keep good notes on the names of the input and output files, as well as all parameters selected.

In addition to using appropriate file names and keeping good notes, it makes good sense to organize your data in a series of folders, much as the data for the exercises in this manual are organized.

A powerful tool to assist you in organizing your data folders is the concept of an **IDRISI Project.** An *IDRISI Project* is a file that keeps track of the *working folders* and *resource folders* for a particular task.   The **working folder** is the main location for the data for your project. It is also the default location for the output for the files created by IDRISI. A **resource folder** is a location where additional files can be stored. For example, in a large project, you might store the original copies of your orthophotography, satellite imagery, and elevation data in separate resource folders.

There is no limit to the number of resource folders used in a single project. Resource folders are listed in file pick lists, and are searched in the orders they are specified (after the working folder) for file names that you type in manually.

In summary, the *IDRISI Project* file determines the default locations where IDRISI will look for data, and the locations to which it will write the output files. Although you can over-ride the *Project* file in determining file locations, it can be tedious to do so, and the chance of becoming confused and making mistakes becomes quite high.

IDRISI Projects may be stored anywhere, however the default folder for projects is located in the *IDRISI Taiga* program folder under the subfolder *Projects*. A single Project Environment file, *default.env*, is automatically created. Some users will find it convenient simply to change the working folder of this default Project Environment file each time they work on a new data set. However, you may wish to set a new *Project* file for each section of this manual, in order to facilitate switching back and forth between the different sections.

Creating a new project file and specifying the working folders with the *IDRISI EXPLORER*
Menu Location: **File – IDRISI EXPLORER**
1. Start the IDRISI EXPLORER from the main menu or toolbar.   2. The *IDRISI EXPLORER* window will open on the left side of the IDRISI workspace. It is anchored to this location, and although you can change the width of the window, you cannot move it to other locations.   3. Practice minimizing the window by clicking on the "-" icon on the top left of the *IDRISI EXPLORER* window. The window will collapse into the left hand side of the IDRISI workspace.   4. Reopen the *IDRISI EXPLORER* by clicking on the "+" icon in the minimized window.   5. Select the *Projects* tab (Figure 1.3.4.a).

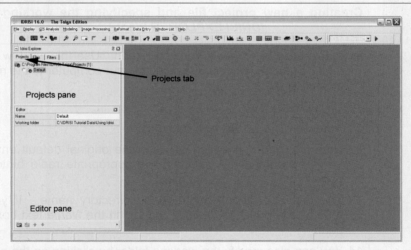

Figure 1.3.4.a   The *Projects* and *Editor* panes in the IDRISI EXPLORER.

Creating a new project file and specifying the working folders with the *IDRISI EXPLORER* (cont.)
6. There should now be two panes within the *IDRISI EXPLORER* window. The first is the *Projects* pane, and below that should be the *Editor* pane (Figure 1.3.4.a). If the *Editor* pane is not shown right click in the *Projects* pane, and select *Show Editor*. (It is possible to close the *Editor* pane by clicking on the red "x" in that pane, hence the need to have a way to open the pane again.)

7. Note also that the boundary between the *Projects* and *Editor* panes can be dragged with the mouse, in order to change the relative size of the two panes. This is convenient if the *Editor* pane is obscuring information in the *Projects* pane.

8. Right click within the *Projects* pane, and select the *New Project Ins* option (Figure 1.3.4.b).

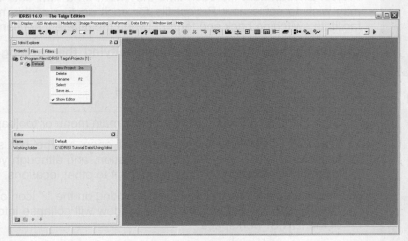

Figure 1.3.4.b   Right click within the *Projects* pane to select the *New Project Ins* option.

Creating a new project file and specifying the working folders with the *IDRISI EXPLORER* (cont.)

9. A *Browse For Folder* window will open. Use this window to navigate to the folder *Chap1-4*, which you copied to your computer to the new *ID_Man* folder, in section 1.3.1.

10. Click *OK*.

11. A new project file will now be created.

12. Note that you can switch between the original default environment and the new environment by selecting the appropriate radio buttons in the *Project* pane.

13. The project's default name is the directory name. If you wish, you can rename the project by editing the text in the *Name* text box, within the *Editor* pane.

14. You can also modify the *working folder* by clicking on the name of the current file listed in the text box next to *Working folder*. This will generate a browse icon (a button with three dots). Clicking on the browse icon will open a *Browse For Folder* window. If we wanted to specify a new file, we would now navigate to that file, and then click *OK*. However, for now, we will leave the existing file, and therefore press *Cancel*.

15. Add a resource folder by right clicking in the *Editor* pane, and selecting *Add folder*.

16. A new line in the Editor pane will open, with the text *Resource folder (1)* in the left cell. Click in the right cell, and a browse icon will appear (a button with three dots). (Figure 1.3.4.c).

17. Click on this browse button, and the *Browse for Folder* window will open. Navigate to the *Raw Images* subfolder, within the *ID Man\Chap1-4* folder on your computer. Click on *OK*. (Figure 1.3.4.c).

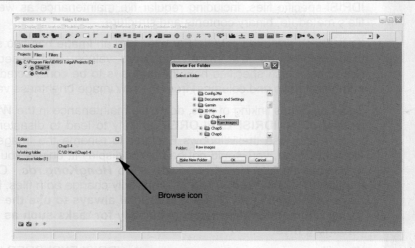

Browse icon

Figure 1.3.4.c   Adding a *Resource Folder*.

Creating a new project file and specifying the working folders with the *IDRISI EXPLORER* (cont.)

18. Once the *Browse for Folder* closes, your project should now be specified. If necessary, you can drag the *IDRISI EXPLORER* window boundary to the right, in order to provide more room to show the compete path file for the folder locations (Figure 1.3.4.d)

The new *project* file now points to the location of the working folder and resource folder for Chapters 1-4 in this manual, as shown in Figure 1.3.4.d. When you exit and re-launch IDRISI, the project file most recently used is retained. Therefore you only need to change the *project* file information when you start a new project. For example, we will create a new *project* file when we start Chapter 5.

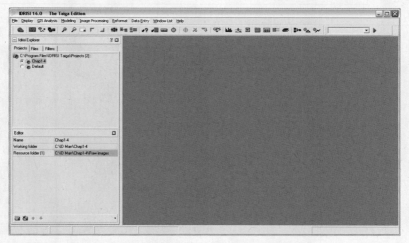

Figure 1.3.4.d   The new project file successfully created.

1.3.5 Basic File Management with the IDRISI EXPLORER

The IDRISI EXPLORER is a powerful tool that has functionality well beyond that of simply managing project files. For example, you can manage all aspects of IDRISI-specific files, including regular file maintenance as well as examining a file's metadata, binary contents and structure.

IDRISI files are often linked. For example, an image has two separate files, one that contains the raw image brightness values, and a second file with the metadata, which specifies how the image is to be constructed (for example, the number of rows and columns) from the raw image brightness values.

Because of this linking of files, doing file maintenance in the *Windows Explorer*, instead of the **IDRISI EXPLORER** is likely to lead to disaster. For example, if you were to use the Windows Explorer to rename the image file *etm1.rst* to *HongKong.rst*, you would not be able to display it, unless you also remembered to change the associated *etm1.rdc* file to *HongKong.rdc*. On the other hand, the IDRISI EXPLORER would automatically change both files, if you changed the name of the *etm1.rst* . **Thus it is crucial always to use the IDRISI EXLORER for all file maintenance work, especially for tasks such as copy, deleting or renaming files.**

We will now examine how we can use the IDRISI EXPLORER to manage files.

Basic file management with the IDRISI EXPLORER

Menu Location: **File – IDRISI EXPLORER**

---

1. If the *IDRISI EXPLORER* window is not already open, open it again.

2. Click on the tab for *Filters* (Figure 1.3.5.a).

3. Observe the list of file types listed. These are only the primary IDRISI extensions. The many different types of file extensions that IDRISI recognizes give some indication of the wide range of functionality that IDRISI offers.

4. Note that it is possible to check which types of files one wants to list in the *Files* pane, an option that we will look at in a moment. The default is to list raster Image files, as well as five other file types.

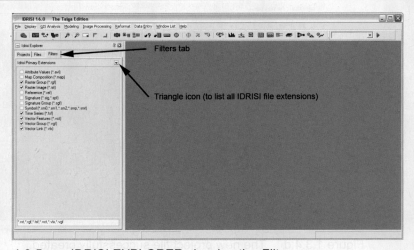

Figure 1.3.5.a   IDRISI EXPLORER showing the *Filters* pane.

Basic file management with the IDRISI EXPLORER (cont.)

5. Click on the small downward pointing triangle on the top right hand side of the pane (Figure 1.3.5.a), representing the icon to switch between the primary and entire list of IDRISI file extensions.

6. After clicking on the downward pointing triangle, observe the much greater list of file types listed.

7. If you want to check all the file types listed, in order to display all the files in the *IDRISI EXPLORER* window, there is a short cut that is much quicker than clicking on each box. Simply right click in the *Filters* pane, and in the resulting pop-up menu click on *Select All*.

8. Before leaving this section of the IDRISI EXPLORER, right click in the *Filters* pane once again, and select *Clear Filter*. This will uncheck all the check boxes.

9. Now scroll to the check box for *Raster Image (*.rst),* and click in the box.

10. Click on the tab for *Files* (Figure 1.3.5.b).

11. Practice clicking on the directory name to show and hide the file names (Figure 1.3.5.b). In many cases when you open the IDRISI Explorer the files may be hidden, and you need to click on the directory to show the files.

12. If necessary, drag the *Metadata* pane boundary up, so that you can see more of the metadata information.

13. Click on the file ***etm1.rst*** in the Files pane.

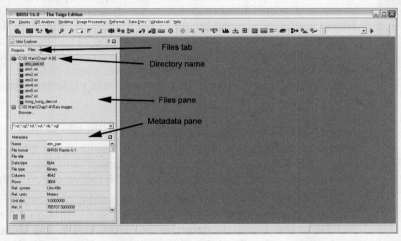

Figure 1.3.5.b   The *Files* and *Metadata* panes in the IDRISI EXPLORER.

The *Files* tab has two panes (Figure 1.3.5.b). The top pane that shows the list of files based on the list of filter selections chosen through the options available via the *Filters* tab, and also listed in the text box above the *Metadata* pane. The lower pane shows the metadata for the file selected in the *Files* pane. The slider bar on the right allows one to scroll through the entire metadata file.

The basic file maintenance routines in the IDRISI EXPLORER window are accessed by selecting one or more files, and then right clicking in the *Files* pane. A pop-up menu will appear (Figure 1.3.5.c). The menu has options for *Copy, Move, Rename* and *Delete*. These functions work in the way you would expect.

Figure 1.3.5.c   The pop-up menu for basic file maintenance commands.

The IDRISI EXPLORER also provides shortcuts for displaying images and also the raw data that underlie an image. When a raster or vector file is selected in the IDRISI EXPLORER, right clicking and selecting the option for *Display Map* will display the image using default options. We will learn about the program DISPLAY LAUNCHER, which allows greater control over how an image is displayed in Chapter 2.

The IDRISI EXPLORER pop-up menu for the *Files* pane also offers options to view the underlying data from in a file. A file may be viewed in its byte-by-byte binary and/or ASCII representation by choosing the *Show Binary* menu option. This is useful for viewing binary raster images to determine their file structure for importing into IDRISI. (Binary is a dense type of coding typically used for images or other large, structured data sets.) Images can also be shown as a grid of pixel values through the *Show Structure* pop-up menu option. The topic of how an image is constructed from a grid of numbers is explored further in the introduction to Chapter 2.

1.3.6 Working with Metadata Using the IDRISI EXPLORER

Note that the last option on the pop-up menu in the *Files* pane of the IDRISI EXPLORER is *Metadata*. You can control whether the *Metadata* pane is displayed by checking or unchecking the *Metadata* option in the pop-up menu.

To investigate further this concept of Metadata, click on the ***etm_pan.rst*** file in the *Files* pane of the IDRISI EXPLORER. Scroll through the metadata values for that file in the *Metadata* pane below. Note that in the Metadata window, each row has two cells. The left cell is a category, for example *Name*. The right cell is the attribute. In order to change the attribute, you simply click in the cell, and type the new value. Be warned, though: if the new values you enter are inappropriate, you can make it impossible to display the file.

Observe the type of data about the image that is recorded in the metadata file: the data type (which determines the potential range of the values stored), number of columns and rows, pixel size, map information, file lineage as well as user-supplied titles, legends and notes. Notice that no title has been specified for the ***etm_pan*** file. In the next exercise, we will add the image title information to the metadata, so that when the image is displayed we will have the option of automatically also displaying a title.

Modifying image metadata with IDRISI EXPLORER

Menu Location: **File - IDRISI EXPLORER**

1. If the *IDRISI EXPLORER* window is not already open, open it again.

2. In the IDRISI EXPLORER, click on the tab for *Files*.

3. If the files are not listed in the *Files* pane, double click on the directory name to display the files.

4. In the *Files* pane, select ***etm_pan.rst***.

5. If the *Metadata* pane is not displayed, right click in the *Files* pane, and select the option for *Metadata*.

6. In the *Metadata* pane, click in the text cell to the right of *File title*, and enter **Hong Kong Landsat Panchromatic Band** (Figure 1.3.6.a).

7. Click on the *Save* icon at the bottom left side of the *Metadata* pane (Figure 1.3.6.a). (Note: the *Save* icon is grayed out most of the time, and is only shown in color when the metadata has been changed, and therefore can be saved.)

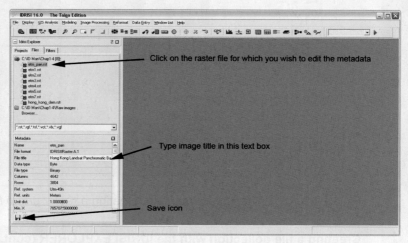

Figure 1.3.6.a   Modifying the metadata of an image.

1.3.7 Working with Collections in the IDRISI EXPLORER

A useful management tool in IDRISI is the concept of collections. A layer collection is a group of layers that are associated with each other, for example the different image bands that together make up a single satellite image. Collections are used to facilitate the input of filenames to dialog boxes. They may also be required as input for particular analytical modules. Finally, raster files that are grouped into a collection and linked when displayed can be viewed in a systematic way, such as through linked zooming and panning.

In this part of the exercise, we will use the IDRISI EXPLORER to create a raster group file with the Hong Kong Landsat data, as a preparatory step for displaying two bands as linked displays in Chapter 2. IDRISI also offers a dedicated program for dealing with collections, available through the menu: *File – Collection Editor.* However, generally, the IDRISI EXPLORER provides a more powerful interface for working with collections.

Creating a file collection with the IDRISI EXPLORER

Menu Location: **File – IDRISI EXPLORER**

1. If the *IDRISI EXPLORER* window is not already open, open it again.

2. Click on the tab for *Files*.

3. Highlight the files **etm1.rst** through **etm7.rst** (note that there is no **etm6.rst** in this data set. The Landsat band 6 is a thermal band, and we will work with that band later, in Chapter 5). You can select multiple bands either by clicking on each file sequentially, while simultaneously pressing the *Ctrl* key. Alternatively, you can click on **etm1.rst** , then, while simultaneously pressing the Shift key, click on the **etm7.rst** file. This will highlight the beginning and end files, as well as all those in between. (Figure 1.3.7.a).

4. Right click in the *Files* pane. Select the menu option for *Create – Raster Group* (Figure 1.3.7.a).

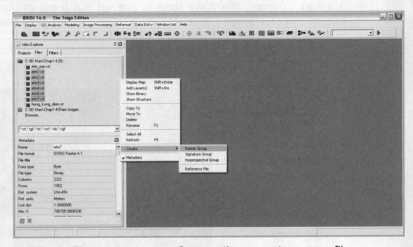

Figure 1.3.7.a   The pop-up menu for creating a *raster group file*.

Creating a file dollection with the IDRISI EXPLORER (cont.)

5. A new file, **Raster Group.rgf**, will be listed in the *Files* pane. Click on this file.

6. In the *Metadata* pane, enter a new name in the right hand cell of the first row, typing over the default name of *Raster Group*. Since this is an entire collection of satellite image bands, we will enter **hk_etm_all** (Figure 1.3.7.b).

7. Press Enter on your computer keyboard.

8. Click on the *Save* icon, at the bottom left hand corner of the *Metadata* pane. The name will immediately be updated in the Files window.

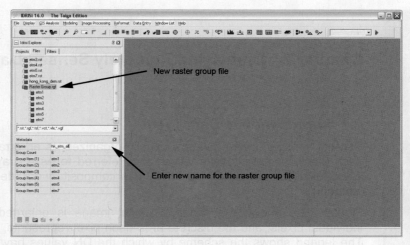

Figure 1.3.7.b   Entering a new name for the *raster group file*.

The *Metadata* pane has additional powerful built-in functionality to add, delete, and reorder the individual layers in the collection. This can be observed by highlighting the ***hk_etm_all.rgf*** raster group file in the *Files* pane, and noting how the *Metadata* pane lists the file names associated with this collection. Now click on the Metadata cell for *etm2*, and then right click. A pop-up menu will list options such as *Remove, Move up* and *Move down* (Figure 1.3.7.c). The latter two options change the order of the layers within the collection. This can be important if the order of the layers in a group file have an associated meaning.

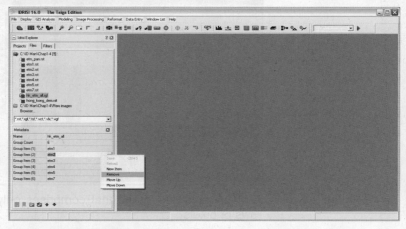

Figure 1.3.7.c   Manipulating individual files in a raster group file.

Chapter 2   Displaying Remotely Sensed Data

2.1 Introduction to Data Types

Remote sensing image data are usually organized as an array of pixels, where each pixel has an intensity value (also referred to as a gray level, brightness value, or digital number (DN)). Pixel is a composite word, derived from "picture element."

Figure 2.1.a shows that when a digital image is enlarged significantly, the individual pixels, and the discrete area each pixel represents, become apparent. The legend shows the scheme by which the DN values have been mapped to image gray tones. Table 2.1.a shows the same information as Figure 2.1, except as numbers instead of gray tones. Note that pixels with dark gray tones in Figure 2.1.a correspond to low DN values in Table 2.1.

The fundamental characteristics of remotely sensed data depend upon the **resolution** of the sensor used to acquire the data (Jensen 2005). There are four types of resolution: radiometric, spatial, spectral and temporal (Warner et al. 2009a).

Figure 2.1.a   A highly enlarged image that comprises only 4 columns and 3 rows of pixels.

Table 2.1.a   The pixel values for the image shown in Figure 2.1.a.

73	86	89	73
50	77	72	43
25	34	34	25

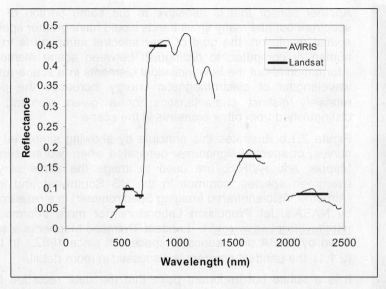

Figure 2.1.b   Simulated spectral curves for a forested pixel as seen by AVIRIS and Landsat sensors.

Radiometric resolution refers to the sensitivity of the sensor to incoming radiance (i.e., how much change in radiance is required to result in a change in recorded brightness value?).   This sensitivity to different signal levels will determine the total range of values that can be generated by the sensor.

Traditionally, **spatial resolution** is considered the minimum distance between two objects that can be differentiated from one another (Sabins 1997, Jensen 2005).   For aerial photography the spatial resolution is usually measured from a test pattern of numerous white and black lines of a defined brightness contrast, but varying thickness.   Resolution can then be measured directly from a photograph of the test pattern as the maximum number of line pairs per millimeter that can be resolved.   In practice, photographic resolution is determined not only by the camera properties, including focal length and configuration determine, but also the aircraft height and stability, as well as the resolution of the film used.

For satellite-borne sensors, resolution is often loosely specified as the dimension of the ground area that falls within the instantaneous field of view of a single detector within the imaging array.   In this terminology, spatial resolution is equivalent to unit pixel size in ground-based units.   However, it is important to realize that this equivalency is not the same as the formal definition of resolution. In fact, using the word resolution to imply the pixel area is somewhat misleading. Most objects that are similar in size to the pixel area will not be large enough to be resolved on the image, since the object is unlikely to be imaged by just a single pixel.   Nevertheless, using the pixel size to refer to resolution is a convenient short hand.

Sensors also are characterized by the wavelength regions of the electromagnetic spectrum for which they record data. A single sensor may record one or more separate measurements per pixel, with each measurement associated with a particular part of the spectrum, usually referred to as a *band,* or sometimes as a *channel*.   An instrument's **spectral resolution** is determined by the number of bands, and the width of the electromagnetic spectrum each band covers. A sensor may detect energy from a wide region of the electromagnetic spectrum, but have poor spectral resolution, if it has a small number of wide bands.

Another sensor that is sensitive to the same portion of the electromagnetic spectrum but has many small bands would have greater spectral resolution. Like spatial resolution, the goal of finer spectral sampling is to enable the analyst, human or computer, to distinguish between scene elements. More detailed information about the how individual elements in a scene reflect or emit different wavelengths of electromagnetic energy increases the probability of finding relatively distinct characteristics for a given element, allowing it to be distinguished from other elements in the scene.

Figure 2.1.b illustrates this principle by showing simulated spectral reflectance curves, or spectral signatures, generated when two sensors, Landsat Thematic Mapper and AVIRIS, are used to image the same pinyon pine forest (an evergreen species, common in the US Southwest and in Mexico). AVIRIS (Airborne Visible/Infrared Imaging Spectrometer) is a research sensor, developed by NASA's Jet Propulsion Laboratory (for more information on AVIRIS see http://aviris.jpl.nasa.gov/). Landsat Thematic Mapper is a satellite borne sensor flown by NASA on a series of spacecraft since 1982. In the following section (2.1.1), the Landsat program is discussed in more detail.

It is a subtle but important point that the data recorded by these sensors is actually radiance (energy) measured at the sensor, not reflectance, which is what is shown in Figure 2.1.b. The radiance measured at the sensor is a function of the reflectance of the ground materials, as well as the solar illumination and atmospheric transmission, which both vary with time of day, season, and atmospheric properties. Therefore, to make the simulated data from the two sensor measurements comparable, it is necessary to convert them to reflectance.

Both Landsat and AVIRIS cover the same broad range of the electromagnetic spectrum, from 400 to 2,500 nm. However, AVIRIS has approximately 210 unique, contiguous bands, each 10 nm wide. (In Figure 2.1.b, AVIRIS bands over the atmospheric moisture absorption regions have been deleted, hence the gaps in the spectrum.) Landsat, on the other hand, has just six bands in the 400 to 2,500 nm region, with a seventh band, not shown, in the thermal region. The Landsat bands are indicated in the figure by horizontal black lines. Each line represents a single band, for which a single radiance value is recorded.

As can be seen from Figure 2.1.b, although both AVIRIS and Landsat capture the overall shape of the spectrum, the AVIRIS curve has much greater detail. For example, in the 2,000 to 2,500 nm region, Landsat has just one band (from 2,080 to 2,350 nm), whereas AVIRIS has approximately 50 bands across this region. In addition, the AVIRIS sensor has another 50 bands in the 900-1,400 nm region, whereas Landsat misses this region entirely. Note that the AVIRIS spectrum has some interesting absorption features (lows) in this region.

The spectral limitations of Landsat may be significant if one were trying to differentiate very similar land cover types. On the other hand, if your main interest is differentiating forest from soil, then the Landsat sampling of the spectrum is more than likely sufficient.

2.1.1 Example: Landsat Data

One of the most important series of satellites for civilian remote sensing is Landsat (Lauer *et al.* 1997). The Landsat Project, which began in the early 1970s, has incorporated a sequence of satellites that have been placed in earth orbit. The most recent of the Landsat series of satellites is Landsat 7 (Figure 2.1.1.a), which was launched on April 15, 1999 and orbits the Earth at an altitude of approximately 438 miles (705 kilometers) with a sun-synchronous 98-degree inclination and a descending equatorial crossing time of 10 a.m.

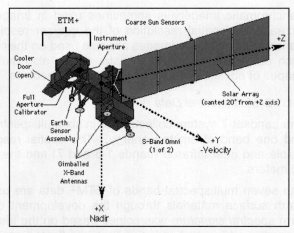

Figure 2.1.1.a   Landsat satellite (from:
http://science.hq.nasa.gov/missions/satellite_48.htm).

Landsat images are spatially referenced by the Landsat World-Wide-Reference system (WRS), which comprises 57,784 scenes, each 115 miles (183 kilometers) wide by 106 miles (170 kilometers) long. Each scene consists of approximately 3.8 gigabits of data. The WRS system is based on the orbital tracks of the satellite (paths, in WRS terminology) and arbitrary rows, in which the tracks are divided into discrete scenes. Thus, Landsat images are usually referenced by WRS path and row.

The Landsat 7 satellite carries the Enhanced Thematic Mapper Plus (ETM+) sensor (Mika 1997). This name was chosen to indicate it was an enhanced version of the earlier Thematic Mapper (TM) instrument, flown on Landsats 4 and 5. (Landsat 6 was destroyed during launch.) The ETM+ instrument acquires two basic types of data: a single band panchromatic image and multispectral images comprising seven bands, each sensitive to a different wavelength, from the visible, through the near and short wave infrared, to the thermal infrared.

Unfortunately the Landsat 7 ETM+ sensor experienced a malfunction in May 2003, and the imagery collected since then is of reduced value because of periodic gaps in each image (USGS 2006). Nevertheless, the large global archive of high quality historical Landsat data are still useful today. In addition, Landsat 5 data, which is not quite as high quality as Landsat 7, is also available.

2.1.1.1 Panchromatic Data

The Landsat ETM+ differs from previous Landsat sensors in that it includes an additional, eighth, band (Mika 1997). This band 8 is a panchromatic band that covers the 0.5-0.9 μm spectrum and has a 15 meter pixel size. The term "panchromatic" traditionally referred to black and white photographic film that is sensitive to the entire wavelength region of visible light. When used, this film was generally filtered to remove blue wavelengths. Likewise, panchromatic digital satellite imagery usually excludes blue wavelengths, in order to minimize the effect of atmospheric scattering, and instead may include a portion of the near-infrared spectrum. By gathering more energy over a wide spectrum, panchromatic sensors can be designed to acquire data with a higher spatial resolution than if those sensors acquired data with multiple bands (i.e. higher spectral resolution) because the signal to noise ratio of the sensor is limited by the amount of energy reaching the detector.

Panchromatic imagery is sometimes used in image processing to sharpen or increase the spatial resolution of the coarser resolution multispectral imagery. Panchromatic satellite images are also used on their own for mapping endeavors such as generating elevation data, and is also quite suitable for detecting the shapes of objects by their boundaries and shadows.

2.1.1.2 Multispectral Data

The Landsat-7 system collects data in six multispectral bands of reflected energy and one band of emitted energy. The spatial resolution is 30 meters for the visible and near infrared (bands 1-5 and 7) and the thermal infrared (band 6) is 60 meters.

The seven multispectral bands of ETM+ data are used to discriminate between Earth surface materials through the development of spectral signatures. The term *spectral signature* was coined based on the idea that for each material, the proportion of incident radiation that is reflected varies by wavelength, and is a characteristic of that material. The basic premise of using spectral signatures is that the signatures, or reflectance patterns, may be sufficiently different to make it possible to distinguish between different classes of materials. The term spectral signature is, however, a somewhat misleading term, as in practice spectral signatures have inherent variability that makes it challenging to separate between them. Thus, automated identification of surface materials based on spectral signatures is almost never 100% accurate.

In displaying multispectral image bands, we can select combinations of individual bands that highlight particular types of signatures. Such multispectral images normally exploit color to provide a visual representation of the earth's surface.

2.1.2 Surface (Elevation and Bathymetry)

A Digital Elevation Model (DEM) is a data set that contains information on the heights or depths of a surface. The format of DEMs can be either a regular grid of points in binary or ASCII format, or an irregular set of points which are typically in an ASCII XYZ file. The United States Geological Survey distributes DEMs for much of the United States that are a regular grid of elevation points in a standard ASCII format.   Other government agencies and commercial providers also provide data in binary format. One of the more common formats, however, is the standard XYZ format where the data are ordered in a three-column ASCII file.

Elevations were in the past almost exclusively produced directly or indirectly by photogrammetric analyses in which images from different vantage points are compared to determine the ground elevations. In the last two decades, two competing technologies have become very common: inteferometric radar (the DEM used in Section 2.3 was originally developed from inteferometric radar) and lidar. Inteferometric radar uses a comparison of two radar images acquired from very slightly different perspectives, whereas lidar uses the measured time it takes for a pulse of light to travel from the sensor, to a reflecting object, and back to the sensor (Maune 2001).

2.2 Satellite Image Display

As discussed in Section 2.1 above, the brightness of a particular pixel in an image is proportional to the pixel DN value. The DN value in turn is related to the intensity of incident solar radiation, and the reflectance properties of the surface material. Thus, a panchromatic image may be interpreted in a manner similar to that of a black-and-white aerial photograph of the same area. A multispectral image consists of several bands of image data. For visual display, each band may be displayed individually as a gray scale image, or in a combination of three bands as a multispectral color composite image.

2.2.1 Preparation

For this section we will be using the Hong Kong Thematic Mapper multispectral and panchromatic data from the *Chap1-4* folder on the CD.

If you have not already copied the data from the CD as described in Section 1.3.1, copy the *Chap1-4* folder from the CD to a new folder in your workspace (e.g. *C:\ID Man\Chap1-4*).

Start IDRISI. In the previous Chapter we set the project file and working folder, however to ensure that nothing has changed since we did that work, we will first check that the data are organized as we expect.

Check project file and working folder with IDRISI EXPLORER
Menu Location: **File - IDRISI EXPLORER**
1. The *IDRISI EXPLORER* window is automatically opened if it was open when you last shut down IDRISI. Therefore it may not be necessary to re-open the *IDRISI EXPLORER*. However, if it is not open, do so.
2. Click on the *Projects* tab to ensure the *Chap1-4* project is listed, and the radio button next to that project has been selected as the current project. If the *Editor* pane is obscuring part or all of the *Projects* information, drag the boundary for the *Editor* pane down to create more room for the *Projects* pane.
3. Confirm in the *Editor* pane that the *working folder* correctly points to the folder you created with the data from the CD (*C:\ID Man\Chap1-4*). (If necessary, return to Section 1.3.4 to review the procedures to create or edit the project file.)
4. Click on the *Files* tab.
5. Check if all the satellite image files (raster) are listed in the *Files* pane.
6. If the files are not listed in the *Files* pane, double click on the directory name to display the files.
7. In order to see the full list of data in the *Metadata* pane it may be necessary to drag the boundary of the *Metadata* pane to make the latter pane smaller. Also, if the space to show the full list of files is not sufficient, you may have to use the slider bar in order to see the entire list of files.
8. There should be 8 *.rst* files present: a DEM (**hong_kong_dem.rst**), one panchromatic image (**etm_pan.rst**), and 6 multispectral images numbered 1-5 and 7 (**etm1.rst** , **etm2.rst** ...**etm5.rst**, and **etm7.rst**) (note that band 6, a thermal band is not included). In addition, if you have completed the exercise in Section 1.3.7, there will also be the **hk_etm_all.rgf**, a *raster group file*.

If the files you expect are not listed in the *Files* pane, then the working folder has not been set correctly. You will need to return to the *Projects* pane, and set the correct folder.

2.2.2 Image Display

In this exercise you will display a single band of a satellite data as a gray scale image, and investigate the nature of a contrast stretch. Panchromatic image data are most commonly displayed as a gray tone image, just like a black and white photograph.

Displaying a panchromatic image with the DISPLAY LAUNCHER

Menu Location: Display – DISPLAY LAUNCHER

1. Start the DISPLAY LAUNCHER program from the main menu, or the tool bar.

2. In the *DISPLAY LAUNCHER* dialog box (Figure 2.2.2.a), start the process to select a file by clicking on the browse button (…) in the center left column.

3. A file *Pick List* window will open. In the new window, if only the directory is listed, click on the plus sign (+) to list the files.

4. Select the ***etm_pan.rst*** raster file (Figure 2.2.2.b) by either double clicking on the file name, or clicking once, and then clicking on *OK*.

5. Select *GreyScale* in the *Palette File* section of the Display Launcher window. (Figure 2.2.2.a).

6. Click on *OK* to display the image.

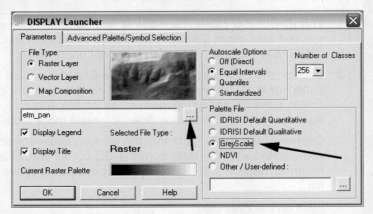

Figure 2.2.2.a   Display Launcher window, with parameters chosen for displaying the ***etm_pan.rst*** image.

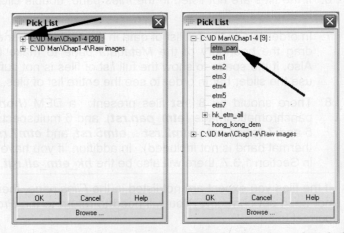

Figure 2.2.2.b   Pick list window. Left: directories can be expanded by clicking on the plus sign. Right, directory with an image file highlighted.

The ***etm_pan*** image is a subset of a panchromatic image from the Landsat Enhanced Thematic Mapper Plus (ETM+) sensor. The image represents green to infra-red radiance (0.5 - 0. 9 µm). This image should therefore at least somewhat correspond to how we view the world, because humans tend to see best in the green to red regions of the spectrum. However, you should be cautious about interpreting this image, because it also includes information from the near infrared (0.7 - 0. 9 µm), for which our eyes are not sensitive.

As a single band image, this image is best displayed in shades of gray. This is true of any single band image. This may be confusing, because you might feel, for example, that an image that represents red radiance should perhaps be displayed in shades of red. Although colors are indeed used when multiple bands are displayed in a single composite image, for the display of single band images, gray shades should be used. This is at least in part due to the fact that the eye is much more sensitive to brightness variation for gray, than the brightness variations within a particular color hue.

Adding further confusion to this issue of how to represent a single band of satellite data, the IDRISI default is to display all single band images with the *IDRISI Default Quantitative* palette. A **palette** in IDRISI terminology is a file that specifies the relationship between the pixel DN values and the colors or gray shades used to represent those pixels on the monitor. The *IDRISI Default Quantitative* palette is a rainbow of colors from blue to red, and although it useful for showing patterns, it is not ideal for most raw images which are best thought of as analogs to black and white photographs. It is for this reason that we specifically selected the *GreyScale* palette file in displaying the image, and you should always make a point of using *GreyScale* for single band images, unless you have a specific reason not to.

Examine the ***etm_pan*** image that you have displayed (Figure 2.2.2.c) and note that the image is dark and has poor contrast. The image is not optimal for visual interpretation. This problem arises because the DISPLAY LAUNCHER automatically applies a stretch to an image based on the minimum and maximum values of the image. However, most images have a rather limited range of values, with a few outliers that are either very dark or very bright. Thus, the stretch applied in this case is not optimal. In the next section, we will investigate this idea of the contrast stretch, including why it is generally necessary and what it means in practice.

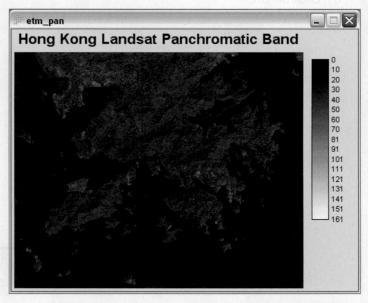

Figure 2.2.2.c   Landsat panchromatic image based on the default stretch.

2.2.3   Image Statistics and a Simple Contrast Stretch

A common format for optical satellite data is for the DN values to be scaled over a potential range from 0 to 255. This range was chosen because it is an efficient way to store numbers in a binary computer file. Computers use a counting system based on the powers of 2, unlike our conventional counting, which is based on powers of 10. The smallest number representation on a computer is a bit, which is location that has a value of 0 or 1. Bits are grouped arbitrarily every 8. This made an 8 bit number (2^8, or 2x2x2x2x2x2x2x2 = 256) a convenient unit of computer storage.

Within this 0-255 range, the optical settings of the sensor are designed to cover the broadest range of possible landscapes, from highly reflective snow and beach sand, to very dark material such as basalt rock, water and shadow. However, any individual scene is unlikely to include the full range of landscape cover types. Thus the range of DN values in a single image is likely to be rather limited. In this section you will adjust the contrast in the image so that the small range of DN values found within a scene is mapped to a wider range of display values, utilizing the full range of 256 brightness levels available for viewing on the computer monitor.

Analyzing the image data distribution with HISTO

Menu Location: **Display - HISTO**

---

1. Start the HISTO program from the main menu or the toolbar.

2. In the *HISTO* dialog box, click on the browse button (…) next to the text box for the *Input file name*.

3. The *Pick list* window will open. Use it to select the **etm_pan** data set.

4. Set the class width to **1**.

5. Leave the remaining parameters set at their default values.

6. Click on *OK*.

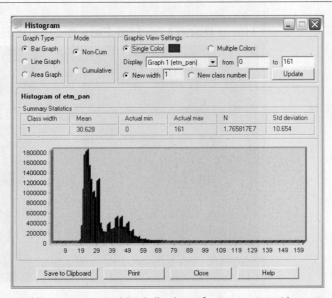

Figure 2.2.3.a   Histogram graphical display of **etm_pan.rst** image.

The frequency histogram is shown as a bar graph (Figure 2.2.3.a). The vertical axis shows the number of pixels in the image that have each particular DN value, as indicated on the horizontal axis.

Note that Figure 2.2.3.a shows that the full 2^8 (0-255) range is not represented in this image, and that the population is not a normal Gaussian distribution (i.e. does not follow a bell-shaped curve). In fact, many satellite images reveal a bimodal frequency distribution, particularly if the scene contains both land and water areas. Also the minimum value and maximum values, 0 and 161, are well outside the range of the majority of pixel values.

Notice how you the graph can be updated dynamically. You can convert the graph to cumulative plot or a line graph by clicking on the appropriate options in the *Histogram* window. You can also set new maximum and minimum numbers for the graph by editing the values in the text boxes for *Display ... from... to....*, and then pressing the *Update* button. For example, you might enter **18** and **80** in these boxes, respectively, and by doing so, obtain a new graph that displays just that part of the histogram.

IDRISI has persistent windows, which means that the dialog boxes that control programs do not close once the program has run. Therefore, the HISTO dialog box should still be open in your IDRISI workspace and available to be run again, though you may need to move the *Histogram* window to one side to see the dialog box.

Analyzing the image data distribution with HISTO (cont.)

7. In the *HISTO* dialog box (i.e. not in the *Histogram* display window, but the original *HISTO* dialog box that produced the *Histogram* window), select the radio button for *Numeric* output, instead of the default *Graphic*.

8. Click *OK*.

This time, because we selected *Numeric* as the output format, the program will generate a text file with the number of pixels for each DN value (Figure 2.2.3.b). From this file, we can learn that there are only 15 pixels with a value of zero, out of a total of 17.7 million pixels. Furthermore, the cumulative frequency of all pixels only reaches 0.001 at a DN value of 17. This means that if you sum all the pixels with a value of 17 or less, they would comprise less than 0.1% of the image.

Figure 2.2.3.b   Histogram numeric output for the ***etm_pan.rst*** image.

Use the slider bar on the right of the *Module Results* window showing the numeric histogram data to observe the DN value associated with a cumulative proportion of 0.999. This should be a DN value of 73. We can therefore summarize our findings to say that only 0.2% of the image DN values lie outside the range 18-73.

Now, using the graphic and numeric histogram data as a guide, let's develop an enhancement of the image contrast that makes the patterns in the majority of the image much clearer. This procedure is called a **contrast stretch**. In carrying out our contrast stretch, we have to accept that we will lose discrimination of changes in DN values at the extremes of the distribution, such as between DN values 0 and 18, and between 73 and 160. However, because there are so few pixels with such values, and overall the image will look much clearer.

At this stage you can close the HISTO dialog box, and the graphic and numeric data windows that program generated.

Contrast Enhancement through modifying the *Display* settings in the *Composer Window*

---

1. If you have closed the image displayed in Section 2.2.2, redisplay the **etm_pan.rst** image using the DISPLAY LAUNCHER and a *GreyScale* palette file (see Section 2.2.2 for further instructions, if necessary.)

2. In the *Composer* dialog box (this window is automatically also opened in the Workspace when an image is displayed), click on the button for *Layer Properties*.

3. The *Layer Properties* dialog box will open (Figure 2.2.3.c). Note that the window has three tabs, with the *Display Parameters* tab as the default.

4. Use the sliders *Display Min* and *Display Max* to set the minimum to **18** and the maximum to **73**, or alternatively, simply type in the appropriate numbers in the text boxes to the right of the sliders.

5. Click on the button for *Apply*, *Save* and then *Close*.

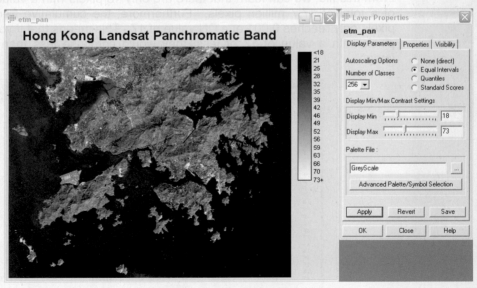

Figure 2.2.3.c   The contrast-stretched **etm_pan.rst** image and the *Layer Properties* dialog box.

Note how the image contrast has improved greatly (Figure 2.2.3.c). This is because we have assigned a black color on the screen to 18, instead of 0, and white to 73, instead of 161. Shades of gray between black and white are assigned linearly from 18 to 73, respectively. Thus middle gray is a DN value of 45 (half way between 18 and 73), instead of the 80, as was the case when we were using a 0-161 stretch. If we refer back to the histogram of the data distribution, we can see that 45 is within the main data distribution, whereas 80 is greater than nearly all the values in the image.

The contrast adjustment we have made so far is not applied to the original data, but only to mapping function for display of the data on the screen. This is a key concept, because it means that the original data are unchanged, which may be important if we are to apply further processing.

By clicking on the button for *Save*, we are storing the minimum and maximum values in the metadata. This means that every time the image is displayed, the enhancement is applied automatically, through the DISPLAY LAUNCHER's *Autoscale* option. In the future, when this image is displayed, the program will automatically use these values to determine the contrast stretch. In the next exercise, we will check the metadata to see where the values are recorded, and the redisplay the image to observe the automatic image stretch.

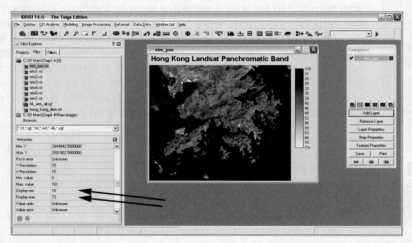

Figure 2.2.3.d   Using the IDRISI EXPLORER to view *Display min* and *Display max*.

Contrast Enhancement (cont.)

6. If the *IDRISI EXPLORER* window is not open, click on the IDRISI EXPLORER icon.

7. Select the *Files* tab.

8. If the files are not listed in the *Files* pane, double click on the directory name to display the files.

9. In the *Files* pane, click on the ***etm_pan.rst*** image.

10. In the *Metadata* pane, drag the slider down until the lines labeled *Display min* and *Display max* are visible.

11. Confirm that the *Display min* text box shows a value of *18* (upper arrow in Figure 2.2.3.d), and the *Display max* text box a value of *73*.

12. Note that it is possible to change these values by simply typing new values in the text boxes.

13. Close the image in the display window, if it is not already closed.

14. Redisplay the **etm_pan.rst** image again. Be sure to select the *GreyScale* palette file, as with any single band satellite image.

The redisplayed image should show a good contrast, as it did when we applied the contrast stretch manually. In this case, however, the contrast is applied automatically.

End this section by closing any windows that are still open in the IDRISI workspace.

2.2.4 Creating False Color Composite Images

In this section, we will create a standard false color infrared composite of three TM image bands (i.e. the ETM+ green band displayed in blue on the screen, the red band displayed as green, and the near infrared band displayed as red).

The concept of a false-color image stems from false color infrared aerial photography. When infrared photography was first developed, an infrared layer was substituted for a blue sensitive layer in the film. However, it was noticed that the vegetation patterns were more obvious if the near infrared was displayed in red colors, and the red and green layers were depicted in green and blue shades, respectively. Today, we refer to any image 3-band composite that uses a color assignment different from that of a natural color composite (i.e. blue, green and red displayed as blue, green and red) as a false color composite. The specific combination we will produce, however, is sometimes known as a standard false color composite, because it is so common.

Creating a false color composite image

Menu Location: **Display - COMPOSITE**

1. Start the COMPOSITE program.

2. In the *COMPOSITE* dialog box, select the browse icon (...) next to the text box for the *Blue image band*. (Figure 2.2.4.a)

3. A *Pick List* window will open. Select the **etm2** raster file. Click twice on the file, or once and click on *OK*.

4. Repeat for the *Green* and *Red image bands*, selecting the files **etm3** and **etm4** files, respectively. (Note: you can also type the names of the files directly in the text boxes.)

5. Enter the *Output image* filename in the text box provided: **etm234_composite**

6. Select the radio button for *Contrast stretch type* as *Linear with saturation points*.

7. In the *Output type* section, select the radio button for *Create 24 bit composite, with original values and stretched saturation points*. (This is the default.)

8. In the Title dialog text box, enter: **Hong Kong False Color Composite**

9. Click *OK* to create and display the false color composite.

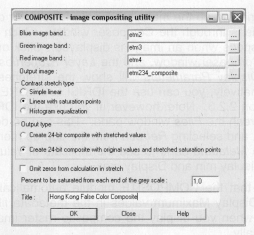

Figure 2.2.4.a   *COMPOSITE* dialog box.

Linear with saturation stretch is much better than a simple linear stretch that uses the minimum and maximum vales as the end points of the stretch.   As we discovered in the previous section, the minimum and maximum values found in the raster data set are not always effective measure for the optimal display.   The linear stretch with saturation determines where the data range encompasses a certain percent of the data (in this case 98%), and use this range in the stretch – much like our determination of the best maximum and minimum vales to use for the panchromatic display in Section 2.2.3

After you have clicked on the OK button in the *COMPOSITE* dialog box, IDRISI will generate the composite image, an automatically display the result.

Figure 2.2.4.b   Landsat false color composite image of Hong Kong, with bands 2,3,4 as blue, green, red (B,G,R).

Try bringing up the metadata for the false color composite. The simplest way to do this is through the *Composer* window, which is always present in the IDRISI workspace when an image is displayed. Click on the *Layer Properties* button in the *Composer* window, and the *Layer Properties* window will open. The tab for the *Display Parameters* will show the stretches applied to each image band. Alternatively, you can use the IDRISI EXPLORER, as we have learned to do in Section 2.2.3. Note, however, if you use the IDRISI EXPLORER you may need to refresh the *Files* window pane. This can be done by right clicking in the *Files* pane, and selecting *Refresh* from the pop-up menu. You will need to scroll down in the *Metadata* pane to see the triplicate of values (one for each band) for both the Display min and Display max.

Note that the COMPOSITE module automatically enters the Display Minimum and Display Maximum values in the metadata file of the color composite. This way, when you display the composite raster image, it will always be enhanced optimally.

2.2.5 Map Annotation

We can also design and create maps within the *Display* window. Maps not only show a representation of the Earth's surface, such as a satellite image, but also include useful and important information such as the reference grid, the north direction, and scale. In addition, maps usually have a title, and provide information about the map projection and data source.

We will now use the Hong Kong false color image as the basis for creating a map composition (Figure 2.2.5.a). The first step in creating a map is to resize your *Display* window so that enough background around the image is available to accommodate our planned map elements.

Map composition construction
Menu Location: **Display - DISPLAY LAUNCHER**

1. Open the DISPLAY LAUNCHER from the main menu or icon bar.

2. Select the raster file ***etm234_composite***.

3. Click on the *OK* button to display the image.

4. Your image should have a title automatically displayed. If not, it means you did not enter a title when you created the image, and you should return to Section 2.2.4, or enter the title through the *Metadata* pane in the *IDRISI EXPLORER*, and then redisplay the image.

5. Resize the *Display* Window by clicking on one of the corners, and dragging the window to an appropriate size to encompass the annotation planned (Figure 2.2.5.a).

6. Double click on the image within the *Display* window.

7. Click and drag the image to center it horizontally beneath the title.

8. Double click on the title in the *Display* window, to select the title. The title will be boxed by a series of black squares, indicating the title box has been selected.

9. Click and drag the title box to a position centered above the image.

10. When you are done, click elsewhere in the *Display* window, to de-select the title box.

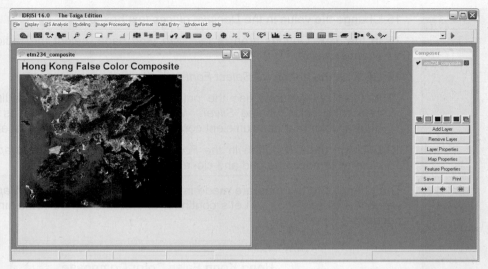

Figure 2.2.5.a   The re-sized display window, with space for planned map elements.

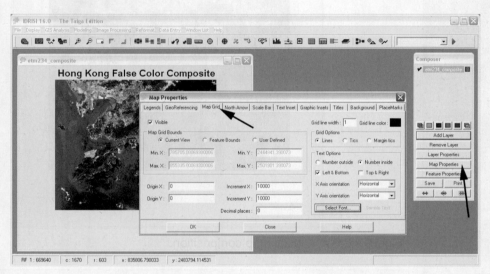

Figure 2.2.5.b   The *Map Properties* dialog box with *Map Grid* pane selected.

We will now create the other components of our map including the map grid, a north arrow, and a scale bar. The tools to create these features are found in the *Map Properties* window.

Map composition construction (cont.): Applying a map grid

11. Open the *Map Properties* window, by either right-clicking on the image in the *Display* window, or by clicking on the *Map Properties* button located in the *Composer* window (Figure 2.2.5.b).

12. Select the *Map Grid* tab to open the *Map Grid* pane (Figure 2.2.5.b).

13. Click to place a check mark in the box labeled *Visible*.

14. In each of the two text boxes labeled *Increment X* and *Increment Y*, enter **10000**.

15. Change the value in the *Decimal places* text box to **0.**

16. In the *Text Options* area of the *Map Grid* pane, select the radio button for *Number inside*.

17. Click on the button for *Select Font*.

18. In the *Font* window, use the pull-down menu under the heading *Color* to select the color labeled *Silver*. We are selecting this color as a relatively neutral color that has sufficient contrast with the image to be discernable.

19. Click on the *OK* button in *the Font* window, and *OK* in the *Map Properties* window to apply the grid and close the *Map Properties* window.

The changes to the map are made immediately after closing the *Map Properties* window (Figure 2.2.5.c). Let's continue, and create all the remaining elements necessary for our map.

Figure 2.2.5.c   Initial map composition.

Map composition construction (cont.): Applying north arrow, scale bar, additional text, and background color

14. Click on the *Map Properties* button in the *Composer* window.

15. Select the *North Arrow* tab.

16. Within the *North Arrow* pane, click in the *Visible* check box.

17. Select the north arrow type you wish to use from the four options. The option you select will be indicated by a black box.

18. Click on the *Scale Bar* tab.

19. Within the *Scale Bar* pane, click on the *Visible* check box.

20. The Units box should indicate *Meters*.

21. Type **20000** in the *Length (in Ground Units)* text box.

22. Click on the *Titles* tab.

23. In the *Titles* pane, click on the *Visible* check box for both subtitle and caption text.

24. Type **Landsat 7 ETM+ Bands 2,3,4 as B,G,R** in the *Subtitle* text box.

25. Click on the *Select Font* button below the *Subtitle* text box.

26. In the *Font* window, set the Font as *Arial*, Font Style as *Bold* and Font Size as *14*.

27. Click *OK* to close the *Font* window.

28. In the *Titles* pane, type **UTM Zone 49N WGS84 Datum** in the *Captions* text box.

29. Use the *Select Font* button below the *Captions* text box to set the Font as *Arial*, Font Style as *Regular* and Font Size as *8*.

30. Within the *Map Properties* dialog box, select the *Background* tab.

31. Within the *Background* pane, click on box labeled *Map Window Background Color*.

32. A *Color* dialog box will open. Select the white color chip in the *Basic colors* section of the window. Click *OK* to close the *Color* dialog box.

33. Click in the check box for *Assign map window background color to all map components*.

34. Click on *OK*.

Note that many of the map components that we just created are located in arbitrary positions that obscure parts of the map. We must now move these elements to a more organized and aesthetically pleasing locations.

Hong Kong False Color Composite

Landsat 7 ETM+ Bands 2,3,4 as B,G,R

Figure 2.2.5.d   The completed Hong Kong Landsat Satellite Image Map.

Map composition construction (cont.): Arranging map elements

35. Double click on the North arrow.

36. Click and hold the cursor over the highlighted North arrow, and move the arrow to the lower left corner. You can resize the arrow, if necessary, by dragging one of the corners of the highlighted box.

37. Double click on the scale bar, so that the scale bar is selected.

38. Click and drag the highlighted scale bar to a location near the bottom-center of the map.

39. Double click on the caption text, *UTM Zone…*

40. Drag the text to a location at the bottom right corner of the image.

41. Double click on the subtitle text, *Landsat 7…*

42. Drag the text to a location at the bottom-center of the map, below the scale bar.

Congratulations! You have now made your first IDRISI map. The map composition should look something like the map in Figure 2.2.5.d.

Now there are several options to save your composition. The simplest is to save it in an IDRISI *map* file format and the other is to save it as a graphic file such as the Windows *Bitmap* (bmp). We will save our composition in both formats.

Map composition construction (cont.): Save to MAP format

43. Select the *Save* button in the *Composer* window.

44. The *Save Composition* dialog box will open.

45. Click on the *Save composition to MAP file* radio button, if it is not already selected.

46. In the text box for *Output file name,* enter **Hong Kong ETM map**.

47. Click on *OK.* The *Save Composition* dialog box will close.

Once saved, a map composition can be redisplayed at any time with the *DISPLAY LAUNCHER*, as we will see in Section 2.2.6 below.

Map composition construction (cont.): Save to BMP format

48. Re-open the *Save Composition* dialog box by clicking on the *Save* button in the *Composer* window.

49. Click on the *Save to Windows bitmap (BMP)* radio button.

50. In the text box for *Output file name,* enter **Hong Kong ETM map**.

51. Click on *OK.* The *Save Composition* dialog box will close.

The BMP file creates a useful graphic for importing into in reports and presentations. Note that you can also use the *Copy to clipboard* option in the *Save Composition* dialog box, to paste a figure directly into another Windows application. However, in our experience this is not always so reliable, and sometimes the resulting image has artifacts. If you find this problem, then you should rather choose the BMP option.

To end this section, close all the files in the IDIRISI workspace.

2.2.6 Printing a Map

The dialog box for printing maps or images from the *Display* window are accessed through the *Composer* window. Importantly, the print function is the only one where you can precisely control the scale of your map. We will now print our Hong Kong image map as a scaled print at 1:500,000.

Printing a map
Menu Location: **Display – DISPLAY LAUNCHER**

1. Start the DISPLAY LAUNCHER.

2. In the *File Type* section of the *DISPLAY LAUNCHER* dialog box, select the *Map composition* radio button.

3. Click on file pick button (…)

4. Select the **Hong Kong ETM map** file we created in the previous section (2.2.5).

5. In the *DISPLAY LAUNCHER* window, click on *OK*

6. Select the *Print* button in the *Composer* window.

7. The *Print Composition* dialog box will open.

8. Click on the *Printer Setup* button. A *Printer Setup* dialog box will open. Make sure that your printer is set for *landscape* orientation. Close the *Printer Setup* dialog box.

9. In the Print Composition dialog box, in the section labeled *Rendering*, click on the radio button for *Highest Quality*.

10. In the *Scaling* section, select the radio button for *Print to scale*.

11. In the *Scale: 1/* text box, type in **500000**

12. Click on the *Print* button.

IDRISI will render and send to your printer a map at the precise scale of 1:500,000. Measure the scale bar to check (it should be exactly 4.0 cm).

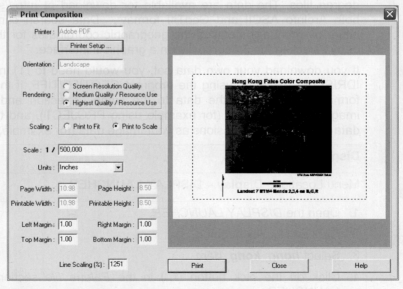

Figure 2.2.6.a   *Print Composition* dialog box.

2.3 3-D Visualizations

IDRISI has a number of modules that allows the user to create three dimensional displays and visualizations. Typically these modules require the use of digital elevation data (DEM) as the basis for the orthographic view. The surface represented can be used to control a palette, or a second file may be draped over the surface. A common choice for the drape files is a satellite image, which results in a perspective view of the Earth's surface. These perspective views can be animated to create fly-through visualizations. We will create such a visualization over Hong Kong.

2.3.1 Preparation

Let us first examine the DEM of Hong Kong supplied with this manual. The DEM is a subset of the nearly global DEM derived from NASA's Spaceborne Imaging Radar-C (SIR-C) Topographic Mission. The Shuttle Radar Topography Mission (SRTM) was an international project that obtained high-resolution digital elevation data on a near-global scale. SRTM consisted of a specially modified radar system that flew onboard the Space Shuttle Endeavour during an 11-day mission in February of 2000. The SRTM DEM was derived from a process known as radar interferometry. In radar interferometry, two images are made of the same scene by two separate radar antennas, separated in the "range" direction, perpendicular to the line of flight. The two radar images have very slight differences between them. These differences allow the calculation of the elevation of the ground surface that was imaged by the radar system. The SRTM experiment aboard the shuttle consisted of one radar antenna in the shuttle payload bay, and a second radar antenna attached to the end of a mast extended 60 meters (195 feet) out from the shuttle.

There are many sources for the SRTM DEM data, including the USGS seamless data distribution system (http://seamless.usgs.gov/) and the Earth Science Data Interface (ESDI) at the Global Land Cover Facility of the University of Maryland (http://glcfapp.umiacs.umd.edu:8080/esdi/index.jsp).

One of the most straightforward sources of SRTM is provided by The Consortium for Spatial Information (CGIAR-CSI) (http://csi.cgiar.org/index.asp). CGIAR maintains a 90m SRTM database of the entire world in mosaicked 5 degree by 5 degree tiles. The data are available for download at http://srtm.csi.cgiar.org in both ArcInfo ASCII and GeoTiff formats. Data search can be accomplished either by manually inputting the geographic coordinates for the area of interest, or by selecting the 5 degree tile on a graphical interface.

If you download your own data set, you would need to (1) import the DEM into IDRISI (for example, using the program GEOTIFF/TIFF, if the image is in TIFF format), (2) reproject the data to the same projection and pixel size as the imagery you are using (for example using PROJECT), and then (3) subset the data to the same dimensions as your image data (for example, using WINDOW).

Display DEM data
Menu Location: **Display – DISPLAY LAUNCHER**

1. Open the *DISPLAY LAUNCHER*.
2. Click on file pick button (…).
3. Select ***hong_kong_dem***
4. Click on the pick button (…) in the *Palette file* section of the *DISPLAY LAUNCHER*.

5. Select the *\IDRISI Taiga\Symbols* folder. (Note that the entire path will be displayed, not just the final folder names as indicated here. The specifics of the entire path will depend on your installation of IDRISI.) (Figure 2.3.1.a.)

6. Scroll down and select the **terrain** palette.

7. Click on *OK* to close the *Palette* window.

8. In the *DISPLAY LAUNCHER*, click on *OK* to display the image.

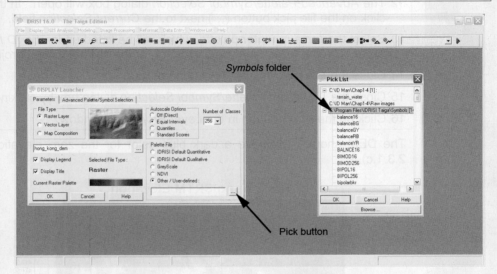

Figure 2.3.1.a   Selecting a palette file from within the */IDRISI/Taiga/Symbols* folder.

Note that the data are a bit noisy with some data drop-outs (Figure 2.3.1.b). The data has yet to be quality checked by NASA and is delivered "as is." The *terrain* palette also shows the zero elevation value as a dark green color. We have included a custom palette along with the DEM data that depicts the zero value (sea level) as a dark blue color. Let's learn how to change the image palette file of a displayed image.

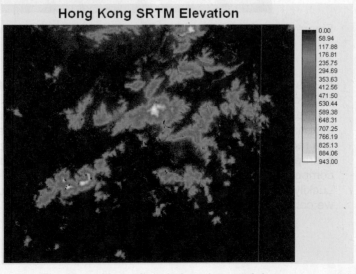

Figure 2.3.1.b   The Hong Kong digital elevation model.

Display DEM data (cont.): Change the palette file

9. In the *Composer* window, select the *Layer Properties* button.

10. The *Layer Properties* window will open, with the *Display Parameters* tab selected.

11. In this new window, click on the *Advanced Palette/Symbol Selection* button.

12. The *Advanced Palette/Symbol Selection* dialog box will open. In this window, click on the file pick button (…) next to the *Current Selection* field.

13. Select the ***terrain_water*** palette, which will be listed under the *ID Man/Ch1-4/* folder, which is your main working folder for the current IDRISI project.

14. Close the *File* pick window by clicking on *OK*.

15. Close the *Advanced Palette/Symbol Selection* dialog box by clicking on OK.

16. Click on the *Apply* button in the *Layer Properties* window.

The DEM should now have a dark blue color for the zero elevations (Figure 2.3.1.c).

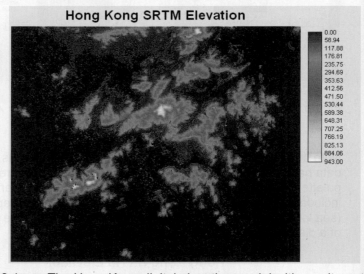

Figure 2.3.1.c   The Hong Kong digital elevation model with an alternate palette.

2.3.2   ORTHO Perspective Display

In this section we will create an orthographic display of Hong Kong using the DEM and Landsat false color raster files. If you were to check the metadata file of the Hong Kong DEM raster data set you would observe that the image dimensions are exactly equal to that of the Hong Kong Landsat raster files. This is a requirement for the orthographic displays and visualizations if we wish to use a drape image. Another requirement for the drape image is that it is either a composite image or a raster file with binary or integer data between 0-255. Luckily for you, we have met all these requirements in our included data sets so we can continue and make our displays.

Orthographic display

Menu Location: **Display - ORTHO**

1. Start the ORTHO program from the main menu.

2. In the *ORTHO* dialog box, double click in the *Surface image* text box. (Figure 2.3.2.a)

3. In the resulting pick list, double click on the file *hong_kong_dem*.

4. In the *ORTHO* dialog box, double click in the *Use drape image* text box.

5. In the resulting pick list, double click on the file *etm234_composite*.

6. In the *Output image* text box, type in the name of a new file: **HK_ortho_1**

7. Click in the *Title* check box.

8. The default resolution is *604 x 480* pixels. If you have a large computer monitor, you can select one of the larger output file sizes by clicking on the appropriate radio button under *Output resolution*.

9. Click on *OK*.

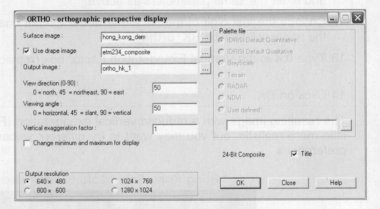

Figure 2.3.2.a   The *ORTHO* dialog box.

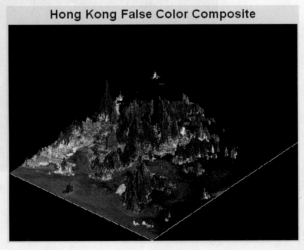

Figure 2.3.2.b   Orthographic image of Hong Kong with a vertical exaggeration factor of 1.

The display window appears with your new orthographic display of Hong Kong from a perspective of a compass direction of 50 degrees (northeast) (Figure 2.3.2.b). One aspect of the display is immediately apparent. The vertical relief looks very unnatural due to an exaggerated display of the terrain. The ORTHO module does not employ a metric scaling, which means that the program does not take into account the units of the DEM values. Therefore the degree of exaggeration is entirely qualitative. The most expedient way to control the degree of exaggeration is to set the viewing angle, and then alter the exaggeration factor to create an appropriate perspective. Specifying an exaggeration factor value of "0.5" will halve the amount of exaggeration, while a value of "2" will double it.

Let's alter our display to create a better orthographic display by modifying the exaggeration factor. We'll try a value of 0.4.

Orthographic display (cont.)

10. Close the *Display* window with the orthographic view.

11. Assuming you have the persistent windows option specified in IDRISI, the *ORTHO* dialog box will still be open. If not, restart the *ORTHO* dialog box, and enter the same parameters as above.

12. Change the last digit of the file name of the Output image from *1*, to a *2*, so the name will now be **HK_ortho_2**.

13. Type **0.4** in the Vertical Exaggeration Factor box (replace the default value of 1)

14. Click on *OK*.

The resulting image with a reduced vertical exaggeration (Figure 2.3.2.c) looks a little more realistic, but you may want to try different values, depending on your preferences.

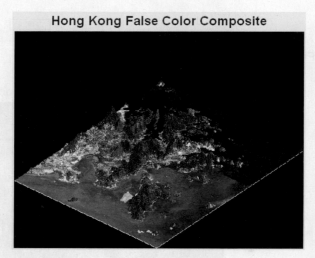

Figure 2.3.2.c.   Orthographic image of Hong Kong with a vertical exaggeration factor of 0.4.

2.3.3 Fly-Through Visualization

The FLY-THROUGH program provides the ability for the user to control interactively the viewing perspective of an orthographic display in real time. This creates a perception of "flying" above and around the surface depicted. Such displays are commonly used as an interesting animation that helps the viewer gain an appreciation for the area depicted.

We will use the same data sets as those in creating our orthographic perspective of Hong Kong. When we open the Fly-Through module, please pay special consideration to the key pad commands, as these are the only means for you to control the display once activated.

Fly-through interactive display
Menu Location: **Display – FLY-THROUGH**

1. Start the FLY-THROUGH program from the menu or the icon bar.

2. In the *FLY-THROUGH* dialog box, click on the pick button (…) to the right of the text box for the *Surface image*. (Figure 2.3.3.a.)

3. Select the **hong_kong_dem** file.

4. Click on pick button (…) to the right of the *Use drape Image* text box, and select the **etm234_composite** file.

5. Select the *Slow* button in the *Initial velocity* section.

6. Use the slider bar to reduce the *Exaggeration factor* to 25%.

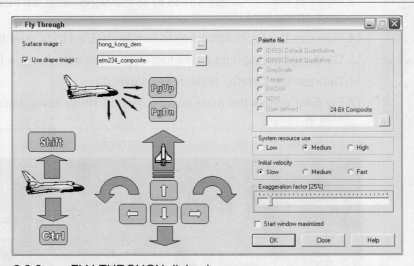

Figure 2.3.3.a   FLY-THROUGH dialog box.

The lower left-hand section of the Fly-Through dialog box shows graphically the keypads that control the view angle, elevation, and direction of movement as you move through the image display (Figure 2.3.3.a).

When we start the FLY-THROUGH display, the initial position is located to the southwest of the surface area. We will try to fly above Hong Kong, making several turns as we go. See if you can use the description in the instruction to fly over the Hong Kong airport, and then over the main part of the city.

Note: If the FLY-THROUGH program gives you an error message when you press *OK* in the instructions below (see for example Figure 2.3.3.b), try following the suggestions in the IDRISI on-line Help. There is a direct link to the Help for this program in the FLY-THROUGH dialog box.

Figure 2.3.3.b   FLY-THROUGH error message.

Fly-through interactive display (cont.)

7. In the FLY-THROUGH window, click on *OK*.

8. A new window, a FLY-THROUGH viewer should open.

9. Hold down the *Up Arrow* Key and watch the display move in the FLY-THROUGH viewer.

10. Tap the *Up Arrow* Key a few times and note how you can move incrementally as well as smoothly.

11. Continue holding the *Up Arrow* Key and as you advance, until some of the first islands you reach have disappeared from view.

12. Press the *Page Down* key to change your view angle downwards.

13. Depress the *Left Arrow* Key to fly to the North West, so that the airport should pass on the right.

14. Now use the *Right Arrow* key to turn North East to fly over the airport.

15. Continue bearing right a little further (this will take you due East).

16. Depress the *Ctrl Key* to decrease elevation.

17. Fly East across the main built up area of Hong Kong, until you reach the far side of image.

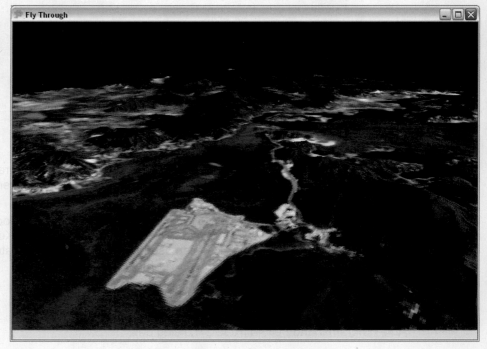

Figure 2.3.3.c   A FLY-THROUGH perspective of the Hong Kong airport.

2.3.4 Recording and playing back fly-through movies

Now that you are familiar with the IDRISI FLY-THROUGH module, you are ready to become your own fly-through movie director! There are two broad ways of creating fly-through movies in IDRISI:

1. Save a path, which the IDRISI FLY-THROUGH program can use to replay a fly-through.

2. Record a fly-through as an .AVI file.

The path approach is attractive because it is very simple, and is a small, text file that takes only minimal disk resources. You can also create the text-file manually, thus giving you tremendous control over creating new movies.

On the other hand, the AVI file recording is also very simple. Once you have created the file, you can play it in any AVI player, such as the Windows Media Player. IDRISI also offers an AVI player, called MEDIA VIEWER. Like many uncompressed video files, AVI files are large, which makes them hard to email. Nevertheless, the advantage of creating and AVI file is that once you have created it, you can play it without access to IDRISI.

In this exercise we will record both a FLY-THROUGH path, and an AVI movie. Before we start, we will create a non-standard false color composite as a base image for our movie. Since we have already used the COMPOSITE program for creating false color composites, the instructions below will be slightly briefer than in Section 2.2.4, where the program was introduced. We will also take advantage of a short cut for selecting files. Instead of clicking on the file browse button (a button with "…" on it, we will simply double click in the text box. In addition, by double clicking on a file, we can insert that file name in the text box. This is demonstrated in the next sub-section.

2.3.4.1 Create a non-standard false color composite

Create a non-standard false color composite image
Menu Location: **Display - COMPOSITE**
1. Start the COMPOSITE program from the main menu, or the main icon bar.
2. In the *COMPOSITE* dialog box, double click in the text box for the *Blue image band.* In the resulting pick list window, double click on the file ***etm3***.
3. Double click in the text box for the *Green image band.* In the resulting pick list, double click on ***etm4***.
4. Double click in the text box for the *Red image band.* In the resulting pick list, double click on ***etm5*** .
5. Enter the *Output image* filename in the text box provided: **etm345_fcc**
6. In the section labeled *Output type*, select the radio button for *Create 24 bit composite, with stretched values*.
7. In the Title dialog text box, enter: **Hong Kong ETM+ 345 as BGR**
8. Figure 2.3.4.1.a shows the *COMPOSITE* window with parameters specified.
9. Click *OK* to create and display the false color composite (Figure 2.3.4.1.b).
10. Close the *COMPOSTE* window, once the new image has been created.

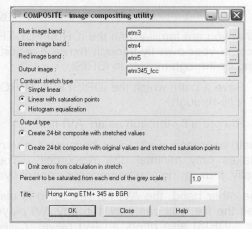

Figure 2.3.4.1.a The *COMPOSITE* window.

Figure 2.3.4.1.b Non-standard false color composite of Hong Kong.

2.3.4.2 *Save a fly-through path*

We will now create a new fly-through, following similar procedures to Section 2.3.3. This time, however, we will use the new non-standard false color composite. You might also try different combinations of settings for starting the FLY-THROUGH program, to see what combination works best for your computer. The settings suggested below are not necessarily the optimal settings for you.

Saving a fly-through path
Menu Location: **Display – FLY-THROUGH**

1. Start the FLY-THROUGH program from the menu or the icon bar.

2. In the *FLY-THROUGH* dialog box, double click in the *Surface image* text box. In the resulting pick list, double click on **hong_kong_dem**

3. Double click in the *Use drape Image* text box, and in the resulting text box, double click on **etm345_fcc**

4. In the System resource use section, select the radio button for *Low*.

5. In the *Initial velocity* section, select the radio button for *Slow*.

6. Use the slider bar to reduce the *Exaggeration factor* to 50%.

7. Click on *OK*.

8. The FLY-THROUGH viewer will open.

9. Move the cursor over the FLY-THROUGH viewer, and right click with the mouse.

10. A pop-up menu will appear. Note the range of options available, and the associated F-key short cuts (Figure 2.3.4.2.a). Some options are grayed out at this stage, but will become available later on.

11. Select *Smooth pixel*.

12. Right click again in the FLY-THROUGH viewer. This time, in the pop-up menu, select *Record*. (Note that the shortcut key **F8** is an alternative for starting to record the movie.)

13. Immediately fly across the Hong Kong image, following the path across the airport as in Section 2.3.3. Change height, perspective and direction, as you wish.

14. When you are done, right click in the viewer, and select *Stop* from the pop-up menu. (Note that the shortcut key **F11** is an alternative.)

15. Right-click in the image, and from the pop-up menu, select *Save path*.

16. A Save as dialog box will open. In the file name text box, enter **flight1**

17. Click on *Save*.

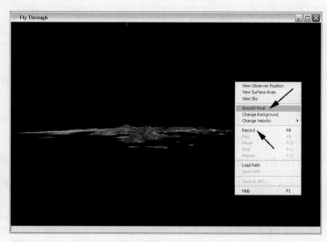

Figure 2.3.4.2.a The FLY-THROUGH pop-up menu.

2.3.4.3 *Play a fly-through based on a saved path*

The process of saving a path also automatically loads it, and makes it available for subsequent use.

Play a fly-through from a previously recorded path

1. The *FLY-THROUGH* viewer should still be open from the *Save as* step in the previous section (2.3.4.2).

2. Right-click in the *FLY-THROUGH* viewer, and from the pop-up menu, select *Play*. (Note that **F9** is an equivalent command.)

3. This should generate a fly-through based on your previously recorded flight path.

Once the fly-through is completed, you can experiment with playing the pre-recorded flight path. Note that the flight path merely specifies the path, and not the images. Thus, if you were to be starting from scratch, you would need to specify the image, and the drape file. In this case, because we are continuing from the previous step, with the fly-through viewer still displayed, there is no need to specify the images once again.

Play a fly-through from a previously recorded path (cont.)

4. Right-click in the image, and select *Load path* from the pop-up menu.

5. In the subsequent pick list, double click on flight_ex1.csv.

6. Right-click in the image, and select *Play* from the pop-up menu.

7. The pre-recorded fly-through path should now play.

2.3.4.4 Record a fly-through as an AVI file

As a final step in this exercise, we will record an AVI file from the flight path recorded in Section 2.3.4.2, above. It is worth noting that it is not necessary to first save the path; you could instead save your recorded path directly to an AVI. However, there is some advantage in first saving the path, as that allows you to preview the movie, prior to generating the movie.

Record an AVI-format fly-through movie

1. The *FLY-THROUGH* viewer should still be open from the *Save as* step in the previous sections (2.3.4.2 and 2.3.4.3).

2. Right-click in the *FLY-THROUGH* viewer, and from the pop-up menu, select *Save as AVI*.

3. A Save as dialog box will open. In the File name text box, type **flight1.avi**.

4. Click on *Save*.

5. The fly-through will play as it is generated and saved in AVI format.

The file, flight1.avi, can be played in IDRISI, through the main menu: **Display – MEDIA VIEWER**. You would then simply open the file, and the movie starts automatically. It is perhaps more useful, however, to see how this movie can be played in a standard AVI format player, such as the Windows Media Player. We provide an example AVI file, **flight_ex1.avi** on the CD, which you can also play.

Play a previously recorded AVI-format fly-through movie

1. Use the *Windows Explorer* to navigate to your data directory (e.g. *C:\ID Man\chap9*)

2. Find the file ***flight1.avi***

3. Double click on the file. This should automatically start the Windows Media Player, and start playing the movie.

4. Alternatively, you can first open the Windows Media Player from the main Windows Start menu, and then open the ***flight1.avi*** file in that program.

Chapter 3   Importing, Georeferencing, Mosaicking and Exporting Images

In this section we will learn how to use IDRISI to import data, georeference the data to our preferred projection, combine data to cover our area of interest, and export it to a general software-independent format. We will use subsets of the four Landsat images required to cover all of Hong Kong, and will end up with a mosaic similar to the Hong Kong images we explored earlier.

3.1 Importing Data into IDRISI

Data formats are numerous and vary widely from those of government and data providers such as the USGS and SPOT Image to software specific such as ERDAS Imagine and ArcInfo. IDRISI comes with a number of import routines for data that cover many of the most common formats. One important format for raster data is the GeoTIFF format. This is probably the closest we have to an international standard for raster data formats.

3.1.1 GeoTIFF Format

Our original Landsat data from Hong Kong was provided by the vendor in the GeoTIFF format, an image format that is growing in popularity. We will use some of this original data to demonstrate the importing of data into IDRISI. A GeoTIFF format is a special case of the Tagged Image File format (TIFF). TIFF is an image format in the public domain, capable of supporting compression, tiling, and extension to include other metadata. GeoTIFF incorporates geographic metadata, such as coordinates and projection type, using compliant TIFF tags and structures.

Let's import a single band (band 3, corresponding to the red spectrum) from subsets of four different Landsat ETM+ scenes of Hong Kong.

Import data
Menu Location: **File – Import – Desktop Publishing Formats – GEOTIFF/TIFF**

1. This program has no associated icon on the main toolbar, so use the menu as described in the title to this instruction box to start the GEOTIFF/TIFF program.

2. The *GEOTIFF/TIFF* dialog box will open. (Figure 3.1.1.a shows the dialog box with the options selected described below.)

3. Note that dialog box has radio buttons for selecting the options for importing and exporting IDRISI files. For this exercise, the default, which is importing files, is what we want.

4. To select an input file, click on the pick button (…) for the *GeoTIFF file name* text box.

5. A *Pick list* window will open. Double click on the *ID Man\Chap1-4\Raw images* subfolder title.

6. The plus sign next to the title will change to a minus sign, and a list of four file names will be displayed.

7. Click on **etm_p121r44_b3**.

8. Click on *OK*, to close the *Pick list* window.

9. IDRISI will automatically put the same name as the potential output filename in the *IDRISI image to create* text box. The IDRISI file has a different extension (**.rst**) from that of the GeoTIFF raw data (.tif), so using the same name will not cause any problems.

10. Click on *OK* to start the import.

Figure 3.1.1.a   The *GEOTIFF/TIFF* dialog box.

The import process is monitored in the status bar. Once the import process finishes, the DISPLAY LAUNCHER is automatically started, and the image is displayed (Figure 3.1.1.b).

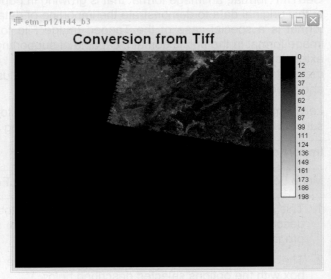

Figure 3.1.1.b.   Successful import of a GeoTIFF Landsat band 3 into IDRISI.

The image is displayed as a gray-scaled image as in Figure 3.1.1.b. As you can see, the actual image only covers part of the display. The TIFF file was generated with bounds that correspond with our area of interest over Hong Kong. More often than not, one's area of interest may span beyond a single frame of imagery. In order to cover the area of interest completely, multiple images are required. In IDRISI it will be necessary to create a spatial composite of the overlapping images in one data file to view the complete area of interest.

Let's see what information was embedded in the GeoTIFF file, by viewing the metadata of the new file. Can you remember how? If so, go ahead and open the metadata. If not, just follow the instructions below, which describe how to open the *Layer Properties* window.   (You can also access the same information through the IDRISI Explorer.)

Import data (cont.): Viewing image metadata

---

11. With the newly created image still open in a display viewer, select the *Layer Properties* button in the *Composer* window

12. Click on the *Properties* tab to open the *Properties* pane (Figure 3.1.1.c).

Figure 3.1.1.c   Imported data layer properties.

Note that the image comes with projection reference information including the UTM zone (UTM-50n), and the bounding coordinates (minimum and maximum X and Y).

Close the *Layer Properties* window before continuing.

Now import the remaining three GeoTIFF images.

Import data (cont.): Import remaining three images

---

13. Because of IDRISI's persistent windows, the GEOTIFF/TIFF dialog box should still be open, though you may need to move or minimize the other windows in the IDRISI workspace. If you do not have the option for persistent windows set, or you have closed the dialog box, use the menu to restart this module.

14. As before, click on the pick button (…) for the *GeoTIFF file name* text box, and select the *ID Man\Chap1-4\Raw images* subfolder title in the *Pick list* window.

15. Select the ***etm_p121r45_b3*** file.

16. Note how once again the output file name automatically changes to the same name as this new input file.

17. Click on *OK* to import the file.

18. Once the status bar indicates the file has been imported, find the GEOTIFF/TIFF dialog box again, and this time select *etm_p122r44_b3* for the *GeoTIFF file name* (input data).

19. Click on *OK* to import this file.

20. Finally, select *etm_p122r45_b3* for the input file, and click on *OK* in the GEOTIFF/TIFF dialog box to import the last data set.

Check the layer properties of each file, as we did for the first image we imported. Note that the path 121 images (i.e. those with *p121* as part of the name) are georeferenced with the UTM50n and the path 122 images (i.e. those with *p122* as part of the file name) are georeferenced with the UTM49n.

Now you can see that the image of Hong Kong that we displayed in the previous section (Figure 2.2.4.b) is actually a mosaic of subsets from four image frames. One can easily see the vertical join line in the original mosaic. The difference in the colors, and thus spectral response, is because the two Western images were acquired on a different date from that of the two Eastern images. However, as we have seen in the importing exercise, the mosaic comprises four images. Can you see any East-West lines that show the remaining joins? The joining of each pair of image subsets from North to South involved data acquired along the same track of the satellite orbit, during the same North to South overpass. Therefore the data can be joined seamlessly since they were acquired under the same conditions.

The similarity or disparity of data spectral qualities during acquisition will influence our choice in the manner that we join data sets. IDRISI offers two modes of spatially joining images, CONCAT and MOSAIC. In the next section, we will utilize the CONCAT module to join the Landsat data with common path acquisition.

3.1.2 Concatenation

Note: The original release of IDRISI Taiga (v. 16.00) has a bug in the CONCAT program. This bug should be fixed in a Service Update release from Clark Labs, available from http://www.clarklabs.org/support/downloads.cfm. Therefore, prior to completing this section (3.1.2) you should first check what version of IDRISI you are running. Use the main IDRISI menu for **Help – About IDRISI 16: The Taiga Edition** to display the program version number (Figure 3.1.2.a). If you are still running 16.00, and an update is available from Clark Labs, you should install the updated program files. Alternatively, you can simply skip this section, and instead complete section 3.1.3, which uses an alternative program, MOSAIC.

Figure 3.1.2.a   The *About IDRISI* window. The version number is indicated by the arrow.

CONCAT is a program module to concatenate, or join, multiple images or vector files to form a larger file. This program may also be used to paste a portion of an image over another image. Some preprocessing may be necessary because all data to be joined must be of the same data type, and have the same spatial resolution (pixel size) and reference system. Since CONCAT does not modify the DN values of the component images, the program works best if the images have comparable spectral characteristics – like along path satellite images – or if the data has been normalized to a standard, for example, elevation data.

Landsat data frames along the same path generally meet the requirement of spectral similarity. Such images are essentially subsets of a single continuous data acquisition along the path of the satellite, and are sub-divided into arbitrary individual images based on the predefined row grid. Thus CONCAT is well-suited to perform the operation of rejoining Landsat images along the same path.

We will use the CONCAT module in IDRISI to join the path images that form each half of the Hong Kong mosaic.

Concatenation of Images with CONCAT

Menu Location: **Reformat – CONCAT**

1. Start the CONCAT program from the main menu.
2. The *CONCAT* dialog box will open.
3. Under *Placement type*, select the radio button for *Automatic placements using reference coordinates*.

The data sets that we will join were originally georeferenced to UTM projection. It is often best to have all data properly georeferenced before joining. This avoids the need for manual placement and also maintains better control of the geographic coordinates of each pixel. When the "Automatic placement" is selected, a new section is created where one can select the images to be joined.

Concatenation of images with CONCAT (cont.)

4. In the *Images to be concatenated* section of the *CONCAT* dialog box, click on the *up* arrow button next to *Number of files*, to set the number of input images to 2 (Figure 3.1.2.b).
5. Click in the first text box under *Filename* (Figure 3.1.2.b). Select the browse files button (…), and the *Pick list* window will open.
6. If necessary, click on the folder name \ID Man\Chap1-4: to list the files in the subdirectory. Select the file **etm_p121r44_b3**, and click OK.
7. Click in the second text box, open the Pick list window, select **etm_p121r45_b3**, and click OK.

Now with the appropriate files selected, one last choice is the manner in which we will deal with the overlap regions of the two files. In the *Concatenation Type* section of the *CONCAT* window, one has a choice of either *Opaque*, or *Transparent*. For *Opaque* concatenation, the first image overwrites the second image, regardless of the values in either image. The second option, *Transparent*, operates in the same way, with the exception of pixels in the first image that have a 0 DN value. These 0 DN pixels are assumed to be null values, and are therefore treated as if they were transparent, allowing the DNs of the second image to be retained, and not overwritten.

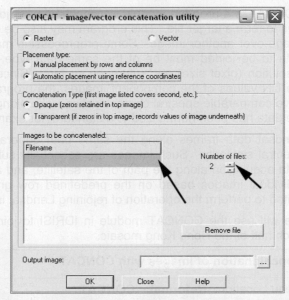

Figure 3.1.2.b   *CONCAT* dialog box, with Automatic Placement option selected.

Generally, image data are almost always transparently joined, whereas for other data that may have negative values or have actual zero values (such as elevation data), we typically use the opaque option. However, we do need to be careful, as many images also have 0 DN values that represent real image data values.

We will now choose the transparent option, and then give an appropriate output name for the concatenated image.

Concatenation of images with CONCAT (cont.)

8. In the *Concatenation Type* of the *CONCAT* dialog box, select the radio button for *Transparent*.

9. In the *Output image* textbox, type the name **etm_p121r44-45_b3**.

10. Click on *OK* to run the CONCAT module.

When the program module has completed the process of concatenating these two images, the image will be displayed automatically (Figure 3.1.2.c). The default for IDRISI for a single band display is a color palette. As we discussed in Section 2.2.2, a gray scale palette is more appropriate for single band images. Therefore, we really should use the *Composer* window to change the palette file for this image to *GreyScale*. However, since we are only interested in checking to see that the file has been joined correctly, we will not worry to change the palette file this time. Also, since the eye is more sensitive to color variations than gray tone variations, you could argue this non-standard representation is useful in this instance.

The joined image shows no seam between the two individual subsets (Figure 3.1.2.c). However, while much of Hong Kong is covered by the image, there still remains a significant portion in the West of the image that is blank. We will need the Path 122 images to cover this region. Therefore, we will need to concatenate the path 122 images just as we did for the path 121 images.

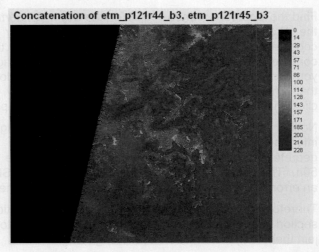

Concatenation of etm_p121r44_b3, etm_p121r45_b3

Figure 3.1.2.c   Landsat Path 121 images joined by concatenation.

Concatenation of images with CONCAT (cont.)

11. The *CONCAT* dialog box should still be open from the concatenation operation. We will use the same parameters, but simply change the input and output files.

12. Click in the first text box under *Filename*. Select the browse files button (…), and the *Pick list* window will open.

13. Select the file ***etm_p122r44_b3***, and click *OK*.

14. Click in the second text box, open the Pick list window, select ***etm_p122r45_b3***, and click *OK*.

15. In the *Output image* textbox, type the name **etm_p122r44-45_b3**. (Note you can simply edit the file name we used the previous time, which only differed in that the path was specified as *p121*, instead of *p122* this time.)

16. Click on *OK* to run the CONCAT module.

Once again the concatenated image will be displayed automatically, with a color palette applied (Figure 3.1.2.d).

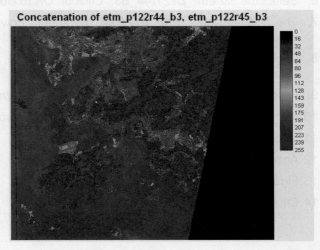

Concatenation of etm_p122r44_b3, etm_p122r45_b3

Figure 3.1.2.d   Landsat Path 122 images joined by concatenation.

Find the *Composer* window, click on the *Layer Properties* button, and then select the *Properties* tab, to examine the metadata for each of the two newly concatenated images. Notice how when you switch the focus between the two concatenated images (i.e. when you click in each image, bringing it to the front), you don't have to reopen the *Layer Properties* window to see the attributes of that window; the attributes are changed automatically. However, you do have to click on the *Property* tab again, as it is not the default pane.

Notice that the concatenated Landsat path images retain the projection information from the original TIFF files. Thus, the path 122 image is georeferenced to UTM-49n, and the path 121 image is georeferenced to UTM-50n. The different projections are a problem in IDRISI in that you will encounter an error if you try to join these images now, to form one single image.

Therefore, let us learn a bit more about map projections and georeferencing in section 3.2 so that we can transform these images to the same projection, and join them to make a mosaic over Hong Kong.

3.1.3 Concatenation using the MOSAIC program

Note: This section is an alternative to section 3.1.2 above. See the note at the start of section 3.1.2 about the choices between sections 3.1.2 and 3.13. You do not need to complete section 3.1.3 if you have successfully completed section 3.1.2.

The MOSAIC program allows us to join two images that are on the same projection.

Concatenation of Images with MOSAIC

Menu Location: **Image Processing – Restoration - MOSAIC**

1. Start the MOSAIC program from the main menu.

2. The *MOSAIC* dialog box will open.

3. In the Images to be processed pane, click in the white area under Filenames. A *Pick list* button will be displayed (…).

4. Click on the *Pick list* button.

5. A *Pick list* window will open.

6. Select the file *etm_p121r44_b3*. Click on *OK* to close the *Pick list*.

7. The first file name, *etm_p121r44_b3*, should now be listed in the *MOSAIC* window.

8. Click in the white space below the first file name. A Pick list button will be displayed.

9. Follow steps 4-7, except this time, chose the file *etm_p121r45_b3*.

10. In the text box labeled *Output mosaicked image*, type **etm_p121r44-45_b3**.

11. Uncheck the option for *Match image grey level*.

12. Accept all other defaults.

13. Figure 3.1.3.a shows the complete dialog box.

14. Click on *OK* to run the concatenation.

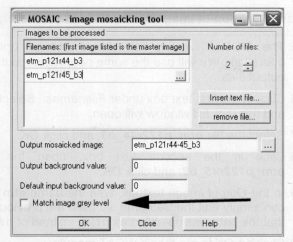

Figure 3.1.3.a. The *MOSAIC* dialog box with parameters chosen for concatenating the two Landsat images. The *Match image grey level check box* should be unchecked.

Figure 3.1.3.b   Landsat Path 121 images joined by the MOSAIC program.

The MOSAIC program offers a powerful tool for matching the histograms of images to try to compensate for brightness differences between images. In this case, however, we do not need the image matching tool because the DN values are equivalent between the images we are joining.

When the program module has completed the process of concatenating or mosaicking these two images, the image will be displayed automatically with a grey scale palette (Figure 3.1.3.b). The joined image shows no seam between the two individual subsets, confirming that there was no need to match the image brightness values with the *Match image grey level* tool in MOSAIC. Although much of the Hong Kong region is covered by the image, there still remains a significant portion in the West of the image that is blank. We will need the Path 122 images to cover this region. Therefore, we will concatenate the path 122 images just as we did for the path 121 images.

Concatenation of images with MOSAIC (cont.)

15. The *MOSAIC* dialog box should still be open from the concatenation operation. We will use the same parameters, but simply change the input and output files.

16. Click in the first text box under *Filenames*. Select the browse files button (…), and the *Pick list* window will open.

17. Select the file **etm_p122r44_b3**, and click *OK*.

18. Click in the second text box, open the Pick list window, select **etm_p122r45_b3**, and click *OK*.

19. In the *Output image* textbox, type the name **etm_p122r44-45_b3**. (Note you can simply edit the file name we used the previous time, which only differed in that the path was specified as *p121*, instead of *p122* this time.)

20. Click on *OK* to run the CONCAT module.

Once again the concatenated image will be displayed automatically (Figure 3.1.3.c).

Figure 3.1.3.c   Landsat Path 122 images joined using the MOSAIC program.

Find the *Composer* window, click on the *Layer Properties* button, and then select the *Properties* tab, to examine the metadata for each of the two newly concatenated images. Notice how when you switch the focus between the two concatenated images (i.e. when you click in each image, bringing it to the front), you don't have to reopen the *Layer Properties* window to see the attributes of that window; the attributes are changed automatically. However, you do have to click on the *Property* tab again, as it is not the default pane.

Notice from the *Layer Properties* window that the mosaicked Landsat path images retain the projection information from the original TIFF files. Thus, the path 122 image is georeferenced to UTM-49n, and the path 121 image is georeferenced to UTM-50n. The different projections are a problem in IDRISI in that you will encounter an error if you try to join these images now, to form one single image.

Therefore, let us learn a bit more about map projections and georeferencing in section 3.2 so that we can transform these images to the same projection, and join them to make a mosaic over Hong Kong.

3.2 Georeferencing

3.2.1 Introduction to Map Projections

Georeferencing is an important, but rather technical topic. Fortunately, much of the complexity of the subject is hidden from us, because IDRISI will take care of the mathematical specifics for us. However, it is necessary for the user to have a qualitative understanding of the principles involved. In the following section we provide a short and highly abbreviated overview of the topic. The reader is encouraged to read further on the topic. For example, the IDRISI manual has an excellent section on georeferencing (Eastman 2009). In addition, most of the texts listed in Table 1.1.2.a have extensive discussions on georeferencing and the issues involved in resampling onto a projection.

A *map projection* is a mathematical procedure which converts between a spherical or ellipsoidal representation of the earth, and a flat planar map surface. Although many projections have been designed over the centuries, just a few are widely used today. The process of geographic referencing of images is known by many names, such as, georeferencing, geocoding, georectification, but they all refer to a process of transforming the image data from a simple matrix reference system (row and column) to a geographic map reference system.

The geographic referencing of individual images allows for the identification of the relative distance and arrangement between features on the image, as well as both the absolute location of features in the imagery, and the comparison of features over time through the overlay of multiple images acquired on different dates. The importance of having an accurate geographic reference system linked to the imagery cannot be overstated. A common coordinate system is the essential element of any GIS database.

No matter how sophisticated the mathematical equations associated with each projection, the Earth's surface can never be converted perfectly to a flat map. There is always some distortion, great or small, in each map.

An important attribute of a projection is the *geodetic datum*. A geodetic datum is the representation of the earth's shape, usually chosen to be an ellipsoid. The geodetic datum therefore includes the parameters that define the ellipsoid, as well as the associated coordinate system origin and orientation. A geodetic datum can be a global datum if it is defined by the center of the Earth, as is the case for WGS84. Otherwise, a local datum defines a specific origin position and azimuth relative to a specific location on the ellipsoid. By locating a datum near one's area of interest, the error associated with projecting onto a flat surface is minimized.

Another aspect of transforming your data to a projection is the decision of how to *resample* or *interpolate* your data to fit the projection grid. Resampling is necessary, because the new grid will have center points for each pixel that differ from the old grid. There are a number of different strategies for estimating the pixel DN values at the new pixel location, including nearest neighbor and bilinear interpolation.

- *Nearest neighbor* is the simplest resampling method. This approach assumes the best estimate of the new pixel value is simply the original DN value of the closest pixel from the input image.

- *Bilinear interpolation* uses the distance-weighted average of the values of the four nearest cells in the input image for the new pixel value.

Choose nearest neighbor whenever it is critical that original pixel values remain unchanged. However, because original pixel values are unchanged, nearest neighbor resampling tends to be very blocky in appearance. Choose bilinear interpolation where averaging seems appropriate for better visual quality. Bear in mind, however, that smoothing will tend to blur the data somewhat.

IDRISI has two modules that may be used for geographic referencing. The first is the module PROJECT, which automatically transforms data from one known geographic projection to another. The second module is RESAMPLE, which allows for the generation of a polynomial equation based on control points picked by the user. Thus, if the data are already georeferenced, but you need to convert the image to another projection, you would use PROJECT. On the other hand, if your data are not georeferenced, you would use RESAMPLE to convert the image to a projection. It is important to note that RESAMPLE requires a georeferenced map or image of the same area to serve as a base map for developing the transformation equation.

3.2.2 Converting Between Projections Using IDRISI-Defined Projections

As discussed above, PROJECT transforms raster images from one known geographic reference system to another known system. IDRISI uses *Reference System Parameter Files* to identify the complete characteristics of a projection, including the datum, origin, units, etc. Thus, to apply the PROJECT module, we will need a *Reference System Parameter File* for both the input and output reference systems.

The IDRISI on-line help gives the source of the algorithms used in the PROJECT module. The projection transformations are based on the formulas of Snyder (1987). Datum transformations are accomplished using the Molodensky transform process, which assumes that the axes of the source and target coordinates are parallel. In the case of conversions between NAD27 and NAD83 within the continental US, IDRISI uses the US National Geodetic Survey's NADCON procedure.

IDRISI incorporates over 500 *Reference System Parameter Files* for a wide variety of projections and datums. These include files for a geodetic system using latitude and longitude and the WGS84 datum, the UTM system (one each for the 60 UTM zones, for both the northern and southern hemispheres) using the WGS84 datum, and, for the United States, the UTM system using NAD27 and NAD83. IDRISI also includes all US State Plane Coordinate (SPC) systems based on the Lambert Conformal Conic and Transverse Mercator projections.

Furthermore, IDRISI allows for the creation of geographic systems by the user, by developing new *Reference System Parameter Files*, which are given the extension *.ref*. Often the best way to create a new *.ref* file is to copy an existing one, and then edit it. The user will need to change the parameters necessary for the new system, and save the file with a new name.

Let us try using the PROJECT module to create maps of our Hong Kong image in different projections. The original Hong Kong images were provided in one of the most common map projections in use today, the Universal Transverse Mercator (UTM) projection. We will transform these images from this projection to a *Geographic* projection that will use latitude and longitude degrees as its coordinates.

Converting between projections using PROJECT
Menu Location: **Reformat - PROJECT**
1. Use the main menu to start the PROJECT module.   2. The *PROJECT* dialog box will open (Figure 3.2.2.a).

3. Use the radio button to specify that the *Type of file to be transformed* is *raster*.

4. Click on the browse button (...) next to the text box for specifying the *Input file name*, and select the **etm1** file from the *Pick list* window.

5. Click on *OK* to close the input file *Pick list*.

6. Note that PROJECT will examine the input raster file's documentation file to determine the reference system in use, and will automatically enter the name of the reference system as it appears in the documentation file in the *Input reference system* text box (*utm-49n*, in this case).

7. Enter a new name for the transformed file in the *Output file name* text box: **etm1_latlong**

8. We will now choose the reference file that defines the grid referencing system for the new output file. To find the list of available reference files, start by clicking on the browse button (...) next to the text box for *Reference file for output result*.

9. The *Pick list* window will open. Double click on *IDRISI Taiga/Georef* to see the files in that folder.

10. Scroll down list and select **latlong**

11. Click the *OK* button to return to the *PROJECT* dialog box.

12. For the *Resample type*, we will use the default option of *Nearest Neighbor*.

13. Likewise, for the *Background value*, we will use the default of *0*.

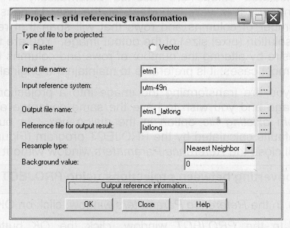

Figure 3.2.2.a   The *PROJECT* dialog box with parameters selected.

The background value is the value that will be used for all new pixel locations that lie outside the bounds of the old image. Because a slight rotation of the image is common in most projection changes, there will likely be regions in the new image for which we don't have data from the old image. Thus, specifying a value for such locations is very important.

Converting between projections using PROJECT (cont.)

14. Click on the *Output reference information...* button.

15. The *Reference Parameters* window will open (Figure 3.2.2.b).

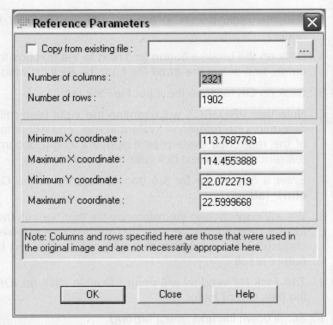

Figure 3.2.2.b   The *Reference Parameters* window.

The PROJECT operation automatically calculates the output boundaries, given the user-selected reference system or the unit distance of the output image. The calculated values are inserted automatically in the *Reference Parameters* window. It is very important for the user to consider carefully the calculated number of columns and rows that will span that region, as this will define the resolution (pixel size) of the output image. You are free to set any resolution you desire by altering the number of rows and columns for the output data; however, in most cases, it is preferable to maintain the original resolution of the data.

If you are transforming the image into a projection already in use by another image and you wish to have the same coverage and resolution, use the *Copy from existing file* option in the dialog box. In our case, we will choose the defaults calculated by the PROJECT program (Figure 3.2.2.a), and therefore we will close the *Reference Parameters* window without changing any parameters.

Converting between projections using PROJECT (cont.)

16. In the *Reference Parameters* window, click on OK to close the window.

17. In the *PROJECT* window, click the *OK* button to start the resampling operation.

The resampling to create the new image will take some time, and therefore it may take a few minutes to generate the new output image. IDRISI will automatically display the new image with a color palette applied (Figure 3.2.2.c). In this case, the color palette shows the rotation very clearly, because the background pixels, which lie outside the boundaries of the original image, are shown in black.

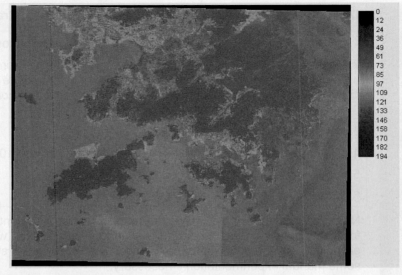

Figure 3.2.2.c   The Landsat image with a geographic projection, and the color palette automatically applied.

This might be a good time to review our skills in modifying a display and creating a map. In the description below, only brief instructions will be provided, since this material has already been covered in Section *2.2.5,* on *Map Annotation*. If you find the instructions below too brief, you will need to review the detailed instructions in *Section 2.2.5*.

Figure 3.2.2.d shows the map we are trying to create.

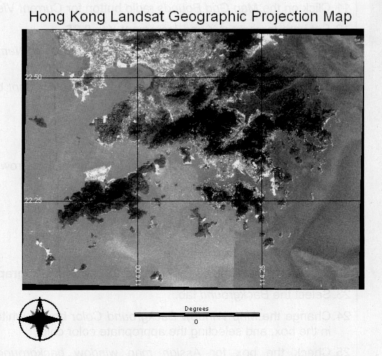

Figure 3.2.2.d   Hong Kong Landsat image map using the *Geographic* projection.

Creating a map: Change the palette file and apply a contrast stretch

1. In the *Composer* window, select the *Layer Properties* button.

2. In the *Layer Properties* window, change the palette file from the default *quant*, by clicking on the browse button (…) next to the *Palette file* text box. The *Pick list* window will open. Open the IDRISI *Taiga/Symbols* folder, and scroll down to select the **greyscale** palette, and click on *OK*.

3. The image should now be displayed in gray tones.

4. Change the *Display Min/Max contrast settings* to 60 and 100.

5. Click on *Apply* to apply the contrast stretch.

6. Close the *Layer Properties* window by clicking on *OK*.

Note that in this example, we have provided appropriate contrast stretch values for the display in order to speed things along. Normally you would run HISTO to get initial estimates of appropriate values for the contrast stretch, followed by some manual experimentation if necessary.

The image should now have a more useful contrast stretch applied, and we can work on the map presentation itself.

Creating a map (cont.): Specify and apply the map annotation

7. In the *Composer* window, click on *Map Properties*.

8. In the *Map Properties* window, select the tab for *Legends*.

9. Uncheck the box for *Visible* (to remove the legend from the display).

10. Select the tab for *Map Grid*.

11. Click on the *Map Grid Bounds* radio button for *Current View*.

12. Set both *Increment X* and *Increment Y* to **0.25**.

13. Under *Text Options*, make sure the radio button for *Number inside* has been selected.

14. Set *X axis orientation* to *Vertical*. Use the *Select Font* button to change the font color to white.

15. Select the tab for *North Arrow*.

16. Make sure the box for *visible* has been checked.

17. Select a *North Arrow* style by clicking on one of the arrow icons.

18. Click on the tab for *Scale Bar*.

19. Make sure the box for *visible* has been checked.

20. Set the *Length (in Ground Units)* to **0.25**.

21. Click on the tab for *Titles*.

22. Type in the *Title* text box: **Hong Kong Landsat Geographic Projection Map**

23. Select the *Background* tab.

24. Change the *Map Window Background Color* box to white, by double clicking in the box, and selecting the appropriate color chip.

25. Check the box for *Assign map window background color to all map components*.

26. Click OK to close the *Map Properties* window.

27. Resize the Display window, so that you have room below the image for the scale bar and north arrow.

28. Drag the individual map components so that the image, scale bar, and title are centered.

29. Note that you can resize the north arrow if necessary.

30. If you are satisfied with the map, you should save it: In the *Composer* window, select the button for *Save.*

31. The *Save Composition* dialog box will open. Select the radio button for *Save composition to MAP file.*

32. Enter a new file name in the text box: **Geographic Projection Map**

33. Click on *OK* to save the file, and close the *Save Composition* dialog box.

The final map composition should look something like Figure 3.2.2.d.   If necessary, you may need to go back and redo some part of the map by altering some parameter in the *Map Properties* window.

Since you have saved the map composition, you can close the *DISPLAY* window.

3.2.3 Converting Between Projections Using User-Defined Projections

Although IDRISI supplies more than 500 specific map projections with specific datum and coordinate origins, occasionally you might need to use a projection that is not included with the software. Fortunately, IDRISI does allow one to specify a new projection, provided that the new projection is a derivative of an existing IDRISI projection, and one knows the datum shift with regards to the datum, spheroid and geographic origins of the IDRISI-supplied projection.

In this exercise, we will create a new projection *reference system parameter file* for the **Hong Kong 1980 grid**. The file will contain all the necessary data for calculating the transformation from a projection based on the WGS84 datum to the HK80 datum.

The Hong Kong grid was created and used by the government of Hong Kong to provide highly accurate positions within that region.   HK1980 Grid is a local rectangular grid system based on the Transverse Mercator projection and Hong Kong 1980 Geodetic Datum. The details of the Hong Kong 1980 grid are:

Reference System:	Hong Kong 1980 Grid System
Projection:	Transverse Mercator
Datum:	Hong Kong 1980
delta WGS84:	162.619 -276.959 -161.764
Ellipsoid:	International 1924
Major s-ax:	6378388 meters
Minor s-ax:	6356911.946 meters
Origin long:	114.17855 degrees
Origin Lat:	22.3121333 degrees
Origin X (False easting):	836694.05 meters
Origin Y (False northing):	819069.8 meters
Scale factor:	1.00
Units:	meters
Parameters:	0

We will use the IDRISI text editor to modify an existing *reference system parameter file* to create the Hong Kong 1980 grid file.

Modifying a *Reference System Parameter File*

Menu Location: **Data Entry – Edit**

1. Use the main menu or icon bar to open the *IDRISI TEXT EDITOR* window.

2. In the *IDRISI TEXT EDITOR* window, use the menu to select *File - Open…*

3. The *OPEN FILE* window will open.

4. Browse to the main IDRISI program directory (for example, *C:\Program Files\IDRISI Taiga,* or possibly *C:\IDRISI Taiga*).   Within the *IDRISI Taiga* folder, double click on the G*eoref* subfolder, to list the files within that directory.

5. Select the *LATLONG.REF* file.

6. Click on *OPEN.*

7. In the *IDRISI TEXT EDITOR* window, use the menu to select *File – Save as…*

8. Once again navigate to the *IDRISI Taiga\georef* folder, and then in the *File name* text box enter **HK80**.

9. Use the information provided about the Hong Kong Grid to change the details of the file to the new projection. Use the original file to guide you as to the appropriate format. For example, observe that the *major s-ax and minor s-ax* fields do not include the designation of the units (meters), only the number. The units are specified later in the file.

10. When you are done, use the *IDRISI TEXT EDITOR* menu to select *File – Save.*

Now that the new projection file has been developed, the procedure to apply the Hong Kong 1980 projection in a REPROJECT operation will be very similar to what we did before in the previous section (Section 3.2.2) using the IDRISI-supplied projection.   Therefore, the instructions will be slightly briefer in this section, as it is assumed that you are familiar with the module steps.

Applying a user-specified projection

Menu Location: **Reformat - PROJECT**

1. Use the main menu to start the PROJECT module.

2. In the *PROJECT* dialog box, use the radio button to specify that the *Type of file to be transformed* is *raster.*

3. Click on the browse button (…) next to the text box for specifying the *Input file name*, and select the **etm1** file from the *Pick list* window.

4. Click on *OK* to close the *Pick list.*

5. Enter a new name for the transformed file in the *Output file name* text box: **etm1_hk80**.

6. Specify the *Reference file for output result* by clicking on the browse button (…) next to the text box. In the resulting *Pick list* window, double click on *IDRISI Taiga/Georef* to see the files in that folder.

7. Scroll down list and select **HK80**.

8. Click the *OK* button to return to the *PROJECT* dialog box.

9. Note that the *PROJECT* dialog box *OK* button is grayed out. IDRISI forces us to check the output parameters. Therefore, click on the button for *Output reference information*.

10. The *Reference Parameters* dialog box will open. Click on *OK* in this dialog box to close it.

11. The *PROJECT* dialog box *OK* button will now be enabled. Click on the button to start the resampling operation.

The final image is now projected with the coordinates consistent with topographic maps published by the government of Hong Kong. When done processing, IDRISI will automatically display the image with a color palette applied. The image should look very similar to the image created with the geographic projection (Figure 3.2.2.c).

See if you can, on your own, create a map display, as we did for the geographic coordinate projection (Figure 3.2.2.d). You can follow the instructions at the end of Section 3.2.2 for creating the map, if you need to be reminded of the steps. However, because this map has a different projection, in the *Map Grid* pane, you will need to choose values of **20000** for the *Increment X* and *Increment Y*, with **0** decimal places. Also, in the Scale Bar pane, you will need to choose **20000** for the *Length (in Ground Units)* parameter. Don't forget to save your map composition when you are done, through the *Save* button on the *Composer* window. The end results should look something like Figure 3.2.3.a.

Hong Kong Landsat HK80 Projection Map

Figure 3.2.3.a   Hong Kong Landsat image map using Hong Kong 1980 national grid projection.

3.2.4   Resample - Transformations with control points

So far we have studied the reprojecting of an image based on the mathematical formulae of the projections themselves, using the PROJECT module. Reprojecting implies the image is already on a map projection, and that we would like to change that projection. However, in many cases the original image is not projected on a formal map projection, but is simply organized based on the view of the sensor at the time of acquisition.

Sometimes, even if the image is already on a projection, we may find that the georeferencing was only approximate, and we need to do a more precise registration of the image. For example, when we do change detection analysis in Chapter 7, in which we will identify and map changes on the landscape, it is essential that we have a very precise co-registration between two images. Likewise, when we mosaic two images, it is very important that the images match well, so there is no obvious misregistration at the join between the two images.

In the circumstances described above, we need to develop an empirical georeferencing, where we calculate our own formula for the relationship for the transformation from the original image orientation to the map projection. In IDRISI, this is done with the RESAMPLE module.

RESAMPLE performs a matrix transformation on a raster file using an equation determined by a series of user-defined **ground control points**. These ground control points are points on both images that correspond to identical ground features. The feature could be a road intersection, or a bridge, or a natural feature like a stream confluence. The amount of error of the transformation can then be regulated by the accurate placement of control points, as well as the order of the polynomial equations.

Using these control points, a set of polynomial equations is developed to describe the transformation of data from its original (input) grid to a new (output) one. Often this is accomplished using least-squares fit to a polynomial of the form:

$$X = a_0 + a_1x' + a_2y' + a_3x'y' + a_4x'^2 + a_5y'^2 \ldots + \varepsilon_x$$

$$Y = b_0 + b_1x' + b_2y' + b_3x'y' + b_4x'^2 + b_5y'^2 \ldots + \varepsilon_y$$

where ε_x and ε_y are residual errors after the transformation. IDRISI includes the option of using the linear, quadratic or cubic mapping functions (the first, second and third orders of the polynomial equation).

The simplest transformation is a static shift of the coordinate system and would only involve the first terms from the equations above (a_0 and b_0). A simple linear transformation would include rotating and shifting the image (the next two terms of the equations, a_2 and b_2) and the second and third order terms of the equations would account for nonlinear transformations that would correct skew, roll, keystone effects, etc. Note that a least-squares polynomial fit cannot and does not correct for parallax caused by topography. To correct for parallax, a process called orthorectification is required, a capability not currently available in IDRISI.

One characteristic of the RESAMPLE operation is that the program does not automatically calculate the output boundaries, reference system or the unit distance of the output image. It is very important for the user to know the minimum and maximum X and Y coordinates of the final output image as well as the number of columns and rows that will span that region. Note that the span of the X and Y coordinates and the number of columns and rows define the resolution of the output image. You are free to set any resolution you desire, however, in most cases it is preferable to maintain the original resolution of the data. Fortunately, one can also copy the reference parameters from an existing file, just as we did in the PROJECT module.

Now that we have some background in the georeferencing of images of an unknown projection, we will apply the IDRISI RESAMPLE procedure to the Hong Kong Landsat ETM+ images. As we have seen already, these images were provided by the vendor in two different projections; the images of path 121 are referenced to UTM 50 and the path 122 images are referenced to UTM 49. We will use the RESAMPLE module to provide an accurate transformation of the *etm_p121r44-45_b3* image to the UTM-49n projection. Although we could also use the PROJECT module in this case, because the images are already on a projection, the RESAMPLE approach is perhaps the best choice because the georeferencing was not a precision correction, but only an approximate correction. Thus, PROJECT will not be able to align the images from two different satellite orbit paths with the accuracy we would like.

Before we begin, we need to set the display minimum and maximum DN values in the metadata of the images we will use, so that the images are optimally stretched in the display process. If this preparatory step is confusing, you may need to review Section 2.2.3.

Specify metada values for an optimal display stretch
Menu location: **File – IDRISI EXPLORER**

1. Open the *IDRISI EXPLORER* window using the main menu or icon bar.

2. In the *IDRISI EXPLORER* window, select the *Files* tab.

3. If the files are not listed in the *Files* pane, double click on the directory name to display the files.

4. In the *Files* pane, click on the *etm_p121r44-45_b3.rst* image.

5. In the *Metadata* pane below the file listing, drag the slider down until the categories of *Display min* and *Display max* are visible.

6. Type **18** in the text box to the right of *Display min* field.

7. Type **100** in the text box to the right of *Display max* field.

8. Click on the *Save* icon (the floppy disk icon) in the bottom left hand corner of the *Metadata* pane.

9. In the *Files* pane, click on the *etm_p122r44-45_b3.rst* image.

10. In the *Metadata* pane, once again drag the slider down until the categories of *Display min* and *Display max* are visible.

11. Type **10** in the text box to the right of *Display min* field.

12. Type **120** in the text box to the right of *Display max* field.

13. Click on the *Save* icon (the floppy disk icon) in the bottom left hand corner of the *Metadata* pane.

14. Close the *IDRISI EXPLORER* by clicking on the red *X* at the top right of the window.

In the instructions above, we have specified optimal display minimum and maximum values to save time. Be aware, however, that normally you would identify the appropriate values by first running the HISTO program to get approximate values, and then selecting values by interactively modifying the values in the *Layer Properties* window, which in turn is accessed through the *Composer* Window.

Georeferencing using RESAMPLE
Menu Location: Image Processing – Restoration – RESAMPLE
1. Use the menu to start the RESAMPLE program. 2. The *RESAMPLE* window will open (Figure 3.2.4.a).

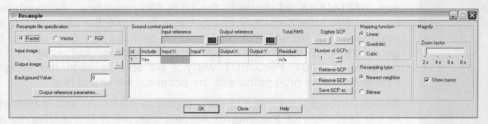

Figure 3.2.4.a The *RESAMPLE* window.

Let's take a moment and examine the *RESAMPLE* window. The window comprises five major sections:

- The *Resample file specification* section defines the input and output file names, as well as the output bounds and resolution.
- The *Ground control points* section allows an interactive designation of the control points by providing displays of the reference image and the image to be transformed.
- *Mapping function* determines the type of equations used in the transformation.
- *Resampling type* gives the option of a bilinear resampling, which involves a smoothing of the data during the transformation, or nearest neighbor resampling, which retains the spectral integrity of the original pixels.
- The *Magnify* section specifies the amount of zoom for the displayed images.

Let's now fill in the *Resample file specification* section.

Georeferencing using RESAMPLE (cont.): *Resample file specification*
3. In the *Resample file specification* section of the RESAMPLE window, click on the browse button (…) to right of *Input Image* text box. 4. From the *Pick list*, select ***etm_p121r44-45_b3***, which you created in Section 3.1 from the two original ETM+ path 121 images. 5. Click *OK* to close the *Pick list*. 6. In the *Output Image* text box enter **etm_p121r44-45_b3_UTM49**. 7. Accept the default value of *0* to use as the *Background Value*. 8. Click on the button for *Output reference parameters...* 9. In the *Reference Parameters* dialog box, click in the check box for *Copy from existing file*.

10. Click on the browse button (…) to the right of the text box for *Copy from existing file.*

11. Select file **etm_p122r44-45_b3** from the *Pick list* window, and then click on the *OK* button to close the *Pick list.*

12. Note that the fields in the *Reference Parameters* window were populated with information obtained from the **etm_p122r44-45_b3** metadata file (Figure 3.2.4.b).

Figure 3.2.4.b   The Reference parameters window with parameters specified from an existing file.

The transformed path 121 image generated by the RESAMPLE program will have the same projection, bounds and resolution as the path 122 image. This will facilitate mosaicking the path 121 and 122 images.

We will now begin to choose our ground control points (GCPs). The GCPs are important because they are used to determine the polynomial equation developed by RESAMPLE and subsequently used in the transformation. The geographic coordinates of the GCPs may be determined by using a GPS system at the locations themselves (hence the name "ground control points"), or by locating the exact same feature in second raster file that has a known and accurate geographic reference system.

For our Hong Kong example, we will use the latter option, that of obtaining the location from another image, in this case the satellite image from the adjacent path. This may seem a bit surprising, since we earlier said that we would use RESAMPLE precisely because the georeferencing for these images is only approximate. Therefore, this would seem to contradict the idea that we can use the adjacent path's image for GCPs. However, in this case, our concern is not absolute georeferencing, but rather obtaining a high quality relative georeferencing of the one image to the other, so that they can be mosaicked without an obvious misalignment at the join.

There are two methods for entering the locations of control points in the *RESAMPLE* dialog box: by image matching or by manually keying in the data. With both methods, a correspondence file is created that records the input and output coordinates for each GCP. Ground control points are entered into the grid on the form. Each line of the grid has text boxes for four numbers. The first two text boxes are used to specify the input X and Y coordinates of a point in the input reference system. The last two text boxes are used to specify the coordinates of that same point in the output reference system.

If points are being digitized for both the input and output reference images, after three control points are entered, subsequent output points will be interpolated linearly, and automatically placed on the output reference grid.

To enter GCPs automatically from image map to image we need to display both the input and output reference files.

Georeferencing using RESAMPLE (cont.): Specifying the reference files

13. Close the *Reference Parameters* by clicking on *OK*.

14. Within the RESAMPLE window, click on the DISPLAY LAUNCHER icon to the right of the *Input reference* text box. This will bring up the *DISPLAY LAUNCHER* dialog box.

15. Within the *DISPLAY LAUNCHER*, select the raster layer ***etm_p121r44-45_b3***.

16. Use the radio button to specify the palette file as *GreyScale*.

17. Click on *OK* to display the image.

18. Within the RESAMPLE window, click on the DISPLAY LAUNCHER icon to the right of the *Output reference* text box. This will once again bring up the *DISPLAY LAUNCHER* dialog box.

19. Select the raster layer as ***etm_p122r44-45_b3***, the palette file as *GreySale*, and click on *OK*.

The displayed images are now linked to the RESAMPLE module for automatic input of locations into the record of GCP locations. However, the displays themselves are not linked to one another, so take care in zooming to create similar zoomed displays.

A potentially useful feature in the RESAMPLE window is the ability to display a zoom window that magnifies the location of your cursor within the main image display. The *Magnify* window gives a detailed view of a portion of the main display, to help locate your control point more precisely. It is very important that each control point be located within one pixel of the correct location, and so the *Magnify* window is very important for obtaining a satisfactory transformation.

We will now modify the zoom window to aid us in placing our ground control points.

Georeferencing using RESAMPLE (cont.): Using the *Magnifier* window

20. In the *Magnify* section of the *RESAMPLE* window, move the *Zoom factor* slider to *4x*.

21. Uncheck the *Show cursor* check box, as we will want a clear view in the zoom window, without the cursor present.

22. Move your cursor over one of the two main displayed images and observe how the *Magnify* display works in creating a zoomed view in the *RESAMPLE* window (Figure 3.2.4.c).

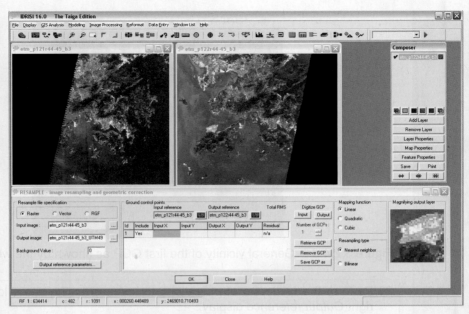

Figure 3.2.4.c   The *RESAMPLE* window, including the *Magnifier* display.

The *Magnifier* magnifies what is displayed in the *DISPLAY VIEWER*, and does not return to the original image to show the full resolution of the data set. Thus, if the image in the *DISPLAY VIEWER* is not at full resolution, then the image in the Magnifier will also not be at full resolution. This is because your screen monitor has a limited resolution, and cannot display the entire image at full resolution. Instead, the DISPLAY VIEWER automatically shows a reduced resolution image, in order to fit the image on the screen. Only by showing a subset of the image, can we see the image at full resolution, as we will see in the next few steps.

Once we have all the displays as we want, let's begin placing GCPs using the *Digitize GCP* option in the top right corner of the *Ground Control Points* section of the *RESAMPLE* window.

Georeferencing using RESAMPLE (cont.): Identifying the first GCP

23. Make the *Input reference* display window (i.e. the left display window showing **etm_p121r44-45_b3**) the focus window by clicking in or on the borders of the window. This will make the window frame a different color, and bring it to the front of any other windows with which it may overlap.

24. We will now need to select an area for the first GCP. Specifically, we'd like a feature that is found on both images, and has a very distinctive shape so we can identify a location down to the specific pixel.

25. Click on the *Zoom Window* icon in the main tool bar.

26. Move cursor into the *Input reference* display.

27. Click the left mouse button, and keeping the button depressed, draw a box around the general vicinity of the first GCP. (Figure 3.2.4.d highlights the region we will select, which is an island in the bay. Make sure you can find the island on both displays, *input* and *output*, before you start zooming in.)

28. If necessary, you can refine the area that you have zoomed in on by repeatedly using the *Zoom Window* icon, or using the Zoom window icon in conjunction with the *Zoom in / Center* and *Zoom out / Center* tools.

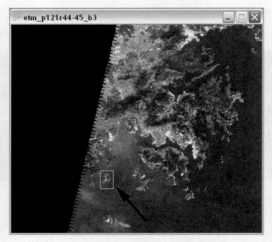

Figure 3.2.4.d   General vicinity of the first GCP as shown by the white box.

29. Perform the same set of operations to zoom in to the same location in the right *Output reference* display.

30. In the *RESAMPLE* window, in the *Ground Control Points* section, and near the words *Digitize GCP*, find the *Input* button, and click on it. A GCP will be appear, located in the center of the *input reference* image, with a numeric identifier (*1*, for this first GCP).

31. Move the GCP to an identifiable location you can find in both displays by selecting the GCP with the cursor and dragging it to the feature. The edge of the breakwater makes a good choice for such a feature.

32. In the *RESAMPLE* window, click on the (Digitize GCP) *Output* button. A GCP with the same numeric identifier as before (1, for this first GCP) will appear in the center of the *output reference* image.

33. Move the GCP to the location of the same feature identified in the *input* display window (Figure 3.2.4.e).

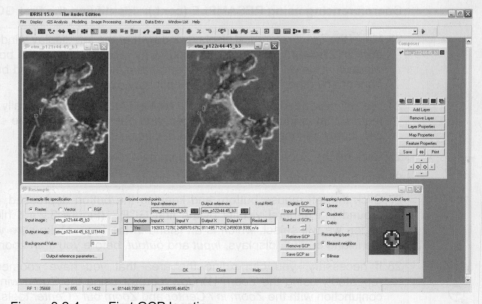

Figure 3.2.4.e   First GCP location.

Note that the RESAMPLE window now has the coordinates of the first GCP recorded on the first line of the *Ground Control Points* form (Figure 3.2.4.e).

Now that we have mastered the capability to locate ground control points, we should pick at least six additional points. By picking at least seven GCPs, we will have a number of redundant points, so that we can get a reasonable estimate of the error in the transformation. If we were using a higher order transformation we would need even more points.

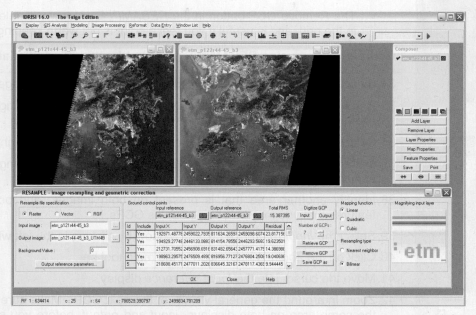

Figure 3.2.4.f   GCPs and RMS error in the *RESAMPLE* window and displays.

Here are some suggestions you should consider as you choose your GCPs:

- You should aim to have the seven GCPs as well-distributed around the images as possible (Figure 3.2.4.f). Thus, in general, try to select each new GCP some distance from the previous GCPs.

- In picking GCPs make sure that you are not confusing boat wakes or other temporary features with permanent features that are likely to be present in both images.

- It can be quite difficult to find suitable objects, so you may want to zoom in slowly, first looking at a general region, and then zooming in a second, and even possibly a third time.

- The best objects to use are road intersections, or other linear objects. Do not use indeterminate objects, for example, the center of an island, unless that island is only 1-2 pixels in size.

- Once three GCPs have been selected, a linear solution is calculated and the total root mean squared error (RMS), and residual error for each point within the GCP table, are all displayed as zero. The next time you pick a GCP in the *input* display, the position of the GCP in the *reference* image is estimated automatically for you. **It is very, very important that you do not simply accept this estimated location.** You must check the location very carefully, and in general you probably will find you need to move the GCP slightly. If you do not conscientiously move the automatically selected points, you will end up with a completely false estimate of the error in your transformation.

- The RMS is an estimate of the average error of the points you have selected. It is important to realize it is only an estimate based on the points you have selected, and not for every pixel in the image. This again emphasizes the importance of a well-distributed set of GCPs so that your estimate of error is representative of most of the image.

- The *Remove GCP* button in the *RESAMPLE* window will delete entire row in the grid, and is useful if you feel a point is not worth keeping.

Georeferencing using RESAMPLE (cont.): Identifying additional GCPs

34. Select *Input reference* display window by clicking in the left image.

35. Return the image to its original zoom and extents by clicking on the *Full extent normal* icon on the main menu bar.

36. Select the *Output reference* display window by clicking in the right image.

37. Return the image to its original zoom and extents by clicking on the *Full extent normal* icon on the main menu bar.

38. Identify another area that is present on both images, and potentially has features that you may be able to use as GCPs.

39. Select the *Input reference* display window by clicking in the left window.

40. Click on the *Zoom Window* icon in the main tool bar.

41. Move the cursor into the *Input reference* display.

42. Zoom in around the general vicinity of the next GCP. Make sure you can find the same area on both displays, *input* and *output*, before you start zooming in.

43. Click on the *Input* button in the Ground Control Points section and a GCP will be located in the center of the input reference image with a numeric identifier.

44. Move the GCP to an identifiable location observed in both displays by selecting it with the cursor and dragging it to a feature that you can identify in both images.

45. Click on the digitize *Output* button. A GCP with the same numeric identifier as that of the *Input reference* image will appear in the center of the *Output reference* image.

46. Move the GCP to the location of the same feature identified in the *Input Reference* display window.

47. Pick at least seven GCPs in total (Figure 3.2.4.f).

Your aim should be for an RMS of less than one half the resolution of the input image. For the Hong Kong image, we have 30 meter pixels, and therefore our aim is for an RMS of 15 or less. If you have an error of 30 or more it means that on average your image registration is one pixel off. We suggest that in this exercise if you error is more than 30 meters, you should review all the GCPs.

One solution to a high RMS is to discard the GCPs that have the highest residuals. These points lie furthest away from the average transformation calculated for the images. You can omit any GCP by changing the *Include* option in the *RESAMPLE* window from *Yes* to *No*. This is done by simply clicking in the appropriate cell from the *Include* column, and using the drop down menu to select *No*. Note that once you change the *Include* attribute of a GCP, the RMS and residuals are automatically recalculated.

It is important, however, that the ground control points cover the image area evenly to control the error. If one were not to pick any control points in an area of the image, the transformation of the image in that area could result in large error even though the overall RMS is within an acceptable range. Therefore, if you have to exclude more than one GCP, or if after excluding even one GCP you find that your points are not longer well-distributed across the image, you should probably add one or more points.

The GCP list can be modified, saved and retrieved. You can save your GCPs at any time using the *Save GCP* button. This will save the GCPs to an IDRISI correspondence file (.cor), which can be retrieved at a later time. Use the *Retrieve GCP* button to retrieve saved GCPs. Let's save our GCPs now in case we wish to use them again.

Georeferencing using RESAMPLE (cont.): Saving GCPs

48. In the *RESAMPLE* window, click on *Save GCP as.*

49. Type in file name as **Hong_Kong_GCP**. (IDRISI will automatically add the .cor extension.)

50. Click on *Save*.

Once you are satisfied with the GCP list and the resulting RMS error, the resample process can be performed. Before performing the resample, however, the last criteria needed are the mapping function and the resampling type to perform on the input files. The mapping function is simply the order of polynomial fit desired: linear (first order), quadratic (second order), or cubic (third order). A lower order of polynomial often provides a reasonable solution since the error associated with poor control point designation increases as the order of equation increases. Since we are simply transforming from adjacent UTM zones in this case, the first order (linear) mapping function is adequate.

The new pixel locations in the geographically referenced grid as determined by the polynomial equations may not align exactly with any existing pixel centers in the original data grid. IDRISI offers two procedures to determine the new pixel location's digital number value, nearest neighbor and bilinear resampling. In a nearest neighbor interpolation, the value of the closest input cell to the position of the output cell is conveyed. In the case of a bilinear interpolation, a linear distance-weighted average of the four closest cells is used. Since we have no need to smooth the data, the nearest neighbor can be chosen.

The reference unit is simply the unit of measure used in the reference coordinate system (e.g., meters). The unit distance refers to the actual ground distance spanned by one reference unit. The unit distance will be 1.0 in most cases. One exception would be the case of a latitude-longitude reference system where the unit distance could be in fractions of a degree.

RESAMPLE (cont.): Running the program

51. Accept the default *Mapping function* of *Linear*.

52. Use the default *Resampling function* of *Nearest Neighbor*.

53. Click on *OK* in the bottom of the RESAMPLE window. This will begin the resample process and the resulting image will be displayed in a new window.

The new path 121 image is displayed automatically with the same bounds, resolution, and projection of the path 122 image. Note that the automatic display uses the default color palette, and therefore will not look quite the same as the Input reference image. This is easily corrected, using the method of changing palette files that we have already experimented with earlier. You are probably quite familiar with the method now, but for completeness sake, we repeat it here.

Change display properties of an image

1. In the *Composer* window, select the button for *Layer Properties*.

2. In the *Layer Properties* window, click on the button for *Advanced Palette/Symbol Selection*.

3. This will open the *Advanced Palette/Symbol Selection* window. In this new window, click on the browse button (…) next to the *Current selection* text box.

4. In the file *Pick list*, click on the *IDRISI Taiga/Symbols* folder, and scroll down to **greyscale**. Click on *OK* in the Pick list, and in the *Palette/Symbol Selection* window.

5. Note that you also need to adjust the display minimum and maximum values in the *Layer Properties* window. Use the values we chose at the start of this section: **18** and **100**.

Now that the two images for paths 121 and 122 are on the same projection, we will join them to create a single mosaic image of Hong Kong in the next section.

3.3 Mosaicking Images

3.3.1 Background

So far we have focused on the geometric challenges of joining images. However, there is an added problem when it comes to joining images. Images acquired at different times typically have different radiometric properties. This means that the DN values for a particular area in one image are not identical to those in another image of the same area. Among the many reasons for this variation in radiometric properties between images are illumination variation due to changes in sun angle as a consequence of the time of day or season, changing atmospheric properties, especially water vapor and pollutants, and sensor differences.

Joining images of dissimilar radiometric properties is a major challenge in image processing. Generally, the goal in mosaicking is to blend adjacent images in an effort to make the join appear seamless. The balancing of the radiometric properties between imagery can be a highly subjective process based on human perception of what a person believes looks "good."

The mosaicking process is relatively effective in areas of sparse development and low terrain relief. However, we should be aware that sometimes there are real differences between images that are not an artifact of the image acquisition. Thus, for example there may be vegetation differences due to seasonal or climate variations, variation in the presence of snow on the ground, changes in the landscape due to fires, agriculture or urbanization, and even differences due to the presence of clouds. Generally, there is very little hope for removing such image differences.

Numerous methods have been developed to make the image join less discernable, for example by blending the overlapping regions, matching the histogram of the images, or using a nonlinear cut line. One approach is to blend the DN values across a join region, rather a sharp line. If a blend region is used, one could average the DN values of the two input images. Alternatively, a feathering could be used, which is a special case of the averaging method. With feathering, the new DN value is a weighted average, where the weights are a function of the distance across the join. Thus the overlap region becomes a progressive blending of the one image into the other.

3.3.2 Mosaicking the Hong Kong data

We did not run into this problem of radiometric matching between images in our concatenation exercise (Section 3.1.2) because when we joined the images that were along the same satellite paths, there was essentially no difference in time, atmospheric conditions or sensor properties between them. However, we have not yet joined the images from the different paths, specifically paths 121 and 122. Since the paths were imaged on different days, we should expect there to be radiometric differences between the images.

In IDRISI, the MOSAIC module creates a new image by spatially orienting overlapping images and balancing the overlap regions by numerically averaging the individual pixels in the overlap region. We will use MOSAIC to join the two path images for Hong Kong. If you have not already done the exercises in Sections 3.1, you will need to do them now, in order to generate the files needed for this section.

MOSAIC
Menu Location: **Image Processing – Restoration – Mosaic**
1. Use the main menu bar to start the MOSAIC program. 2. The *MOSAIC* dialog box will open. In the *Images to be processed* section of the dialog box, click in the first text box below *Filenames*, to bring up the browse button (…). 3. Click on the browse button. 4. Select the path image generated using the RESAMPLE program, ***etm_p121r44-45_b3_utm49***. 5. Click *OK*. 6. Click in the second text box below *Filenames,* to bring up the browse button (…). 7. Click on the browse button. 8. Select the path image, ***etm_p122r44-45_b3***. 9. Click *OK*.

Note that the module allows for different background values to be selected. The *Output background value* is the DN value the program will assign to pixels that lie outside the bounds of the two images we are joining. A DN of 0 is the default, and the most common background value used. The *Default input background value* is the DN value which will be regarded as not part of the input images. This is a very important option, because our images have large blank areas, which we expressly do not want the MOSAIC program to regard as part of the data to be used in the mosaicking process.

The *MOSAIC* dialog box has as a default procedure for the radiometric matching between the images. If this option is deselected, then the MOSAIC module operates much like the CONCAT module in that no radiometric adjustment is applied.

There are two options for determining the output pixel DN values in the overlap region: *Cover* and *Average*. We will test both options to see which works best for us in this case.

MOSAIC (cont.): *Cover* option for *Overlap Method*
11. Type **HK_b3_mosaic_cover** in the *Output mosaicked image* text box.
12. Leave remaining options at their default settings (Figure 3.3.2.a).
13. Click *OK* to run MOSAIC.

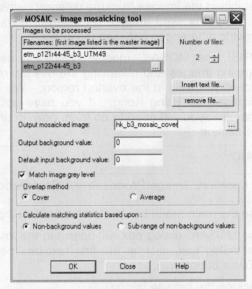

Figure 3.3.2.a   *MOSAIC* dialog box with initial parameter selection.

The image is automatically displayed after the processing is complete. In this case, the mosaic has a GreyScale palette applied, which is appropriate for the data. However, remember to adjust the contrast stretch values. In the *Composer* window, click on the *Layer Properties* button, and in the *Layer Properties* window, set the *Display min* and *Display max* to **18** and **100**, respectively. Figure 3.3.2.b shows the image after the contrast stretch has been applied.

The first thing that is obvious upon examining the output image is that there is a sharp line at the boundary between the two images. However, this line is only evident in the water part of the image. For the land part of the image, the two images appear to be well balanced and almost seamlessly joined. This suggests that the image differences in the sea portion of the mosaic represent a real difference in water quality between the two images. For example, the amount of sediment in the ocean might be different between the two dates.

Figure 3.3.2.b   Hong Kong Landsat mosaic.

This difference between the two images in the sea portion of the mosaic could possibly be minimized by further processing or more involved mosaicking procedures not available in IDRISI. However, it is doubtful that these differences could totally be overcome.

Overall, one could be satisfied with this mosaic. However, let's try the *Average* cover option for the overlap region to see if it yields any improvement.

MOSAIC (cont.): *Average* option for *Overlap Method*
14. Because of IDRISI's persistent windows, the MOSAIC window should still be open in your IDRISI workspace.
15. Type **HK_b3_mosaic_average** in the *Output mosaicked image* text box.
16. Change the *Overlap method* to *Average*, by clicking on the radio button.
17. Leave remaining parameters as before.
18. Click on *OK* to run MOSAIC.

Once the program has finished processing the image, don't forget to change the display min and display max to **18** and **100** in the *Layer Properties* dialog box.

The resulting image (Figure 3.3.2.c) has perhaps a less noticeable join in the water part of the image. However, there is a striking diagonal pattern across the left side of the image.   This artifact is due to the characteristics of the preprocessing of the original data. The edge effects on the left side of the path 121 image are due to the jagged scene edges and shutter intrusion at the end of each scan. The jagged edges have non-zero data and thus are not ignored in the average option, unlike the background areas.

Figure 3.3.2.c   Hong Kong Landsat mosaic using "average" option.

Thus, while the *Average* option did indeed help create a smoother join in the water areas, averaging changes the actual radiometric values of the images and may cause difficulties in classifying the imagery later.

3.4 Exporting Images

At the start of this chapter (Section 3.1) we saw that IDRISI could be used to import images into IDRISI. IDRISI also supports the exporting of data and composite imagery into many formats. The main bar menu divides these formats into three group, each with their own submenu.

- **General Conversion Tools** are utilities for converting image DN values into text files of various formats.

- **Desktop Publishing Formats** are modules for exporting raster data, and include GeoTIFF as well as JPEG and BMP formats. The Desktop Publishing Formats work well with the composite images created in IDRISI.

- **The Software-Specific Formats** are modules that export the IDRISI format to those of other remote sensing and GIS programs. This group of programs generally works best for single band data, rather than the composite images.

We will now try an export of our newly created Hong Kong mosaic file to a GeoTIFF format, using one of the modules in the Desktop Publishing Formats category.

EXPORT
Menu Location: **File – Export – Desktop Publishing Formats – GEOTIFF/TIFF**
1. Use the main menu to start the GEOTIFF/TIFF module. 2. The *GEOTIFF/TIFF* dialog box will open.

3. Select the radio button for the *Idrisi to GeoTIFF/Tiff* option.

4. Click the browse button (…) next to the *Idrisi file name* text box.

5. Select **hk_b3_mosaic** and click *OK*.

6. Note that IDRISI automatically inserts the same name in the output GeoTIFF file to create text book. Because the output file will have a **.tif** extension, there will be no confusion between the IDRISI format file and the TIFF format file. However, if you wish to change the name of the output file, you can do so at this time.

7. Click the browse button (…) next to the *Palette to export with image* text box.

8. Select the *\Idrisi Taiga\Symbols* folder (the folder name will include the full path, the specifics of which will depend on your IDRISI installation) .

9. Scroll down till you see, and can select, the file **greyscale**.

10. Click *OK*.

11. Review in the parameters for the dialog box to see they are all correctly specified (Figure 3.4.a).

12. Click on *OK* in *GeoTIFF/TIFF* window to start the export routine.

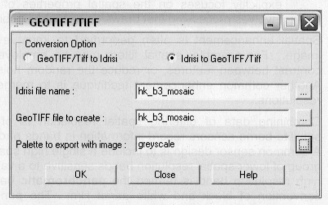

Figure 3.4.a   The *GEOTIFF/TIFF* dialog box.

The file is exported when the lower left pane in the main window is clear. The file has now been exported successfully and you can easily read it into any image display software or word processing software.

To end this chapter, close all DISPLAY windows and dialog boxes.

Chapter 4   Enhancing Images Spatially

This chapter, as well as the subsequent two chapters, deals with the enhancement of images. The term enhancement is used in remote sensing to imply image processing to make patterns in the data stand out more clearly. Contrast enhancement, which we already covered in Section 2.2.3, and which manipulates the look up table used for image display, is a good example of a basic enhancement technique.

In this manual, we separate enhancement techniques into two categories: spectral and spatial.

- **Spectral enhancement** is covered in Chapters 5 and 6, and involves various mathematical combinations of image bands, usually with each pixel treated independently of its neighbors.

- **Spatial enhancement**, the topic for this chapter, includes processing that explicitly focuses on the spatial properties of an image, and typically involves processing that draws on a local neighborhood of pixels.

Spatial enhancement is often performed to improve the visual quality of an image. For example, spatial filters may be employed to either increase the contrast between features, or reduce the random noise inherent in the image. Another common enhancement technique is to merge data of differing spatial resolutions.

Combining data of differing spatial resolution is of interest because many satellite-borne sensors record information in bands of different spatial resolution. A common sensor design is to include a single high spatial resolution band and a group of lower spatial resolution bands sensitive to a variety of wavelengths. The high resolution band is termed the **panchromatic** band, following the naming convention of black and white aerial film. The panchromatic band provides detailed spatial information. The lower resolution bands are termed the **multispectral** bands, and they provide the spectral information, or, by analogy, the color information. The aim in a multi-spatial resolution merge is to combine the spatial information from the panchromatic band with the spectral information from the multispectral bands, to obtain a multi-band, high resolution image.

In this chapter we will examine the ways we can spatially enhance the Hong Kong Landsat image. We will initially develop a so-called high-pass filter that enhances spatial features in a single band image. We will then merge the high-resolution panchromatic band with a combination of multispectral bands to form a multi-resolution product.

4.1 Convolution

A convolution filter is a local image processing operation, which involves the use of moving windows. A **window** is a local group of pixels, for example, one pixel and its eight immediate neighbors (Figure 4.1.a), and is by definition a subset of the image. Windows can be of any size; Figure 4.1.a shows an example of a 3x3 window, with three rows and three columns of pixels. An important part of the concept of the moving window is that the template that defines the local neighborhood can be moved sequentially across the image, so that each pixel is the center of a local group of pixels. Pixels from the edge of the image require special handling, as they do not have neighbors on all sides.

b	b	b
b	a	b
b	b	b

Figure 4.1.a   A 3 x 3 window of pixels (a = center pixel, b = neighbors).

In convolution, some mathematical operation is used to combine the DN values in the window. The result of this local analysis is written to a new image, the convolution image. Specifically, the convolution value is usually written out to the new image at the pixel location equivalent to the center of the window as it was placed over the old image. The precise nature of the mathematical combination performed in the convolution operation is controlled by the relative values stored in the **matrix kernel**. Specifically, the convolution output value is the sum of the products of each pixel value and its corresponding kernel value. Then the matrix is moved by one pixel location, and the operation is repeated. The filter operation can be **normalized** by dividing the result by the sum of the kernel values.

4.1.1 Smoothing Filters

Noise suppression and/or removal can be accomplished with convolution filtering. The simplest type of smoothing filter is the **low pass filter**, also known as a **mean** filter, which simply adds all the pixel values in the matrix kernel and divides the sum by the matrix size (or number of pixels used in the summation). In this particular case, the matrix kernel has a value of 1/9 in each kernel location (Figure 4.1.1.a), since no pixel is given a greater weighting than another. Note that there is no significant difference between a 3 x 3 kernel with values of 1/9 in each location, and one with values of 1 in each location, except that the former would have DNs that were on average nine times that of the original image. It is for this reason the normalization of the filter is often applied to ensure the output image has a similar radiometric range to the input image.

1/9	1/9	1/9
1/9	1/9	1/9
1/9	1/9	1/9

Figure 4.1.1.a.   A kernel for a smoothing filter.

IDRISI offers a wide variety of filters in the FILTER module. For example, the *Gaussian* filter is a more sophisticated smoothing filter than the simple uniform averaging of the type illustrated in Figure 4.1.1.a. The *Gaussian* filter fits a

Gaussian or bell curve to the kernel. The Gaussian filter thus gives the greatest weight to the value at the center of the kernel, and the pixels further out from the center are given a progressively lower weighting. Another filter offered, the *median* filter, can be useful for noise suppression, as is the *adaptive box* filter, which is good for correcting "salt-and-pepper" random noise.

We are now ready to investigate our first filter operation. The data for this chapter is the same as we used for Chapters 1-3. Therefore, if you have been working through the manual sequentially, there is no preparatory work you need to do, as the data should already be available, and the resource folder set up. If not, you will need to follow the instructions in Chapter 1 to copy the data from the CD, and set up a resource folder (see Section 1.3). You will also need to set the *Display Min* and *Display Max* in the **etm_pan.rst** metadata, as was described in Section 2.2.3.

Let's begin by displaying the Hong Kong Landsat panchromatic data, **etm_pan**. If you need to, you can refer back to Section 2.2.2 to refresh your memory on how to display an image. However, be sure to display this image with a *GreyScale* palette. If, after you have displayed the file, the image has a color palette, then you forgot to set the palette file correctly, and you should simply redisplay the image with the correct *GreyScale* palette.

We will use the display of the **etm_pan** image to compare with our results from filtered version of the image, generated through the FILTER module.

Low pass filter
Menu Location: **Image Processing – Enhancement - FILTER**
1. Use the main menu bar to start the FILTER module. 2. The *FILTER* dialog box will open (Figure 4.1.1.b).

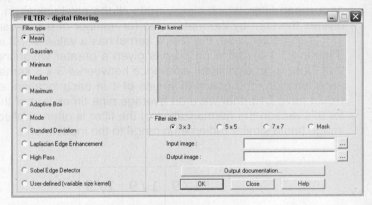

Figure 4.1.1.b   The *FILTER* dialog box.

The *FILTER* dialog box shows a list of pre-defined filters on the left, on the upper right a view of the values of the matrix kernel selected (though note that initially no values are shown), and in the middle radio buttons for selecting different kernel sizes.

The default filter is the *Mean* filter. In order to see the kernel values for the *Mean* filter, click on the radio button for *Gaussian*, and then again on the button labeled *Mean*. The values should now appear in the Filter kernel window (Figure 4.1.1.c). The kernel should now be filled with 1/9 values, similar to Figure 4.1.1.a.

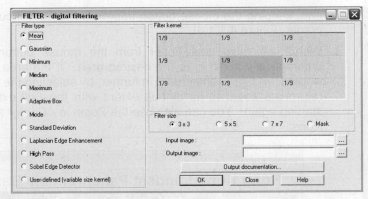

Figure 4.1.1.c   The *FILTER* dialog box with the Mean filter selected.

As already discussed, mean filtering is commonly applied to smooth an image and remove some of the random noise. We will now apply the *Mean* filter to our Hong Kong panchromatic data.

Low pass filter (cont.)

3. In the FILTER dialog box, specify the *Input image* by clicking on the browse button (…) next to the appropriate textbox, and then double clicking on the *etm_pan* file in the *Pick list* window.

4. In the *Output image* text box, type the name of the file we will generate: **pan_mean3x3**.

5. In the *FILTER* dialog box, click on *OK* to generate the filtered image.

When the program is done, the image will be displayed automatically with the appropriate *GreyScale* palette. However, bear in mind that the program does not automatically set a contrast enhancement similar to that of the unfiltered data. You will therefore need to set the contrast enhancement for the new image.

Change contrast enhancement of an image

1. Make sure the new *pan_mean3x3* image is the focus of the IDRISI workspace by clicking in the image.

2. Find the *Composer* window, and select the button for *Layer Properties.*

3. In the *Layer Properties* window, enter in the *Display Min* and *Display Max* text boxes the values for the contrast stretch we used for the *etm_pan* image, namely **18** and **73**.

4. Still in the *Layer Properties* window, click on the buttons for *Apply*, *Save* and *OK*.

Once the contrast stretch has been applied, the original *etm_pan* and the filtered *pan_mean3x3* should look fairly similar. This is in part because of the scale that we are using to look at the data. In order to see the effects of the filter operation, which is a local operation, we need to see the image in greater detail.

Zooming in to an already displayed image

1. Click on the *Zoom* icon from the main icon bar.

2. Draw a box in the *etm_pan* Display window around the Hong Kong airport by using the left mouse button to click on the top left corner of the desired box

and, keeping the mouse button depressed, drag the cursor to the lower right corner (Figure 4.1.1.d).

3. When you raise your finger from the mouse button, the display should automatically zoom in to the desired area. If the area is not quite what you wanted, you can either zoom in further, by selecting the zoom button again, or return the zoom to its default extent with the *Full extent normal* icon, and starting again. You can also use the *Zoom in / Center* and *Zoom out / Center* icons.

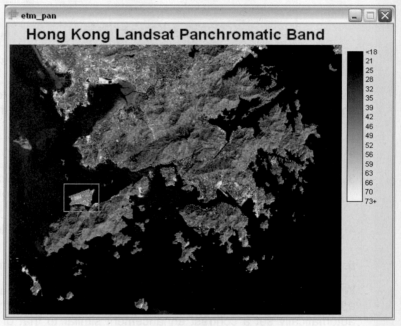

Figure 4.1.1.d   Drawing the zoom box around the Hong Kong airport.

When you are satisfied with the zoomed window for the ***etm_pan*** image (Figure 4.1.1.e), repeat the zoom operation for the filtered ***pan_mean3x3*** image (Figure 4.1.1.f).

Compare the two zoomed in images (Figures 4.1.1.e and 4.1.1.f). Note the *Mean* filter reduces the grainy texture of the original image, thus reducing the internal variability in each cover class. This would be an improvement for image classification (Chapter 6). However, the reduction in variability is not without a cost: the detail of the features found within the airport, particularly associated with the terminal building, is clearly reduced.

4.1.2 High-pass and Edge Filters

Fundamentally, a **high pass** filter is a type of **edge detector** that emphasizes abrupt changes relative to regions of gradual change within the image. Specialized filters available in IDRISI that focus on edge effects include *Laplacian Edge Enhancement* and the *Sobel Edge Detector*.

4.1.2.1 High pass filter

The high pass filter generates an image that indicates where abrupt boundaries are found in an image. Other, non-spatial information, such as the average brightness information, is lost in generating a high pass image. An image with

Hong Kong Landsat Panchromatic Band

Figure 4.1.1.e   Original Panchromatic image of the Hong Kong airport.

3 x 3 Mean filter of etm_pan

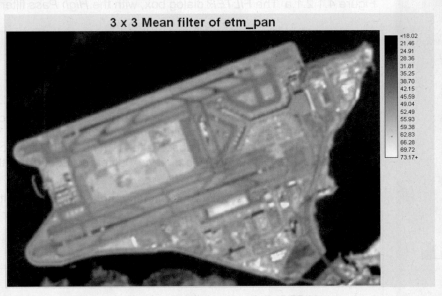

Figure 4.1.1.f   *Mean* filtered Panchromatic image of the Hong Kong airport.

only the boundaries shown can be useful, however, and we will see such an example in Section 4.2, dealing with a multi-resolution merge, below. We will now try this filter, and see what it does to the Landsat Panchromatic image of Hong Kong.

High pass filter

Menu Location: **Image Processing– Enhancement - FILTER**

1. The *FILTER* dialog box should still be open from the Low Pass Filter operation. If not, use the main menu to open the *FILTER* dialog box, and specify the input file as ***etm_pan***.

2. In the *FILTER* dialog box, select the radio button for the *High Pass* filter. (Note that there is a strange quirk in this program. If *High Pass* is the first filter you click on when opening the window it may be necessary to first click on another filter, such as *Gaussian*, in order to see the kernel values.)

After you select the *High Pass* filter, note the values in the matrix kernel (Figure 4.1.2.1.a). You will see that the value of the center pixel is positive while all the other values are negative.   The high pass kernel calculates the difference between the center pixel and the average of its surrounding neighbors.

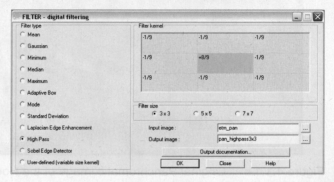

Figure 4.1.2.1.a The *FILTER* dialog box, with the *High Pass* filter selected.

High pass filter (cont.)

3. Type **pan_highpass3x3** in the *Output image* text box.

4. Click on *OK*.

After the program has completed processing, it will automatically display the resultant image. The image should appear almost featureless, with a dominant middle gray image tone. If you observe the legend, you will notice the values are centered on a DN of zero. This is a very different result from that of the *Mean* filtered image.

Let's display the image histogram to understand the filtered results better.

Analyzing the image data distribution with HISTO

Menu Location: **Display - HISTO**

1. Start the HISTO program from the main menu or the toolbar.

2. In the *HISTO* dialog box, click on the browse button (…) next to the text box for the *Input file name*.

3. The *Pick list* window will open, and use it to select ***pan_highpass3x3***.

4. Set the class width to **0.5**.

5. Click on *OK*.

The result of the HISTO program shows that the mean of the filtered image is centered on zero (Figure 4.1.2.1.b). The reason the result of the *High Pass* filter is so different from that of the *Mean* filter can be understood by looking in detail at the values of the filter kernels. Add up the kernel weights in the *Mean* filter and compare the result to the sum of the kernel weights in the *High Pass* filter. The *Mean* filter kernel sum is equal to 1 (9 x 1/9 = 1), whereas the sum of the values in the *High Pass* kernel is equal to 0 (8 x [-1/9] + 8/9 = 0).

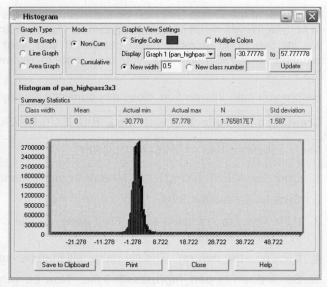

Figure 4.1.2.1.b Histogram of 3x3 *High Pass* filtered Panchromatic image.

The sum of the values in the kernel is essentially a measure of how much information of the original image is retained in the filtered result. The *Mean* filter retains most of the image statistical information – the mean and standard deviation are similar to the original image – but the image is smoothed and boundaries blurred. On the other hand, the *High Pass* filter, with its zero-sum kernel, removes most of the original image brightness information. The *High Pass* has a mean centered on zero, and a narrow standard deviation. Figure 4.1.2.1.b shows that the *High Pass* image has some large outliers (anomalous DN values), and this may partly explain the lack of contrast we observed in the displayed image. Therefore, let's adjust the contrast of the high-pass filtered image so that we can better see what the filter did to the image.

Apply a contrast enhancement to an image

1. Make sure the new *pan_highpass3x3* image is the focus of the IDRISI workspace by clicking in the image.

2. Find the *Composer* window, and select the button for *Layer Properties.*

3. In the *Layer Properties* window, enter in the *Display Max* and *Display Min* text boxes the values of **-7** and **7**, respectively.

4. Click on the buttons for *Apply, Save* and *OK.*

The result should show more contrast, but still appear to be mainly noise. In order to see the details, we need to zoom into a scale where the edges become more apparent. However, we are faced with a challenge – how do we find the airport in this rather featureless image? One way to do this is to carefully note the location of the airport in the *etm_pan* image, and then zoom in on the same general region in the *pan_highpassx3* image. Another more precise method, which we will try in the next section, zooms in on a file using the zoom of a companion image, based on the IDRISI *Group Link* concept.

4.1.2.2 IDRISI Group Link Display

In order to take advantage of the *Group Link* we need to create a *Raster Group File* that links the files. The images are displayed using their *Raster Group* identities. If the *Group Link* icon on the main tool bar is then depressed, zooming in on one file will result in a similar zoom for the other linked files. This procedure will be described in more detail below. If you want additional discussion on creating *Raster Group Files*, you may wish to review the material in Section 1.3.7.

Before you start this section, close any currently displayed images.

Creating a file dollection with the IDRISI EXPLORER

Menu Location: **File – IDRISI EXPLORER**

---

1. Open the *IDRISI EXPLORER* window from the menu or the main icon toolbar.

2. Click on the tab for *Files*.

3. If the files are not listed in the *Files* pane, double click on the directory name to display the files.

4. Click on **etm_pan.rst**. The file name will then be highlighted.

5. Scroll down to **pan_highpass3x3** file. Now be very careful. Hold the *CTRL* key down, and click on the **pan_highpass3x3** file, thus highlighting it simultaneously with **etm_pan.rst.**

6. Remove your finger from the *CTRL* button. Press the right mouse button.

7. A pop-up menu will appear. Within this menu, scroll down to *Create*, and then select *Raster Group*.

8. This will create a new file called **Raster Group.rgf**. Click on this file name in the *Files* pane.

9. In the *Metadata* pane of the *IDRISI EXPLORER*, delete the **Raster Group** text in the *Name* text box, and type: **filter**, then press *Enter* on the computer keyboard.

10. Click on the *Save* icon in the bottom left hand corner of the *Metadata* pane.

Now that we have created the *Raster Group File*, we can display the two images within the context of the *Raster Group File*. IDRISI calls this displaying the images "with their full "dot-logic" filenames." The logic of these terms will become clearer in a moment.

Displaying images that form part of a Raster Group File

Menu Location: **Display – DISPLAY LAUNCHER**

---

1. Open the DISPLAY LAUNCHER using the main toolbar or main menu.

2. Within the *DISPLAY LAUNCHER* window, click on the browse button (…).

3. The *Pick List* will open. Scroll down to **filter**. Click on the plus sign (+).

4. The plus sign will change to a minus (-), and the two files, **etm_pan** and **pan_highpass3x3** should both be listed below. Note that both image files are actually listed twice in the *Pick List* window, once independently, and once as part of a *Raster Group File* (Figure 4.1.2.2.a).

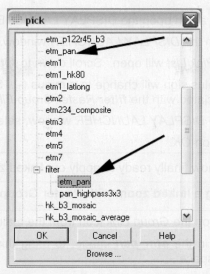

Figure 4.1.2.2.a The *Pick List* showing the image ***etm_pan*** listed independently, and also as part of the ***filter*** *Raster Group File*.

Displaying images that form part of a Raster Group File (cont.)

5. Select the ***etm_pan*** image associated with the ***filter*** *Raster Group File* from the *Pick list* window, and click on *OK*.

Observe the name of the file we have just selected, as listed in the DISPLAY LAUNCHER (Figure 4.1.2.2.b). The file is listed as ***filter.etm_pan***. Thus the format of the image is *Raster Group File name* "dot" *image file name*. The dot in this context specifically implies that the etm_pan image is a part of the raster group. When the image is identified with its full name, indicating the image and the raster group it is a part of, it is termed as the image file name "with full dot logic."

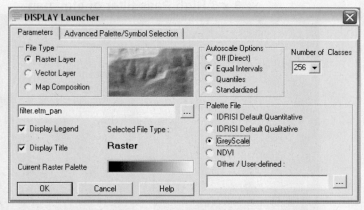

Figure 4.1.2.2.b The *DISPLAY LAUNCHER* showing the image file name associated with a *Raster Group File*.

Displaying images that form part of a Raster Group File (cont.)

6. In the *DISPLAY LAUNCHER* window, select a *GreyScale* palette.

7. Click on *OK*.

8. Once again open the DISPLAY LAUNCHER using the main toolbar.

9. Within the *DISPLAY LAUNCHER* window, click on the browse button (…).

10. The *Pick List* will open. Scroll down to *filter*. Click on the plus sign (+).

11. The plus sign will change to a minus (-). Select the ***pan_highpass3x3*** image associated with the ***filter*** *Raster Group File*, and click on *OK*.

12. In the *DISPLAY LAUNCHER* window, select a *GreyScale* palette.

13. Click on *OK*.

We are now finally ready to apply our linked zoom.

Applying a linked zoom with Raster Group File images

1. Click on the *Group Link* icon from the main menu bar.

2. Click in the ***etm_pan*** image, to bring this window to the front of the IDRISI workspace.

3. Click on the *Zoom* icon from the main menu bar.

4. Draw a zoom box around the airport by clicking at the upper left corner of the airport, and dragging the mouse to the bottom right corner of airport.

5. Both images should zoom in to the same place and extent. You may need to move the ***etm_pan*** image display, to see the ***pan_highpass3x3*** image.

The zoomed image shows that the *High Pass* filter highlights the boundaries between features by creating contrasting negative and positive pixels (Figure 4.1.2.2.c). Look closely at the boundary between the airport and the sea. Note that the boundary is marked by a dark line, with an adjacent parallel white line. This distinctive result emphasizes the edges of the features in the image. Also, observe how image noise within the image is heightened. High-pass filters tend to enhance any noise present in the image, since any variability, especially variation that is not correlated spatially, is enhanced.

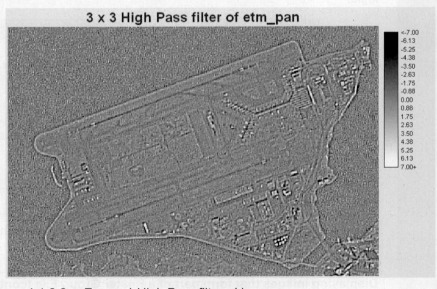

Figure 4.1.2.2.c Zoomed *High Pass* filtered image.

4.1.2.3 Sobel Edge Detector

Another edge filter, called the *Sobel Edge Detector* filter, is very useful in highlighting long continuous linear features in your imagery. Linear features in imagery, commonly called **lineaments**, are sometimes used in geological studies. Natural geomorphic features that exhibit relatively linear patterns may indicate structural features, such as faults or fracture systems controlled by joints. We will use the *Sobel Edge Detector* filter to highlight linear features found in the ***etm_pan*** image.

Sobel edge detector FILTER

Menu Location: **Image Processing– Enhancement - FILTER**

1. The *FILTER* dialog box should still be open from the Low Pass Filter operation. If not, use the main menu to open the *FILTER* dialog box, and specify the input file as ***etm_pan***. (If necessary, review Section 4.1.1.)

2. Select the *Sobel Edge Detector* radio button.

3. In the *Output Image* text box, type **pan_Sobel**.

4. Click on *OK* to generate the filtered image.

After the processing, the image is automatically displayed with an appropriate *GreyScale* palette. However, we do need to set the appropriate contrast.

Apply a contrast enhancement to an image

1. Click in the ***pan_Sobel*** window.

2. Find the *Composer* window, and click on the *Layer Properties* button.

3. In the *Layer Properties* window, type **20** in the *Display Min* text box, and **45** in the *Display Max* text box.

4. In the *Layer Properties* window, click on the buttons for *Apply*, *Save* and *OK*.

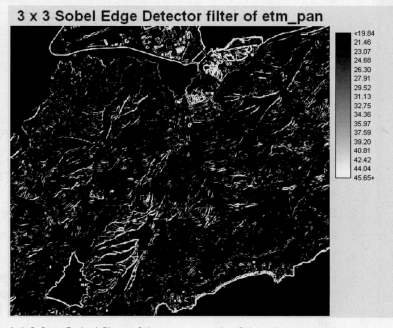

Figure 4.1.2.3.a Sobel filter of the area south of the airport.

Now zoom in on the Sobel Edge Detection image around the airport, and especially the adjacent island, Lantau (Figure 4.1.2.3.a). Note the strong NE trending linear features. These features suggest a distinctive NE structural geology trend.

<u>Note</u>: In working through this exercise you may have decided to redisplay one or more of the images. For example, you may have closed the **pan_mean3x3** image, and may wish to view it again to compare it with the subsequent images. If so, be sure to use the *GreyScale* palette each time you display the image. However, if you have saved the *Display Min* and *Display Max* settings you have entered, it should not be necessary to reapply the contrast stretch.

4.1.3   <u>Sharpening Filters</u>

For the satellite optical data such as Landsat data, convolution filtering is typically employed to sharpen the image. Often referred to as high-pass filtering, this operation is somewhat analogous to focusing a lens – it enhances the boundaries between features of distinctly different digital values. The difference between sharpened images and typical high-pass and edge filtered images is that most of the image information is retained in the final sharpened image.

In addition to the preset filters, IDRISI allows the user to define custom values for the kernel. We will now use this capability to define a filter that will sharpen our image without losing most of the image content. To retain the image content, we will design a matrix kernel whose sum is equal to 1 keep the results comparable with the mean filter kernel.

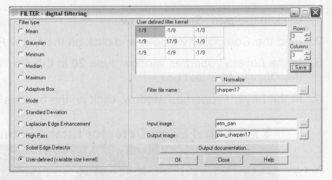

Figure 4.1.3.a   *FILTER* dialog box for custom filter creation.

Custom filter

Menu Location: **Image Processing– Enhancement - FILTER**

---

1. The *FILTER* dialog box should still be open from the Low Pass Filter operation. If not, use the main menu to open the *FILTER* dialog box, and specify the input file as **etm_pan**.

2. Select the radio button for *User-defined filter (variable size kernel)*.

3. In the *User-defined filter kernel* area, click on the center kernel position.

4. Type **17/9**

5. In the surrounding 8 kernel positions, click and type **-1/9** in each cell. You may find it easier to type the value in one cell, copy it (press the keys *Cntrl* and *c* simultaneously), and paste the value (*Cntrl* and *v)* in each subsequent cell.

6. Make sure that the normalize option is <u>not</u> selected (we have already normalized the kernel by dividing it by the number of kernel positions, i.e. 9).

7. In the *Filter file name* text box, type **sharpen17**.

8. Click on the *Save* button above and to the right of the *Filter file name* text box.

9. In the Output image text box, type **pan_sharpen17**.

10. Figure 4.1.3.a shows the *FILTER* dialog box with the parameters specified.

11. Click on *OK*.

The filtered image retains most of the image information of the original image, and shows a similar range of values. Therefore we now need to set the contrast once again.

Change contrast enhancement of an image

1. Make sure the new ***pan_sharpen17*** image is the focus of the IDRISI workspace by clicking in the image.

2. Find the *Composer* window, and select the button for *Layer Properties.*

3. In the *Layer Properties* window, enter in the *Display Min* and *Display Max* text boxes the values for the contrast stretch we used for the ***etm_pan*** image, namely **18** and **73**.

4. Still in the *Layer Properties* window, click on the buttons for *Apply*, *Save* and *OK*.

The image should now have much better contrast.

Zoom in on the airport and compare the filtered results with the original panchromatic image (Figures 4.1.3.b and 4.1.3.c). (If you need to redisplay the panchromatic image, remember to use a GreyScale palette.) The sharpen-filtered image shows better definition to the features in the airport such as the fuel tank field, the variations of the internal field, and the jets at the terminal. However, the filtered image also appears noisier.

Figure 4.1.3.b   Sharpened image of Hk_etm_pan.

Figure 4.1.3.c   Hong Kong Landsat Panchromatic data.

4.2 Multiresolution Merge

Another approach to enhancing images spatially is to merge high-resolution panchromatic data with multispectral imagery of lower spatial resolution. As noted previously in Section 2.1.1, multispectral imagery, which because of its multi-band nature can be displayed in a false color composite format, tends to have a lower spatial resolution than single band panchromatic data. An ideal merge of the two data sets would result in retaining the spectral integrity of the multispectral bands, while incorporating the spatial resolution of the panchromatic data. In this section we will learn how to use two methods to merge data of differing resolution. The first method will draw on color theory, and the second will take advantage of spatial filters and mathematical operators to merge the data sets.

In performing this resolution enhancement, it will be necessary to perform many steps to obtain the final product. The step-by-step processing can be very time consuming and laborious, especially if we need to repeat the process due to some adjustment required somewhere along the process stream. Thus, we will learn how to employ a very useful feature of IDRISI, the MACRO MODELER.

This MACRO MODELER has a number of significant benefits:

- It provides an excellent way to develop a sequence of program steps.

- It tends to be a more efficient way of running programs, especially those that are sequential.

- It provides a record of a processing sequence.

- The sequence of processing steps can easily be adapted to apply to a new data set, thus making it possible to develop "canned" procedures.

- It is easy to repeatedly run through a processing sequence, thus facilitating scenario modeling, where for example, multiple alternative values in some key processing parameter are compared.

4.2.1 Building a simple model in the MACRO MODELER

The Macro Modeler is a graphical user interface in which the user can easily develop and execute multiple operations in a sequential fashion. In essence, the interface allows the user to plan complex operations by creating a process stream that includes data inputs, operations, temporary file outputs as well as final outputs. Let's begin and work on becoming acquainted with this interface.

MACRO MODELER
Menu Location: **Modeling – Model Deployment Tools - MACRO MODELER**
1. Start the MACRO MODELER either from the main menu or the icon bar. 2. The *MACRO MODELER* graphical interface will open (Figure 4.2.1.a).

The Macro Modeler window has a standard pull-down menu and an icon toolbar. We will be using the icon toolbar exclusively so let's see what is available. Run your cursor over each icon, and note the brief name that pops up as you read the summary information below on the groups of icons.

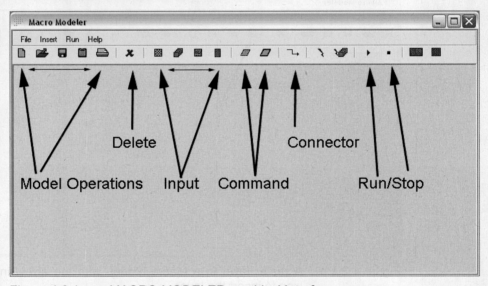

Figure 4.2.1.a   *MACRO MODELER* graphical Interface.

- **Model Operations**. The blue model operations icons on the left include commands to create a new model, open a model file, save the model to a file, copy the graphical representation of the model to the windows clipboard, and print the graphic representation of the model.

- **Delete**. The red x icon allows the user to delete elements of the model.

- **Input**. The green icons are the data elements that are inputs into processing modules, including raster files, raster group files, vector files, as well as attribute data (the latter two are for GIS operations).

- **Command Elements**. The next two icons in red are the command elements of a module and a sub-model. Sub-models are previously constructed modules that can be used within a larger model. When a command element is placed into the model, an output file is automatically connected to the module of the appropriate data type and with a default temporary file name.

- **Connector**. The next icon, the blue arrow, creates connections between model elements. Connectors control the flow of input data to the command modules.

- **Start/Stop**. The red triangle and square icons are for running and stopping the model. (The other icons will not be used here.)

In order to demonstrate the Macro Modeler's capability, let's first build a simple one-step model before we attempt building more complicated models. Let's build a model that creates a color composite image from three separate data layers.

MACRO MODELER (cont.)

3. Click on the *Raster Layer* icon to insert a data input into the model. (Figure 4.2.1.b shows the icon and the result of the operation described here.)

4. In the *Pick* window, select the data layer ***etm2***.

5. Click on *OK*.

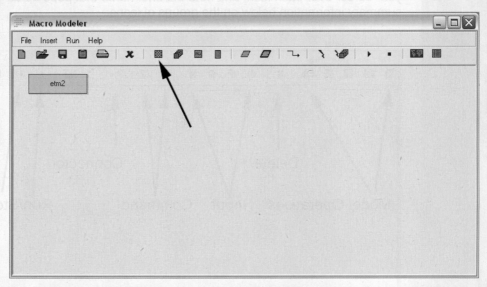

Figure 4.2.1.b   A raster layer in a Macro Model, with the arrow indicating the icon to insert the layer.

The Macro Modeler creates a blue rectangle as the graphical representation of a data input layer and places the name of the input file inside the rectangle (Figure 4.2.1.b). Click on the rectangle and the rectangle's border becomes a bold line indicating that the data input is selected. You can also move the element by selecting the element, hold the mouse click down and dragging it to your desired location. Continue now to add the other two data inputs.

MACRO MODELER (cont.)

6. Click on the *Raster Layer* icon to insert a data input into the model.

7. In the *Pick* window, select the data layer ***etm4***.

8. Click on *OK*.

9. Click on the *Raster Layer* icon to insert a data input into the model.

10. In the *Pick* window, select the data layer ***etm5***.

11. Click on *OK*.

Now we will add the command module.

MACRO MODELER (cont.)

12. Click on the *Module* icon to insert a command module into the model.

13. In the *Pick* window, select the module *composite*.

14. Click on *OK*.

The MACRO MODELER adds the command module, which is represented in the model by a pink parallelogram with the label *composite* (Figure 4.2.1.c). Notice that the modeler automatically creates an output file with the name **tmp000** (**tmp** followed by a series of numbers), and shows the connection from the *composite* module.

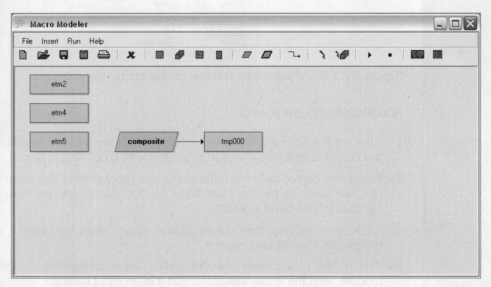

Figure 4.2.1.c   The model with three input data sets and the *composite* module specified.

We will now need to establish the connection and sequence of the input files to the *composite* module. First, we must learn the order that the *composite* module expects the input files, and then we can establish the connectors. The MACRO MODELER establishes the order of the data input files into a command module by the sequence in which you connect the data to the module. So it is very important to know before what order to physically connect the inputs to the module. Let's try with the model we are building.

MACRO MODELER (cont.)

15. Place your cursor over the pink *composite* module parallelogram, and right click.

16. A *Parameter* window appears for the *composite* module (Figure 4.2.1.d). This window shows the input files, output file name, and the parameters used in creating the output.

17. Notice the inputs are arranged from top to bottom as *Blue band*, *Green band*, and *Red band*. This is the sequence that the module expects the input files to be connected.

18. Try clicking in the fields for the inputs and output. Notice that you cannot change these attributes.

19. You can, however, change the values in the section labeled *Additional parameters*. Click on each parameter attribute to view the possible options. For this exercise, leave the options unchanged (default options)

20. Click on the *OK* button to close the *Parameters* window.

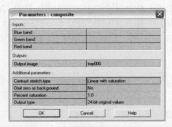

Figure 4.2.1.d   *Parameters* window for the *composite* module.

MACRO MODELER (cont.)

21. Click on the *Connect* icon, and move your curser into the model. Notice that the cursor shape has changed to a hand with a pointing finger.

22. Place the cursor over the blue rectangle representing the input raster layer that we want to be the blue band for the *composite* module, namely the Landsat ETM+ band 2, **etm2**.

23. Click, and holding the mouse button down, drag the cursor over to the *composite* module and release.

24. The model now shows the **etm2** data layer connecting to the *composite* module, with the arrow indicating that it is an input data file.

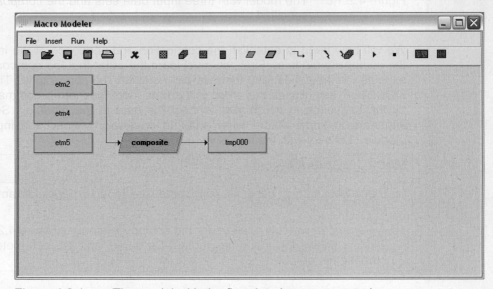

Figure 4.2.1.e   The model with the first data layer connected.

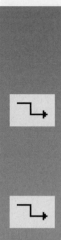

MACRO MODELER (cont.)

25. Right click with the cursor over the *composite* module to bring up the *Parameters* window once again. Note that the *Blue band* field now indicates **etm2,** indicating that you have successfully connected the data layer to the module. Let's continue and add the other data inputs.

26. Click on the *Connect* icon and move your curser into the model.

27. Place the hand cursor over the rectangle representing the **etm4** raster layer input.

28. Click, and keeping the mouse button depressed, drag cursor over to the *composite* module, and release.

29. Click on the *Connect* icon and move your curser into the model.

30. Place the hand cursor over the rectangle representing the **etm5** raster layer input.

31. Click, and keeping the mouse button depressed, drag cursor over to the *composite* module, and release.

One final step before we will run our model is to create an output data layer with an appropriate name. The **tmp** (temporary) filename prefix is typically used for intermediate data layers rather than final products. The model creates data layers for all the outputs and doesn't automatically clean up the temporary files. We should clean up these temporary files after we run the model by either manually deleting the files or by using the *Delete all temporary files* command found in the *File* pull-down menu. Let's continue and name our output.

MACRO MODELER (cont.)

32. Place you cursor over the **tmp001** data output and right click.

33. A *Change layer name* window appears, with the original name in the field.

34. Type in new file name as **etm542**.

35. Click *OK*.

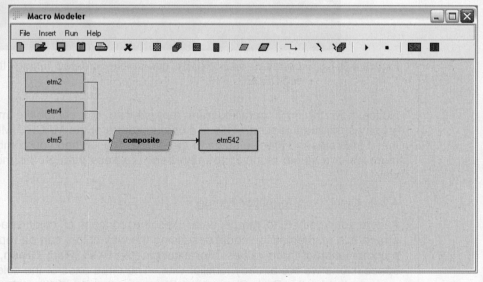

Figure 4.2.1.f   The model completely specified.

One aspect of the MACRO MODELER that we need to consider is the standard output directory for all the data layers created when you run the model. All data are automatically written to the standard output directory in the *Working Folder*. One can always use the IDRISI file explorer to move the final data layers to another folder location if necessary.

Finally, let's save and run our new model.

MACRO MODELER (cont.)

36. Click on the *Save* icon.

37. Specify the Model file name **composite542**.

38. Click *OK*.

39. Click on the *run* icon.

40. A window will open in which you are warned that the files created by the model will overwrite any existing files of those names. Click on *Yes to all*.

41. Your new raster file is created and displayed (Figure 4.2.1.g).

Figure 4.2.1.g   Landsat 542 (RGB) composite created using the MACRO MODELER.

Notice how the pink parallelogram representing the *composite* module turns green as the module runs. This is a useful feature of the MACRO MODELER, in that it indicates the precise stage of the processing. When you combine multiple modules in a single module, you can track progress through the module in this way.

4.2.2 Color Transformation Merge

A common method to merge data uses the concept of color spaces. **Color space** is a mathematical model describing the way colors can be represented as a combination of three values. For example, the **RGB (Red, Green, Blue)** color space is one we are already familiar with. The three axes of the color space are represented by the Red, Green, and Blue components of the color. Based on fact that the impressions of almost all the colors we perceive with our eyes can be evoked by mixing these three components, a point in the RGB color space will represent a distinctive color.

RGB is not the only possible representation of color. An alternative color space is the **HLS (Hue, Lightness, Saturation)** model. In this case, Hue, Lightness, and Saturation are the axes of the color space, just as Red, Green and Blue are the axes in the RGB model.

- **Hue** refers to the characteristic tint of a color. For computer-based color, the color wheel is based on the RGB model and includes secondary colors of cyan, magenta, and yellow. Since the color wheel is circular, the number assigned to the Hue value is typically an angle, from 0° to 360° (Figure 4.2.2.a). IDRISI will normalize this 360-degree value to an 8-bit range (0-255).

- **Lightness** refers to the brightness, which extends from black to white.

- **Saturation** refers to the purity of the color, so that low saturation colors tend to gray, and have a typically pastel quality, whereas high saturation colors are the purest colors. With no saturation at all, the hue becomes a shade of gray equivalent to lightness (Figure 4.2.2.b).

Sometimes HLS system is referred to as IHS, for **intensity** (instead of lightness), **hue**, and **saturation**. Soil scientists refer to this system by the terms **hue**, **value** (for lightness) and **chroma** (for saturation). For this exercise we will use the terms used in IDRISI, i.e. HLS.

Interestingly, there are in fact additional color spaces, which sometimes are used in preference to either the RGB or HLS models. The reader seeking additional information about color spaces should refer to a text such as Jensen (2005).

Transformations between color spaces are essentially matrix rotations of the data between the different color space axes. The differences between the RGB and HLS color spaces can be visualized in Figure 4.2.2.b.

The Lightness component in the HLS space is the useful component for merging datasets of different resolutions. In Landsat ETM+ data, the panchromatic band has four 15 m pixels for every one 30 m pixel of the multispectral bands. The panchromatic band, which is sensitive to 0.5-0.9 µm electromagnetic radiation, gives a good average reflectance of the pixel. We will use IDRISI's color space transformation functions to merge the Landsat panchromatic band with the multispectral Landsat bands 5, 4, and 2.

We will use the MACRO MODELER to develop the multi-step merge procedure. The model will first transform three multispectral bands from RGB to HLS color space. We will then expand the resolution of the resulting Hue and Saturation outputs to match that of the panchromatic band. The panchromatic band will be substituted for the Lightness data, and then the data will be transformed back to RGB color space. The final step will be to create the color composite image to view the merged image.

HLS resolution merge with the MACRO MODELER
Menu Location: **Modeling – Model Deployment Tools - MACRO MODELER**

1. Start the MACRO MODELER either from the main menu or the icon bar.

2. In the MACRO MODELER window, use the menu to select *File* and then *Delete all temporary* files.

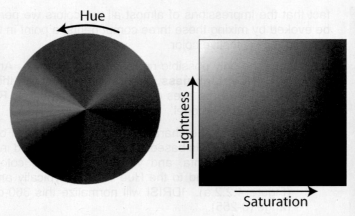

Figure 4.2.2.a   Left: Hue color wheel.   Right: Lightness and saturation variation associated with a red hue.

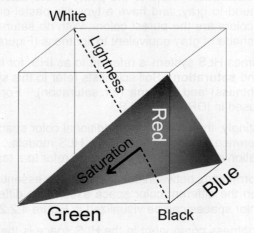

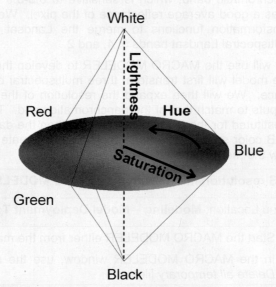

Figure 4.2.2.b   RGB color space and HLS color space.

3. Click on *File* and select *Set/Reset temporary file counter*.

4. The *Set/Reset TMP File Counter* window will open. Click on *Reset*.

5. If the value for Current counter value is not *0*, change the value in the *Set next counter window* to **0**. Click *OK* to close the *Set/Reset TMP File Counter* window.

6. Click on the *Raster Layer* icon to insert a data input into the model.

7. In the *Pick list* window, select the data layer **etm5**.

8. Click on *OK*.

9. Repeat the above three steps to insert raster layer **etm4**, and again to insert raster layer **etm2**.

10. Click on the *Module* icon to insert a command module into the model.

11. In the *Pick list* window, select the module *colspace*.

12. Click on *OK*.

13. Right click with the cursor over the *colspace* module to bring up the *Parameters: colspace* window.

14. Within the *Parameters* window, note that the input images are listed as *hue image band*, *lightness image* band and *saturation image band*.

15. Find the *Additional Parameters* section. In that section, the *Conversion type* should list the default option of *HLS to RGB*.

16. Click in the *HLS to RGB* field, and select *RGB to HLS* from the popup menu (Figure 4.2.2.c).

17. Note that the input images are now listed as *Red image band*, *Green image band* and *Blue image band*, in that order (Figure 4.2.2.c). Therefore, we will want first to connect the Landsat band that will be displayed as red, then green, then blue.

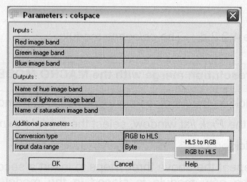

Figure 4.2.2.c   The *colspace Parameters* window after the *RGB to HLS* option has been selected.

HLS resolution merge with the MACRO MODELER (cont.)

18. Click on *OK* to close the *Parameters* window.

19. Click on the *Connect* icon and move your curser into the model.

20. Place cursor over the red band for the *colspace* module, which will be **etm5**. Click, and keeping the left mouse button depressed, drag the cursor over to the *colspace* module, and release.

21. The model now shows the **etm5** data layer as connecting to the *colspace* module with the arrow indicating that it is an input data file.

22. Repeat the previous three steps to connect **etm4** to the *colspace* module, and the **etm2** to the *colspace* module, in that order.

Your model should now show the three input Landsat ETM+ images connected to the *colspace* module (Figure 4.2.2.d). The colspace module provides for three outputs that currently have default names, such as **tmp003**, **tmp004** and **tmp005**. These files represent, in order, hue, lightness and saturation. We will next expand the resolution of the hue and saturation data to match the Landsat panchromatic image.

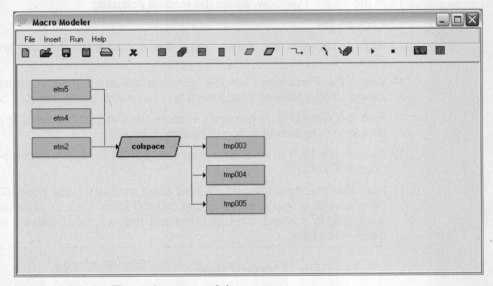

Figure 4.2.2.d   The *colspace* module.

HLS resolution merge with the MACRO MODELER (cont.)

23. Click on the *Module* icon to insert a command module into the model.

24. In the *Pick list* window, select the module *expand.*

25. Click on *OK.*

26. Repeat the above three steps to insert a second *expand* module in the model. (The new module is placed in the model somewhere to the right of the existing model elements. You may need to scroll over to find them.)

27. Drag each of the *expand* modules and their outputs to line up with the first and third raster file outputs from *colspace*, which correspond to the *hue* and *saturation* outputs from the module (for example **tmp003** and **tmp005** in Figure 4.2.2.d).

28. Use the connector icon to connect the first and third raster output files from the *colspace* module to *expand* modules.

29. Right click on the first *expand* module. The *Parameters* window will open.

30. In the blank text box next to *Expansion factor*, type **2** (Figure 4.2.2.e).

31. Click *OK*.

32. Right-click on the output file icon from this expand operation, currently indicated with a temporary name such as ***tmp006***. The *Change layer name* window opens. Change the file name to **hue_expand**.

33. Repeat steps 29-31 to specify an *Expansion factor* of **2** for the second *expand* module. Rename the output file **sat_expand** (sat is short for saturation) (Figure 4.2.2.e).

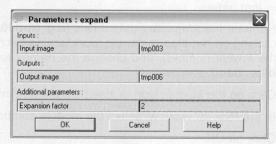

Figure 4.2.2.e   Entering the expansion factor of **2** in the *expand* module.

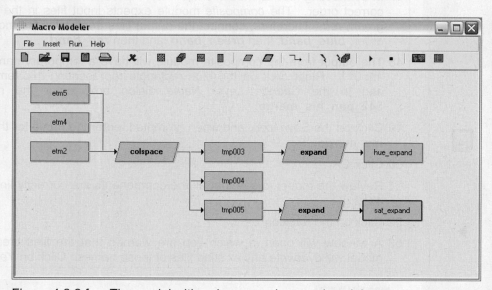

Figure 4.2.2.f   The model with *colspace* and *expand* modules.

Now we will insert the panchromatic band into the model, substituting it for the lightness data in the reverse of the color space transform, from HLS back to RGB. The final step will be to construct a composite for viewing our results.

HLS resolution merge with the MACRO MODELER (cont.)

34. Click on the *Raster Layer* icon to insert a data input into the model.

35. In the *Pick list* window, select the data layer ***etm_pan***.

36. Click on *OK*.

37. Line up raster file ***etm_pan*** between the expanded *hue* and *saturation* raster files (***hue_expand*** and ***sat_expand*** in Figure 4.2.2.f).

38. Click on the *Module* icon to insert a command module into the model.

39. In the pick window, select the module *colspace*.

40. Click on *OK*.

41. This time we need to convert from HLS to RGB, which we saw above was the default option in colspace. Therefore we can directly connect the input files to the new *colspace* module.

42. Use the connector icon to connect the expanded hue output (***hue_expand*** in Figure 4.2.2.f), ***etm_pan***, and the expanded saturation output (***sat_expand***), *in that order*.

43. Rename the temporary output files (e.g. **tmp008**, **tmp009**, **tmp010**), by right-clicking on the blue rectangle representing each file (starting with the file with the lowest number), and change the names to **red_band**, **green_band** and **blue_band**, respectively.

44. Click on the *Module* icon to insert a command module into the model.

45. In the *Pick list* window, select the module *composite*.

46. Click on *OK*.

47. In connecting files to modules it is very important to connect the files in the correct order. The *composite* module expects input files in the order *blue, green, red*. Therefore, connect the output files from *colspace* module in this order: ***blue_band***, then ***green_band***, and then ***red_band***.

48. The output from the composite module will have a temporary name, such as tmp011. Right click on the blue rectangle representing this temporary file, and in the *Change Layer Name* dialog box, enter the new name, **542_pan_hls_merge**.

49. Click on the *Save* icon, and when prompted, enter the name for the model as **hls_merge**.

50. Click *OK*.

51. Review the model to see that all the components are correctly linked (Figure 4.2.2.g).

52. Click on the *run* icon.

53. A window will open in which you are warned that the files created by the model will overwrite any existing files of those names. Click on *Yes to all*.

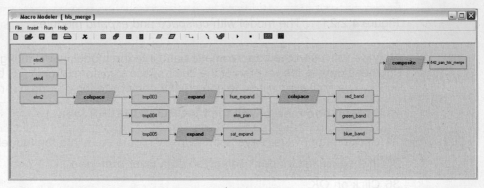

Figure 4.2.2.g   HLS resolution merge model.

As the model runs, the progress through the various steps is clearly illustrated by the sequence of modules that turn green. After the program is completed, the merged image will be displayed automatically.

Let us now compare the standard false color composite of bands 2, 4 and 5 we created in Section 4.2.1 with the merged image comprising bands 2, 4 and 5 with the panchromatic band.

Use the DISPLAY LAUNCHER to display the **etm542** image. Select an area, for example the east end of Deep Bay (the significant embayment to the north of the airport), and zoom into the same area in both images (Figure 4.2.2.h and Figure 4.2.2.i). Note how the detail is sharpened in the merged image. The spectral quality, however, is slightly changed in the merged image. Both the water areas and agricultural areas have different shades of blue from the original. This slight mismatch in the spectral quality is due to the fact that the Landsat panchromatic data are statistically different from the 542 lightness band. The simple substitution of the panchromatic data for lightness results in a slightly different spectral character to the resulting RGB image.

Before starting the next section, close all files, including the MACRO MODELER.

Figure 4.2.2.h   Landsat 5,4,2 (RGB) false color composite image of the eastern end of Deep Bay with 30 m resolution.

Figure 4.2.2.i   HLS merge of Landsat bands 5,4,2 (RGB) and the panchromatic band, with approximately 15 m resolution.

4.2.3 Multiplicative Merge

We saw in section 4.2.2 that some multiresolution merge methods change the relative spectral values, and colors are consistent between a regular false color composite and one made using the merged bands. Therefore, our aim in this section will be to develop a merge procedure that does not change the relative spectral properties. One way to do this is to use a multiplicative approach that uniformly enhances the lower resolution spectral bands with the panchromatic band.

Rather than simply multiply directly the panchromatic bands with the multispectral bands, we will first filter the panchromatic band. If you remember from our earlier exercise in filtering, a high pass filter will emphasize the edges of features, while simultaneously removing much of the average brightness signal associated with the feature. By using a high pass filtered image as an input into the image merge, we will sharpen the boundaries of features, while also retaining the integrity of the spectral characteristic of the feature. Let's create the model and compare the results to the HLS merge.

Note: In this model, we will assume you have gained familiarity with the MACRO MODELER, and therefore the instructions will be shortened somewhat for commands that we have already used a number of times. If necessary, you can always refer back to Section 4.2.2 to see more detailed instructions for these commands.

Multiplicative resolution merge with the MACRO MODELER
Menu Location: **Modeling – Model Deployment Tools - MACRO MODELER**

1. Start the MACRO MODELER either from the main menu or the icon bar.

2. In the MACRO MODELER window, click on *File* and select *Delete all temporary* files.

3. Click on *File* and select *Set/Reset temporary file counter*.

4. The *Set/Reset TMP File Counter* window will open. Click the *Reset* button. If the value for Current counter value is not *0*, change the value in the *Set next counter window* to **0**. Click *OK*.

5. Use the *Raster Layer* icon to insert data layer **etm2** into the model. Repeat to insert **etm4** and **etm5** into the model, in that order.

6. Use the *Module* icon to insert the *expand* command module into the model. Repeat to insert two more *expand* modules, to create a total of three *expand* modules.

7. Arrange the *expand* modules, one each in front of the three input file, **etm2**, **etm4** and **etm5**.

8. Use the *Connector* icon to connect each of the three blue rectangles representing the raster layers, **etm2**, **etm4** and **etm5**, to an *expand* module (Figure 4.2.3.a) (*Note that your temporary output names may have different numbers, e.g. **tmp002** where the figure shows **tmp000**. This is not significant. The important issue is how the files are connected, and for some program modules, such as composite, the order in which they are combined.*)

9. Sequentially right-click in each *expand* command module, and each time the *Parameter* window opens, set the *Expansion factor* to **2**.

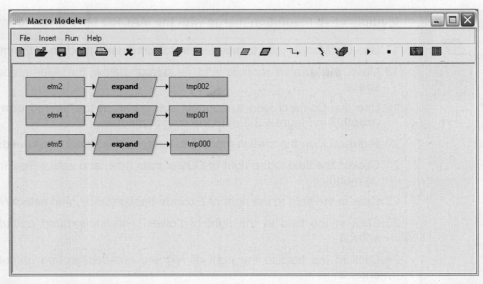

Figure 4.2.3.a   The initial model with three *expand* modules.

Having added the Landsat multispectral bands and expanded them to the same resolution as the Landsat panchromatic band, we will now add the panchromatic band to the module, and filter it to highlight feature boundaries. Once we have filtered the panchromatic band, we will scale it so that its histogram and mean are centered on one.

Multiplicative resolution merge with the MACRO MODELER (cont.)

10. Use the *Raster Layer* icon to insert data layer **etm_pan** into the model.

11. Arrange the etm_pan rectangle, in line under the other input data layers.

12. Use the *Module* icon to insert the *filter* command module into the model.

13. Use the Connector icon to connect the **etm_pan** layer to the *filter* module.

14. Right-click on the *filter* module to bring up the *Parameters* window.

15. Right-click in the field to the right of the *filter-type,* and select *High-pass* (Figure 4.2.3.b) .

16. Click on *OK* to close the *Parameters* window.

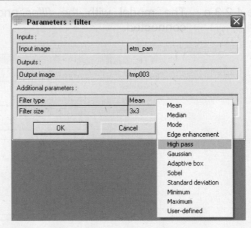

Figure 4.2.3.b   Setting the *Filter type* to *High Pass*.

Multiplicative resolution merge with the MACRO MODELER (cont.)

17. Use the *Module* icon to insert a *stretch* command module in the model.

18. Move the *stretch* module and its output below the *filter* module, to save space.

19. Use the *Connect* icon to connect the output of the filtered ***etm_pan*** image (***tmp003*** in Figure 4.2.3.c) to the *stretch* module.

20. Right-click on the *stretch* module to bring up the *Parameters* window.

21. Click in the field to the right of *Output data type*, and select *Real* from the pop-up menu.

22. Click in the field to the right of *Exclude background?,* and select *No*.

23. Click in the field to the right of *Lowest non-background output value*, and enter **0**

24. Click in the field to the right of *Highest non-background output value*, and enter **2**

25. Leave the remaining fields with their default values (Figure 4.2.3.d), and close the window by clicking on *OK*.

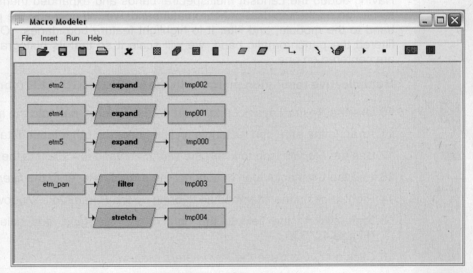

Figure 4.2.3.c   The model with the *filter* and *stretch* modules added and connected.

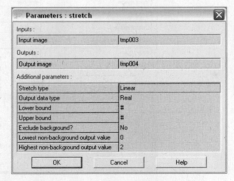

Figure 4.2.3.d   The stretch module *Parameter* window.

The Parameters window for stretch (Figure 4.2.3.d) had # symbols in the fields for Lower bound and Upper bound. For this module, # is used to indicate that the program should use the appropriate values from the image itself. Thus, in this case, the input image will be queried, and the stretch will extend from the minimum value in the image to the output value.

For the fields *Lowest non-background output value* and *Highest non-background output value*, we chose values of *0* and *2*, so that the average value after the stretch would be approximately 1.0 (i.e. half way between the two extremes).

We are now ready to combine the filtered and stretched panchromatic band with the multispectral bands by a simple multiplication. Since the filtered panchromatic band is centered on approximately 1.0, the only changes in the multispectral bands will be on the edges of features, and these will be made slowly lower or higher, thus accentuating those edges.

Multiplicative resolution merge with the MACRO MODELER (cont.)

26. Click on the *Module* icon and insert an *overlay* command module.

27. Repeat the previous step twice, to create a total of three *overlay* modules in the model.

28. Line up each pink parallelogram that represents an *overlay* module with an output temporary file from the three *expand* modules.

29. Use the *Connect* icon to connect each output temporary file from the *expand* modules to the adjacent *overlay* module.

30. Use the *Connect* icon another three times to connect the output file from the stretch module (**tmp004** in Figure 4.2.3.e) to each *overlay* module.

31. Right-click on the first *overlay* module to bring up the *Parameters* window.

32. Click on the field to the right of *Operations*, and select *Multiply* from the pop-up menu.

33. Repeat the previous two instructions for each *overlay* module, so that each module is set to *Multiply*.

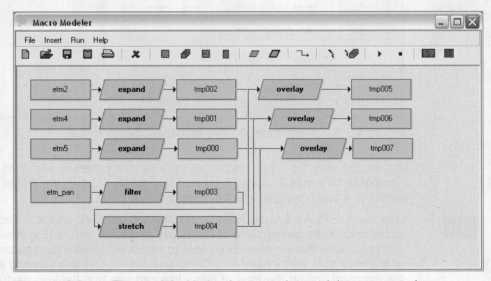

Figure 4.2.3.e   The model with the three *overlay* modules connected.

We are now ready to create a false color composite image of the merged data.

Multiplicative resolution merge with the MACRO MODELER (cont.)

34. Use the *Module* icon to insert the *composite* command module in the model.

35. Connect the temporary raster files from the *overlay* modules so that if you follow along a row, the result of the expansion and overlay operation for the **etm2** file is connected first, then **etm4**, and finally **etm5**. In Figure 4.2.3.f, this would be in the order **tmp005**, **tmp006** and **tmp007**.

36. The output from the *composite* module will have a temporary name, such as **tmp008**. Right click on the blue rectangle representing this temporary file, and in the *Change Layer Name* dialog box, enter the new name, **542_pan_mult_merge**.

37. Click on *OK*.

38. Click on the *Save* icon.

39. Specify the Model file name **mult_merge**.

40. Click on *OK*.

41. Review the model to see that all the components are correctly linked (Figure 4.2.3.g).

42. Click on the *run* icon.

43. A window will open in which you are warned that the files created by the model will overwrite any existing files of those names. Click on *Yes to all*.

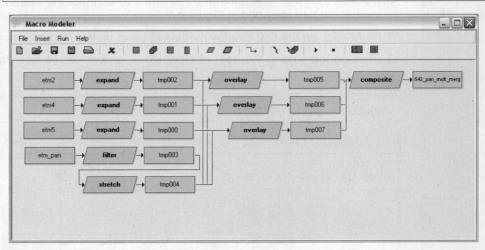

Figure 4.2.3.f   The multiplicative resolution merge model.

As we did with the HLS merge, let us now compare the standard false color composite of bands 2, 4 and 5 created in Section 4.2.1 to the image comprising bands 2, 4 and 5 merged with the panchromatic band.

Use the DISPLAY LAUNCHER to display the **etm542** image. Zoom into the same area of the eastern end of Deep Bay as we did before (Figures 4.2.3.g and 4.2.3.h). Note that we have been able to match accurately the spectral character of the mud flats that extend into Deep Bay, as well as the spectral signature of the exposed soil on the tops of hills. We can see that we successfully retained the relative spectral characteristics of the image. Also, look at the urban areas in the zoomed images and we can see a definite sharpening of the roads and buildings.

Figure 4.3.2.g   Landsat 5,4,2 (RGB) false color composite image of the eastern end of Deep Bay with 30m resolution.

Figure 4.2.3.h   Multiplicative merge of Landsat bands 5,4,2 (RGB) and the panchromatic band, with approximately 15m resolution.

Chapter 5　Image Ratios

5.1 Introduction to Image Ratios

In this chapter, we will explore three different applications of band ratios. We will start with one of the most common ratios used, that of a vegetation index. We will then look at how a ratio might be designed to separate snow from clouds. In the final section of the chapter we will look at ratios in a more in-depth fashion. We will design three ratios to highlight different mineral compositions, and use the ratios in a false color composite.

5.2 Copy Data for This Chapter

Starting with this chapter, we will use different data sets for each chapter, and even for different sections within each chapter. Thus, in this chapter we will work with three different image sets, one for each for vegetation, snow and rock ratios. Therefore, you should now copy the *Chap5* folder from the CD, and paste it as a new subfolder within the *ID Man* folder on your computer.

After you have copied the folder, you should remove the Read-Only attribute from this new folder on your computer. This is done by right-clicking on the *Chap5* folder name, selecting *Properties* from the pop-up menu. A dialog box will open, labeled *Chap5 Properties* (if you apply this procedure to the entire *ID Man* directory, then the dialog box will be labeled *ID Man Properties*). Now clear the check mark from the *Read Only* check box, by clicking in the box. You should then click on the button for *Apply*, and in the subsequent *Confirm Attribute Changes* dialog box, accept the default *Apply changes to this folder, subfolder and files*, and click on *OK*. You will need to also click on *OK* in the *Chap5 Properties* dialog box.

Note: Section 1.3.1 provides detailed instructions on how to copy the data from the CD, and also on how to remove the *Read-Only* attribute from the data. Also, the procedure for setting up the *ID Man* folder on your computer is described.

5.3 Vegetation Indices

5.3.1 Background

5.3.1.1 The normalized difference vegetation index (NDVI)

Some enhancement techniques help the analyst explore a data set, and do not require any preconceived ideas about the potential spectral properties of the objects in the scene. Sometimes, however, the analyst would like to enhance a specific land cover, such as vegetation. There is a very long history in the remote sensing literature of using ratios as a method of estimating vegetation abundance (i.e. biomass estimates) and greenness associated with the seasonal cycle of deciduous vegetation.

Green vegetation is particularly well suited for spectral enhancement because the pigment, chlorophyll, absorbs blue and red wavelengths strongly, and thus the reflectance of leaves at these wavelengths is very low (Figure 5.3.1.1). On the other hand, leaves typically reflect strongly at near infrared wavelengths, providing a very strong contrast between the red and near infrared. It is this contrast that the vegetation ratios capitalize on. In this section we will see how a contrast in spectral properties between two different wavelengths provides a much more reliable method of distinguishing a particular land cover than just a single wavelength does.

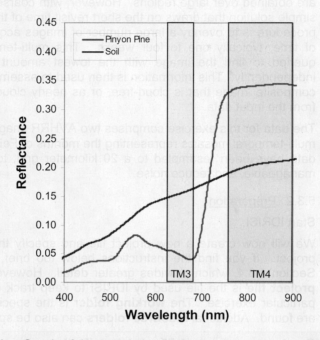

Figure 5.3.1.1.a Graph of the spectral reflectance of vegetation and soil, with the locations of TM bands 3 (red) and 4 (near infrared) shown.

The ratio we use is the **normalized difference vegetation index**, or **NDVI**. This ratio is defined:

NDVI = (Near Infrared – Red) / (Near Infrared + Red).

NDVI is a variant of the simple ratio of Near Infrared/Red. However, by constructing the ratio as the difference of the two wavelengths over the sum of the two wavelengths, NDVI is normalized, so that the range falls between -1 and +1, and the middle value is zero. Furthermore, NDVI is designed such that high values of the ratio (close to +1) indicate abundant green vegetation, and values near zero or less indicate an absence of vegetation.

5.3.1.2 Background on the data used in this exercise

The data for this exercise is from the National Oceanic and Atmospheric Administration (NOAA) Advanced Very High Resolution Radiometer (AVHRR). The AVHRR sensor has been flown on NOAA satellites since the 1970s, and therefore there is a large archive of AVHRR data, providing a very rich source of information for multi-temporal studies. AVHRR data are usually classified as coarse resolution, as the nominal pixel size at nadir is 1.1 kilometer. However, the sensor has a relatively broad field of view (approximately 2400 kilometers), thus facilitating the construction of global image mosaics. Although different AVHRR sensors have had slightly different band combinations over time, all AVHRR sensors have included a red band (band 1, which measures 0.58-0.68 μm radiation) and a near infrared band (band 2, 0.72-1.10 μm), in addition to channels in the 3-5 μm and 8-12 μm ranges. For this exercise, we will only work with AVHRR bands 1 and 2.

In continental or global scale analyses of the terrestrial earth, the presence of clouds is a particular problem, because it is extremely rare that cloud free scenes are obtained over large regions. However, with coarse resolution data there is a simple solution that draws on the short revisit time of the sensor. In essence, the procedure is to overlay a large number of images acquired within a short period of time, typically one to four weeks. This multi-temporal stack of images is queried to find the image with the lowest amount of cloud, for each pixel independently. This information is then used to assemble a single multi-temporal composite image that is cloud-free, or as nearly cloud-free as can be achieved from the input data.

The data for this exercise comprises two AVHRR images of Africa. The data are multi-temporal mosaics representing the months of February and July 2001. The data have been resampled to a 20 kilometer grid, to make the file size more manageable, and reduce noise.

5.3.2 Preparation

Start IDRISI.

We will now create a new project file and specify the working folders for that project. If you find the instructions below too brief, you may need to review Section 1.3.4, which provides greater detail. However, just to remind you, the **project file** is the file used by IDRISI to keep track of the data locations for a particular exercise. The **working folder** is the specific folder where your data are found. Additional **resource folders** can also be specified.

Create a new project file and specify the working folders with the IDRISI EXPLORER

Menu Location: **File – IDRISI EXPLORER**

1. Start the IDRISI EXPLORER from the main menu or toolbar.

2. The *IDRISI EXPLORER* window will open on the left side of the IDRISI workspace. At the top left of the *IDRISI EXPLORER* window will either be a plus (+) or a minus (-) symbol. If the symbol is a plus sign, click it to expand the window.

3. Select the *Projects* tab.

4. If the *Editor* pane obscures the listing of project files, drag the boundary of the Editor pane down, to show the *Projects* pane (Figure 5.3.2.a).

5. Right click within the *Projects* pane, and select the *New Project Ins* option.

6. A *Browse For Folder* window will open. Use this window to navigate to the *ID_Man* folder, which is the folder you created on your computer for the data for this manual. Now navigate to the *Chap5_3* subfolder, within the *ID Man/Chap5* folder.

7. Click *OK* in the *Browse For Folder* window.

8. A new project file *Chap5_3*, will now be listed in the *Project* pane of the IDRISI EXPLORER. The working folder will also be listed in the Editor pane. (Figure 5.3.2.b).

9. Note that you can switch between the *Chap1-4* project and this new *Chap5-3* project by selecting the appropriate radio buttons in the *Project* pane of the IDRISI EXPLORER.

10. Close the IDRISI EXPLORER by clicking on the red *x* in the upper right corner of the *IDRISI EXPLORER* window.

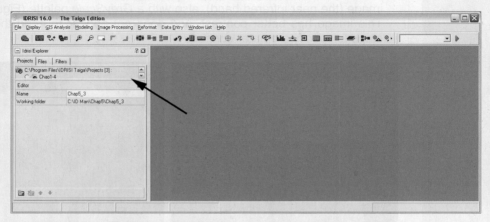

Figure 5.3.2.a   *Editor* pane obscuring the *Projects* pane.   Arrow points to the boundary of the *Editor* pane.

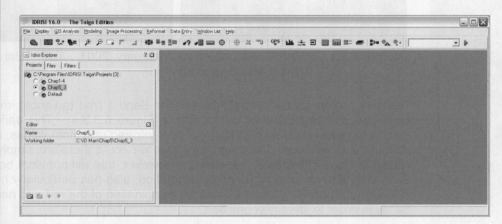

Figure 5.3.2.b   *Projects* and *Editor* panes visible, new project specified.

5.3.3 Exploratory investigation of the AVHRR data of Africa

Initial display and enhancement of AVHRR images

1. Start the DISPLAY LAUNCHER.

2. In the *DISPLAY LAUNCHER* window, click on the browse button (…) to select the file name for display.

3. Select the ***feb_b1*** image (the AVHRR red band) from the *Pick list* window, and click on *OK* to close that window.

4. In the *DISPLAY LAUNCHER* window, select a *GreysScale* palette.

5. Click on *OK* to display the image.

6. Find the *Composer* window in the IDRISI workspace. In the *Composer* window, click on the *Layer Properties* button.

7. In the *Layer Properties* window, adjust the *Display Max* slider so that the image has more contrast, and the pattern in the Sahara Desert (North Africa) is clearer. A value of **675** appears to provide a good contrast (Figure 5.3.3.a).

8. In the Layer Properties window, click on *Save* button, and then *OK*.

9. Now repeat the above steps 1-5 to display in another viewer the *feb_b2* image (the near infrared band), also with a *GreyScale* palette (Figure 5.3.3.a). This image has better contrast, and does not appear to need the additional steps to specify a greater contrast.

 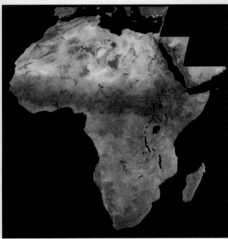

Figure 5.3.3.a   AVHRR data of Africa, February 2001. Left: Band 1 (red). Right: Band 2 (near infrared).

The dark region across central Africa in the Band 1 (red radiance) image is the dense tropical vegetation of central Africa (Figure 5.3.3.a). This dark region is associated with relatively high Band 2 (near infrared radiance) values, a common attribute of vegetation. We might think that we could therefore simply use high values in Band 2 to identify vegetation. However, this will not work because the Sahara desert, an area of very little vegetation, also has particularly high values in the infrared band. Clearly we need a combination of the red and near-infrared bands in order to identify vegetation.

One simple way of combining two bands is to create a false color composite. The creation of a false color composite was introduced in detail in Section 2.2.4, and that section should be consulted if you find the instructions too brief here.

Create a false color composite image

Menu Location: **Display - COMPOSITE**

1. Start the COMPOSITE program using the main menu or tool bar.

2. In the *COMPOSITE* dialog box, specify the file name for the *Blue image band* by clicking on the adjacent browse button (…), and in the resulting *Pick list* selecting *feb_1*. Click on *OK* to close the *Pick list*.

3. Repeat the previous step for the *Green image band*, specifying the *feb_2* image.

4. Again, repeat the previous step for the *Red image band*, this time specifying the *feb_1* image (i.e. the same as for the *Blue image band*).

5. Enter the *Output image* filename in the text box provided: **feb_fcc**.

6. Enter in the *Title* text box: **February False Color Composite (R,B = red, G = IR)** .

7. Accept all other defaults, and click *OK* to create and display the false color composite (Figure 5.3.3.b).

Figure 5.3.3.b   Africa February AVHRR false color composite image.

In the above steps, we are forced to use one of the two bands twice because we only have two AVHRR bands, instead of the three we need for a false color composite. Nevertheless, the results are quite impressive, especially compared to the original black and white images. You should be able to discern a very distinct east-west boundary between the lush green along the West African coast, and the dry interior, transitioning to the very arid Sahara Desert. This transition region is known as the Sahel.

However, although the false color composite is very useful to look at, it retains a great deal of detail that is not relevant to vegetation, including patterns associated with dunes and mountain ranges in the Sahara. Furthermore, color is inherently subjective. Thus, we could not easily identify one or more thresholds that differentiated between relatively dense and less dense vegetation regions. On the other hand, a ratio such as NDVI is well-suited for such tasks.

5.3.4 NDVI image of Africa

IDRISI offers a built in program, VEGINDEX for calculating 19 different vegetation ratios. We will use this program to calculate one of the simplest and most enduring ratios, NDVI.

Calculating NDVI with VEGINDEX
Menu location: **Image Processing – Transformation - VEGINDEX**

1. Start VEGINDEX from the main menu.

2. The *VEGINDEX* dialog box will open.

3. Select the radio button for *NDVI*.

4. Click on the browse button (…) next to the *Red band* text box, to identify the input file ***feb_1***.

5. Click on the browse button (...) next to the *Infrared band* text box, to identify the input file as ***feb_2***.

6. In the *Output image* text box, type **feb_NDVI**.

7. Click on OK to generate and display the image.

8. After the program has finished processing, find the *VEGINDEX* dialog box again, which may be hidden by the displayed image.

9. Change the file specified for the Red band to ***july_1***.

10. Change the file specified for the Infrared band to ***july_2***.

11. Type a new *Output image* filename: **july_NDVI**.

12. Click on *OK*.

The two images should show the vegetation patterns quite well. However, to be able to compare between the images, it is necessary to adjust the display properties so that a particular DN value has the same associated color in both images. The current images have default stretches, based on the minimum and maximum values in each image. The fact that the two images have different stretches is immediately apparent when you compare the ocean background areas.

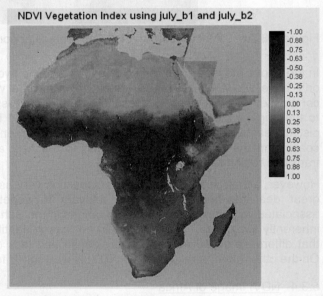

Figure 5.3.4.a   Africa NDVI for February.

Setting the image contrast

1. Find the *Composer* window, which is automatically present when any image is displayed.

2. Click in the ***feb_NDVI*** image, and then click on the *Layer properties* button in the *Composer* window.

3. In the *Layer Properties* window, clear the *Display Min* text box, and then enter **-1**.

4. Clear the *Display Max* text box, and then enter **1**.

5. Click on *Apply*, and then *Save*.

6. The image should now have a legend that extends from -1 to +1.

7. Click in the **july_NDVI** image, and then click on the *Layer properties* button in the *Composer* window.

8. In the *Layer Properties* window, clear the *Display Min* text box, and then enter **-1**.

9. Clear the *Display Max* text box, and then enter **1**.

10. Click on *Apply*, *Save*, and then *OK*.

In comparing the February and July (Figure 5.3.4.a) data, note how the band of high values (deep green) just south of the Sahara Desert has moved north in July. In contrast, Southern Africa, with the exception of the tip of Africa, near Cape Town, is now relatively dry. These two images capture the major seasonal patterns of Africa and, in particular, show how the seasons follow the sun.

In January, the sun's rays are most intense in the southern hemisphere. The low pressure belt and heavy rainfall caused by the rising air due to intense heating is south of the equator, and the Sahel region is relatively dry. By July, however, the latitude of the sun's most intense illumination has migrated to the northern hemisphere. Likewise, the low pressure belt also moves north, bringing welcome rains to the Sahel. For the island of Madagascar, off the south east coast of Africa, only the east coast is relatively wet in July. On-shore easterly winds and local orographic precipitation bring moisture in an otherwise dry region.

5.4 Discriminating Snow from Clouds

5.4.1 Overview

One of the most basic image enhancement procedures is the false color composite. The combination of three bands, each assigned to a different primary color, is a powerful method for visualizing the spectral information in an image. As the number of spectral bands in a data set increases, the potential number of combinations of bands as false color composites increases exponentially. It is therefore important to consider what factors make a good false color composite, and how the colors in the image can be interpreted if fundamental information is available regarding the spectral properties of the surfaces in the image.

In this exercise, we will choose a band combination to separate snow and clouds, and also predict the associated colors based on the band combination and color assignment we choose. We will then develop a snow ratio, or index, and use that to set a threshold that maps snow. Thus, this exercise will start with enhancement, and end with a simple classification. The procedure we will follow is loosely based on Dozier (1989).

5.4.2 Snow and Cloud Properties

We know from everyday experience that both fresh snow and clouds are typically very bright in the visible part of the spectrum. In fact, snow and clouds have a reflectance close to 100% in the visible (Figure 5.4.2.a). However, their spectral properties beyond the visible, in the short wave infrared, are very different. Clouds are also bright in the short wave infrared, but snow has very low reflectance beyond 1.4 µm (Dozier 1989).

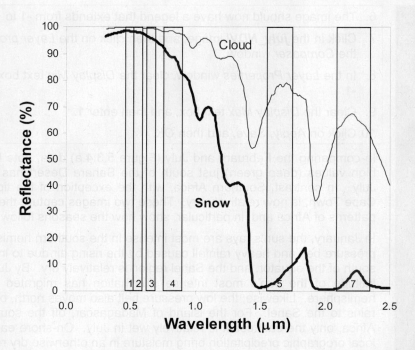

Figure 5.4.2.a   Comparison of the spectral reflectance of snow and cloud, as well as the Landsat spectral band passes. (Snow modeled as 200 μm radii grains, cloud as 5 μm radii water droplets, modified from Dozier 1989).

Based on Figure 5.4.2.a, we can see that with careful selection of the spectral bands it should be possible to create a false color composite that shows snow and cloud as different colors. A false color composite has the advantage of combining information from different wavelengths. For example, although Figure 5.4.2.a appears to suggest that a single band, such as the 1.55 – 1.75 μm TM band 5, can potentially differentiate snow and clouds, we need to remember that there are usually other spectral classes that may confuse our interpretation. Thus, snow is not the only substance that has a low reflectance in band 5; water also has a low reflectance in that band. Adding further complexity is the effect of varying illumination on slopes of different steepness and topographic aspect. Furthermore, mixed pixels dilute the characteristic spectral properties of the cover classes. Combinations of bands, including both false color composites for visual interpretation, and ratios of bands for either visual or more quantitative interpretation, can in many cases overcome these problems.

5.4.3 Preparation

For this section we will use Thematic Mapper data from the Cascade Mountains of Washington State, USA. In Section 5.2 you should have already copied the data from the CD. However, we still need to set the *Project* and *Working Folders* for this new data set.

Before starting you should close any dialog boxes or displayed images in the IDRISI workspace.

Create a new project file and specify the working folders with the IDRISI EXPLORER

Menu Location: **File – IDRISI EXPLORER**

1. Start the IDRISI EXPLORER from the main menu or toolbar, if it is not already open.

2. In the *IDRISI EXPLORER* window, select the *Projects* tab.

3. Right click within the *Projects* pane, and select the *New Project Ins* option.

4. A *Browse For Folder* window will open. Use this window to navigate to the *ID_Man* folder, which is the folder you created on your computer for the data for this manual. Now navigate to the *Chap5_4* subfolder, within the *ID Man/Chap5* folder.

5. Click *OK* in the *Browse For Folder* window.

6. A new project file *Chap5_4*, will now be listed in the *Project* pane of the IDRISI EXPLORER. The working folder will also be listed in the Editor pane.

7. Close the IDRISI EXPLORER by clicking on the red *x* in the upper right corner of the *IDRISI EXPLORER* window.

5.4.4   A Color Composite to Discriminate Snow from Clouds

We will first create a simulated natural color composite of the TM data. We call this a natural color composite because it somewhat replicates the colors we might see with our eyes, if we were to fly over the landscape. We should remember, however, that the TM bands are not perfect matches for the wavelengths the eye is sensitive to, and furthermore, each band is stretched in the composite generation. Therefore the colors will not be identical to natural colors.

Create a simulated natural color composite image

Menu Location: **Display - COMPOSITE**

1. Start the COMPOSITE program using the main menu or tool bar.

2. In the *COMPOSITE* dialog box, specify the file name for the *Blue image band* by clicking on the browse button (…), and in the resulting *Pick list* selecting **TM_casc_b1**. Click on *OK* to close the *Pick list*.

3. Repeat the previous step for the *Green image band*, specifying the **TM_casc_b2** image.

4. Again, repeat the previous step for the *Red image band*, this time specifying the **TM_casc_b3** image.

5. Enter the *Output image* filename in the text box provided: **123comp**.

6. Enter in the *Title* text box: **Simulated Natural Color Composite**.

7. Accept all other defaults, and click *OK* to create and display the false color composite (Figure 5.4.4.a).

Figure 5.4.4.a   Simulated natural color Landsat TM image of a mountain with snow and clouds in places.

In the simulated natural color image (Figure 5.4.4.a), snow and clouds are both white. However, the presence of shadows to the northwest of each cloud (the image is oriented that north is approximately in the "up" direction) makes it possible for a human interpreter to differentiate the clouds from the snow. However, in this image there are some patches of snow and small clouds that make the use of shadows alone challenging for snow and cloud differentiation. Furthermore, a spatial rule is difficult to implement using automated image processing, and most remote sensing enhancement is usually spectrally based.

Referring back to the graph shown in Figure 5.4.2.a, it is apparent that the standard false color composite has a major limitation in that it does not include a short wave infrared band, where snow and clouds have contrasting reflectance. Therefore, a better choice would be a false color composite produced from bands 2, 4, and 5.

For this reason, we will now create another false color composite. This time we will assign bands 2, 4 and 5, to blue, green and red, respectively.

Create a false color composite image

Menu Location: **Display - COMPOSITE**

1. If necessary, start the COMPOSITE program using the main menu or tool bar.
2. Specify the file name for the *Blue image band* as ***TM_casc_b2***.
3. Specify the file name for the *Green image band* as ***TM_casc_b4***.
4. Specify the file name for the *Red image band* as ***TM_casc_b5***.
5. Enter the *Output image* filename in the text box provided: **245fcc**.
6. Enter in the *Title* text box: **False Color Composite (2,4,5 as BGR)**.
7. Accept all other defaults, and click *OK* to create and display the false color composite.
8. Click *Close*, to remove the *COMPOSITE* dialog box.

For this false color composite image, we can predict the colors snow and clouds should be, based on a comparison of the expected relative intensities in each of three bands used (2, 4 and 5), as shown in Figure 5.4.2.a., and the color assigned to those bands in the image (blue, green and red, respectively). In addition, we need some information about the mixing of colors of light, based on the additive mixing system that applies to computer monitors (Figure 5.4.4.b).

- Clouds, which are bright in all three bands of this false color, should be represented by high red, green and blue values in the false color composite. A combination of red, green and blue makes white in the additive color scheme used on computer monitors (Figure 5.4.4.b).

- Snow, on the other hand, is bright in only the first two bands (2 and 4, represented by blue and green in the false color composite), but not the third band (5, represented by red). The combination of blue and green makes cyan (Figure 5.4.4.b).

Thus, in summary, for the TM Bands 2, 4, 5 false color composite, we predict clouds will be white, and snow cyan.

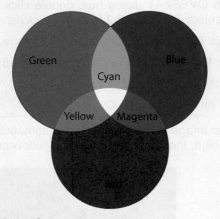

Figure 5.4.4.b   Additive colors.

The non-standard false color composite (Figure 5.4.4.c) does indeed show snow in cyan, and clouds in white. In addition, vegetation is shown in green because of their strong near infrared (band 4) radiance, which is assigned to the monitor's green gun.

Figure 5.4.4.c   Washington State false color composite. Bands 2,4,5 as BGR.

5.4.5   A Ratio to Discriminate Snow

The false color composite shown in Figure 5.4.4.c draws on the distinctive spectral reflectance pattern of snow: strong absorption in the short wave infrared TM band 5, and strong reflectance in the visible and near infrared, including TM bands 2 and 4. This contrast lends itself to the development of a snow ratio. One possible ratio is (Band 2 – Band 5)/ (Band 2 + Band 5) (Dozier, 1989). This is not a ratio that IDRISI offers as a prepared program. However, the program OVERLAY provides a simple way of implementing any ratio.

Calculating ratios with OVERLAY
Menu location: **GIS Analysis – Mathematical Operators – OVERLAY**
1. Start the OVERLAY program from the main menu or the icon tool bar.   2. In the *OVERLAY* dialog box, double click in the text box next to *First image*, and select **TM_casc_b2** from the *Pick list*. Click *OK*.   3. Select **TM_casc_b5** for the *Second image*, and click *OK*.   4. Enter the *Output image* name: **snow2by5**.   5. Select the radio button for *First – Second / First + Second*.   6. Click on *OK*, and then *Close*.

The ratio image will be displayed automatically (Figure 5.4.5.a). Ratio values that are high, those shown in red and yellow colors, indicate snow.

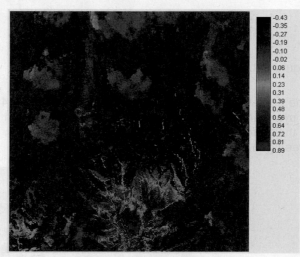

Figure 5.4.5.a   TM (Band 2 – Band 5) / (Band 2 + Band 5) ratio image. The higher DN values (assigned to red colors in the figure) indicate areas of snow.

Finally, to make the location of the snow most clear, we will make a map that indicates where snow is located. This map could be used, for example, as a mask, to blank out any snow-covered areas. To create our map, we need to identify a threshold value in the snow ratio image that differentiates snow. The value we select is somewhat arbitrary, since the boundary is actually a fuzzy one; there will be a complete gradation from 100% snow-covered pixels to pixels without any snow at all. We will choose our threshold by examining the ratio image histogram. We observe that snow makes up only a relatively small proportion of the image. Therefore, in the ratio image, it should comprise the anomalously high values.

Compute the histogram of DN values with HISTO

Menu location: **GIS Analysis – Database Query – HISTO**

1. Start the HISTO program from the main menu or the toolbar.
2. Double click in the *Input file name* text box, and select ***snow2by5***. Click on *OK*.
3. Select the radio button for *Numeric*.
4. Accept all other defaults.
5. Click on *OK*.

Observe the resulting table of data. Note that the fourth column represents the histogram frequency, or the number of pixels in the image within the range of DN values specified in the second and third columns. The frequency values peak at 20,208 for DN values between -0.276 and -0.263, and then decline rapidly. The frequency values reach a local minimum of 215 between the values of 0.320 and 0.333, and then increase slightly again. We therefore will select 0.333 as a threshold, on the assumption that the slight increase is the influence of the snow pixels.

Thresholding is an operation of dividing a single band image into a small number of classes, in this case, just two. We will set up a rule, such that any input DN value below the threshold will be classed as 0, and any DN above the threshold, will be classed as 1.

Applying a threshold to an image with RECLASS

Menu location: **GIS Analysis – Database Query - RECLASS**

1. Start the RECLASS program from the main menu or toolbar.
2. The *RECLASS* dialog box will open.
3. Double click in the text box for *Input file,* select ***snow2by5*** from the *Pick list*, and click *OK*.
4. Enter a name for the *Output file*: **snowmap**.
5. Below the Output file name is the table of *Reclass parameters*. Complete the first line of the table as follows:
   Assign a new value of: **0**
   To all values from: **-1**
   To just less than: **0.333**
6. Complete the second line of the table:
   Assign a new value of: **1**
   To all values from: **0.333**
   To just less than: **1**
7. Check that the dialog box has been completed correctly (Figure 5.4.5.b).
8. Click on *OK*.
9. IDRISI will generate a warning notice: *Warning the input file contains real values. Would you like to convert the output file to integer?*
10. Click on *Yes* to accept this default of an integer output file.

Figure 5.4.5.b   *RECLASS* dialog box with parameters entered.

The output image will be displayed automatically. Compare the image to the false color composite (Figure 5.4.4.c). On the whole, the thresholded image provides a good map of the snow.

Figure 5.4.5.c   Snow map from the snow ratio image.

We can calculate the area that the snow covers in this image, by using the HISTO program one more time.

Compute the histogram of DN values with HISTO
Menu location: **GIS Analysis – Database Query – HISTO**
1. Start the HISTO program from the main menu or the toolbar, if it is not already open.

2. Double click in the *Input file name* text box, and select **snowmap**. Click on *OK*.

3. Select the radio button for *Numeric*.

4. Accept all other defaults, and click on *OK*.

Observe the resulting tabular data (Figure 5.4.5.d). The **Lower Limit** is the minimum DN value, the **Upper Limit** should be interpreted as "just less than." Since our data are integer, Class 0 will therefore only include pixels with a DN of 0, and class 1, pixels with a DN value of 1. The **Frequency** column (fourth from the left), gives information on the number of pixels in each category. Thus, we see that there are 240,140 pixels with a DN value of 0, and 10,861 with a DN value of 1. (Your numbers should be similar, unless you chose a different threshold for discriminating snow.) Summing the non-snow and snow pixels gives us 251,001. This latter sum is equal to the total number of pixels in the image, 501 rows by 501 columns (501 x 501 = 251,001).

```
Histogram of snow map


Class  Lower Limit  Upper Limit  Frequency  Prop.   Cum. Freq.  Cum. Prop.
-----  -----------  -----------  ---------  ------  ----------  ----------


   0      0.000        1.000       240140   0.957     240140      0.957
   1      1.000        2.000        10861   0.043     251001      1.000


Class width        =       1.000
Display minimum    =       0.000
Display maximum    =       2.000
Actual minimum     =       0.000
Actual maximum     =       1.000
Mean               =       0.043
Stand. Deviation   =       0.203
df                 =     251000
```

Figure 5.4.5.d   HISTO output for the **snowmap** image map.

We can now estimate the area of snow. One pixel represents 30 meters by 30 meters or 0.09 hectares (30 m x 30 m = 900 m^2, 1 hectare = 10,000 m^2). Therefore, 10,861 x 0.09 ha = **977.5 ha of snow**.

5.5 *Mineral Ratios*

In the Section 5.3 we saw how the NDVI index is an excellent way to enhance information about vegetation in an image, and in the previous section we saw that snow could be mapped quite reliably with a custom "snow index." In this section we will explore the idea of ratios further. We will investigate what makes a good ratio, and how ratio data can be combined to enhance different mineral types.

Our study area is a volcanic region near Puna de Atacama, Bolivia. The rocks in this region have been altered extensively by hydrothermal fluids. Hydrothermal fluids consist of hot ground water. As these hot ground waters circulate, they chemically alter the surrounding rock. Hydrothermal fluids often carry dissolved chemicals that may precipitate, and may eventually form economic mineral deposits. Thus hydrothermally altered regions make very good mineral exploration targets.

Early work using MSS data, which as just four spectral bands, showed that ratios could be used to enhance mineral alteration in Nevada (Rowan *et al*, 1974.) In addition to enhancing subtle spectral differences, ratios tend to suppress topographically-caused illumination differences in a scene. (We saw this topographic normalization to a certain extent in the snow ratio data.)

A ratio is created by dividing brightness values, pixel by pixel, of one band by another. The primary purpose of such ratios is to enhance the contrast between materials by dividing brightness values at **peaks** and **troughs** in a **spectral reflectance curve**. Specifically, the absorption feature (trough) should be used for the denominator of the ratio, and the peak brightness (peak) as the numerator. This combination of peak and trough will tend to result in higher numbers for the ratio when the class of interest is present.

It is very important that image analysts who use ratios understand the theory behind them, and have specific absorption features in mind for the analysis. Figure 5.5.a can be used to illustrate why the ratios identified in Table 5.5.a can be used to highlight the types of minerals listed. Figure 5.5.a also shows the band passes of the Landsat TM sensor, and thus serves to remind us that it is only possible to use ratios in regions for which we have data. Kaolinite has an absorption feature at 1.4 μm, but Landsat has no spectral band in this region, and thus it cannot be used in an analysis using Landsat TM data. In addition, we need to keep in mind that the bands integrate all the energy across the entire width. Thus, although the mineral jarosite has a deep absorption feature within the band pass of Landsat Band 7 (2.3 μm), the Band 7 DN value for a pixel of pure jarosite would be a single number, and would include radiance from the adjacent, relatively high reflectance regions. Therefore, the signal of jarosite in Band 7 would not be as distinctive as might be expected at first.

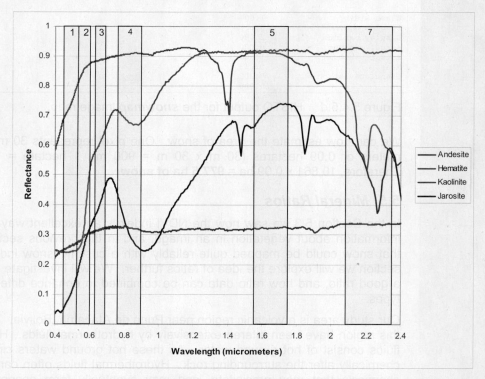

Figure 5.5.a   Spectra of selected rocks and minerals and Landsat spectral band passes. (Source of spectra: Andesite: Johns Hopkins Spectral Library, Hematite & Jarosite: USGS Spectral Library (Clark *et al.* 2003), Kaolinite: JPL Spectral Library).

Table 5.5.a   Typical Landsat TM Mineral Ratios

Ratio (Bands)	Material typically highlighted	Example mineral
5/7	Clay minerals	Kaolinite
5/4	Ferrous iron minerals	Jarosite
3/1	Ferric iron minerals	Hematite

The Andesite spectrum (Figure 5.5.a) is typical of the country rock in our study area in Bolivia. It is a relatively flat spectrum, with few spectral features. Therefore, the andesite might be a spectrum in contrast to which we hope to highlight the other minerals.

The spectra shown in Figure 5.5a suggest that a ratio of band 5 by band 7 will result in a relatively large value for kaolinite, and also, to a lesser extent, for jarosite. Jarosite, however, will have a very high value for a 5 by 4 ratio. Several minerals will have strong 3 by 1 ratios, but the ratio will be particularly strong for hematite, because its strong red color (high band 3 values) contrast against the lower band 1 (blue-green) values. In developing the link from Figure 5.5.a to the image we will produce in this exercise we need to remember that the spectra are library mineral spectra, and the image spectra are composites of many minerals. In some cases there are non-linear mixing effects, especially when dealing with iron minerals. Non-linear mixing effects add further to the difficulties of predicting the results.

The next section is a purely hypothetical example, to illustrate the idea of ratios further, and should be completed prior to working with the real data.

5.5.1 Hypothetical Ratio Example

Figure 5.5.1.a presents two hypothetical spectral curves that might be collected from a field spectrometer for two materials, A and B. Note that the vertical axis is on an arbitrary 8 bit scale, instead of the more normal reflectance, which has a 0-1 scale. The figure also shows the spectral band passes of a 3-band imaging sensor, with 0.1 µm wide bands centered on 0.6, 0.8 and 1.0 µm.

Now, we will investigate the ratios from the three band sensor that would give us the best separation of cover type A from B. The first step is to complete Table 5.5.1.a, estimating the value that the sensor would record for each cover type, in each band. You will simply estimate an average value for the curve, within the sensitivity region of the band you are dealing with. To provide an example, the first row, for the 0.6 µm band, has been completed for you. In the image band (or channel) centered on 0.6 µm, material A has a reflectance response that starts at 175 and peaks at about 195, but the sensor only records a single number, representing an average. In this case the average is probably close to 185. The value recorded for material B is similar, but a little higher on average.

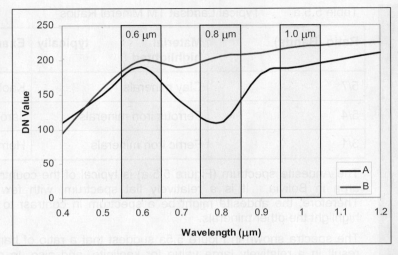

Figure 5.5.1.a   Hypothetical field-collected spectral reflectance curves image sensor wavelength bands.

Table 5.5.1.a   Table of expected DN values for the two cover types as imaged by the three band sensor (compare to Figure 5.4.1.a).

Band	Integrated D.N Values for Band	
Wavelength (µm)	Material A	Material B
0.6	185	200
0.8		
1.0		

Once you have completed the remaining two rows of Table 5.5.1.a, you are ready to try developing your own ratio by completing Table 5.5.1.b. Specifically you should try to develop a ratio *that highlights cover type A in bright tones, and B in dark tones*. As an example, the first row has been completed using the ratio **1.0 µm / 0.6 µm**. The DN values used in the figure are derived from the table you will develop of the integrated values for each band (Table 5.5.1.a).

The **1.0 µm / 0.6 µm** ratio wasn't very successful, because the values obtained are very similar, 1.0 and 1.1. If we look at Figure 5.5.1.a, we can see that this is not surprising, because at those wavelengths cover type **A** does not have any distinctive absorption features. Instead, we need to select two wavelengths, for one of which **A** has an absorption feature, and **B** doesn't. For the second wavelength both **A** and **B** should have relatively high reflectance. Remember to put the wavelength that has the absorption feature for cover type **A** in the denominator of the ratio you choose.

See if you can get a better result with a more carefully chosen set of band rations, *based on the absorption features in Figure 5.5.1.a*.

Hints for completing Table 5.5.1.b: There are two possible ratios that give a high value for **A**, and a low value for **B**. Both choices give a ratio for **A** that is about 50% higher than the value obtained for **B**. If your ratio is higher for **B** than **A**, then your ratio has the wrong wavelength band in the denominator.

Table 5.5.1.b   Worksheet for developing a ratio that highlights A relative to B.

Band Ratio	A		B	
(Band$_X$ / Band$_Y$)	DN Values DN$_X$ / DN$_Y$ (Obtain values from Table 5.4.1.a)	Resulting Ratio Value	DN Values DN$_X$ / DN$_Y$ (Obtain values from Table 5.4.1.a)	Resulting Ratio Value
1.0 μm / 0.6 μm	185 / 185	1.0	220 / 200	1.1

5.5.2 Preparation

For this section we will use Thematic Mapper data from a volcanic region in Puna de Atacama, Bolivia. In Section 5.2 you should have already copied the data from the CD. However, we still need to set the *Project* and *Working Folders* for the Bolivian data.

Before starting you should close any dialog boxes or displayed images in the IDRISI workspace.

Create a new project file and specify the working folders with the IDRISI EXPLORER

Menu Location: **File – IDRISI EXPLORER**

1. Start the IDRISI EXPLORER from the main menu or toolbar.

2. In the *IDRISI EXPLORER* window, select the *Projects* tab.

3. Right click within the *Projects* pane, and select the *New Project Ins* option.

4. A *Browse For Folder* window will open. Use this window to navigate to the *ID_Man* folder, which is the folder you created on your computer for the data for this manual. Now navigate to the *Chap5_5* subfolder, within the *ID Man/Chap5* folder.

5. Click *OK* in the *Browse For Folder* window.

6. A new project file *Chap5_5*, will now be listed in the *Project* pane of the IDRISI EXPLORER. The working folder will also be listed in the Editor pane.

7. Close the IDRISI EXPLORER by clicking on the red *x* in the upper right corner of the *IDRISI EXPLORER* window.

5.5.3 Exploratory Investigation of the Puna de Atacama TM Data

For this section we will use TM data. Table 5.5.3.a lists the wavelengths of the TM bands.

We will start by creating a simulated natural color composite of the TM data, just as we did for the Washington State image, used in Section 5.4. We will use the program COMPOSITE, and assign bands 1, 2 and 3 to blue, green and red, respectivley.

Table 5.5.3.a   Thematic Mapper bands

Band Number	Wavelength Region	Wavelength Interval (µm)
1	Blue	0.45-0.52
2	Green	0.52-0.60
3	Red	0.63-0.69
4	Near Infrared	0.76-0.90
5	Mid Infrared	1.55-175
6*	Thermal	10.4-12.5
7	Mid Infrared	2.08-2.35

*Note that Band 6 is not included with the data for this exercise.

Create a simulated natural color composite image

Menu Location: **Display - COMPOSITE**

1. Start the COMPOSITE program using the main menu or tool bar.

2. In the *COMPOSITE* dialog box, specify the file name for the *Blue image band* by clicking on the browse button (…), and in the resulting *Pick list* selecting **landsat1**. Click on *OK* to close the *Pick list.*

3. Repeat the previous step for the *Green image band*, specifying the **landsat2** image.

4. Again, repeat the previous step for the *Red image band*, this time specifying the **landsat3** image.

5. Enter the *Output image* filename in the text box provided: **123bolivia**.

6. Enter in the *Title* text box: **Simulated Natural Color Composite**.

7. Accept all other defaults, and click *OK* to create and display the false color composite (Figure 5.5.3.a).

Figure 5.5.3.a   Simulated natural color composite of Puna de Atacama TM data.

Figure 5.5.3 illustrates that a simulated natural color composite works well in this arid environment to show the hydrothermal alteration. Note the central bright area, which is the main region of hydrothermal alteration, and which provides a strong contrast against the dark volcanic rocks. Erosion products from the hydrothermal area are resdistributed to the northeast and southwest along stream courses.

5.5.4 Calculating Ratios

We will calculate three ratios to highlight the different minerals present in these rocks: Band 5 / Band7, Band 5 / Band 4, and Band 3 / Band 1 (Table 5.5.a). We will use the program OVERLAY.

As with the snow ratio of Section 5.4., we will generate a normalized difference ratio (First – Second)/(First + Second), rather than a simple ratio (First / Second), because the former gives a more balanced range of values, from -1, to +1, with 0 representing the middle value, namely a flat spectrum. For simplicity sake, however, we will refer to each ratio as if it were a simple ratio. Thus, (Band 7 – Band 5) / (Band 7 + Band 5) will be referred to as Band 7 / Band 5.

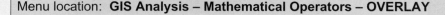

Calculating ratios with OVERLAY

Menu location: **GIS Analysis – Mathematical Operators – OVERLAY**

1. Start the OVERLAY program from the main menu or the icon tool bar.

2. In the *OVERLAY* dialog box, double click in the text box next to *First image*, and select **landsat5** from the *Pick list*. Click *OK*.

3. Select **landsat7** for the *Second image*, and click *OK*.

4. Enter the *Output image* name **5by7**.

5. Select the radio button for *First – Second / First + Second*.

6. Click on *OK*.

The resulting image does not look impressive. Partly this is because ratios are very noisy. A ratio suppresses the majority of the information, which derives from variation in illumination due to topography, and enhances a minor part of the signal, the spectral differences between bands. Another reason why the image looks rather unimpressive is that the default palette is the *quant* palette. This ratio would make more sense as a black and white image. Therefore, follow the instructions below to change the palette and increase the contrast.

Change palette and contrast enhancement of an image

1. Make sure the new **5by7** image is the focus of the IDRISI workspace by clicking in the image.

2. Find the *Composer* window, and select the button for *Layer Properties.*

3. In the *Layer Properties* window, select the browse button (…) next to text box blow *Palette File*.

4. In the *Pick list* window, click on the plus sign next to the *IDRISI Taiga\symbol* folder.

5. Scroll down, until you can select **GreyScale**. Click on *OK* to close the *Pick list* window.

6. Back in the *Layer Properties* window, enter in the *Display Min* text box **-0.05**.

7. Enter in the *Display Max* text boxes **0.20**.

8. Still in the *Layer Properties* window, click on the buttons for *Apply*, *Save* and *OK*.

The resulting image (Figure 5.5.4.a) should show the central hydrothermally altered area very distinctly.

Figure 5.5.4.a   Ratio of Landsat bands 5 / 7, with *greyscale* palette and contrast enhanced.

Having produced the first ratio, now run the OVERLAY operation two more times to create the remaining two ratio combinations (Band 5 / Band 4 and Band 3 / Band 1).

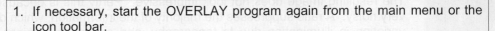

Calculating ratios with OVERLAY

Menu location: **GIS Analysis – Mathematical Operators – OVERLAY**

1. If necessary, start the OVERLAY program again from the main menu or the icon tool bar.

2. In the *OVERLAY* dialog box, double click in the text box next to *First image*.

3. The *Pick List* window will open. Select ***landsat5*** from the *Pick list*. If necessary, click on the plus symbol (+) to see the names of the individual bands within the *Chap5_5* folder. Click *OK* to close the *Pick list*, if necessary.

4. Select ***landsat4*** for the *Second image*, and click *OK*.

5. Enter the *Output image* name **5by4**.

6. Select the radio button for *First – Second / First + Second*.

7. Click on *OK*.

8. The image will display automatically, with a *quant* palette file.

9. Now alter the file names to create the third and last ratio.

10. In the *OVERLAY* dialog box, double click in the text box next to *First image*, and select ***landsat3*** from the *Pick list*. Click *OK*.

11. Select ***landsat1*** for the *Second image*, and click *OK*.

12. Enter the *Output image* name **3by1**.

13. Click on *OK*.

Once you have the three ratio images, you can combine them in a false color composite, with the program **COMPOSITE**. Use the Band 5 / Band 7 ratio for blue, Band 3 / Band 1 for green, and Band 5 / Band 4 as red.

Create a color composite image
Menu Location: **Display - COMPOSITE**

1. Start the COMPOSITE program using the main menu or tool bar.

2. In the *COMPOSITE* dialog box, specify the *Blue image band* as **5by7.**

3. Specify the *Green image band* as **3by1**.

4. Specify the *Red image band* as **5by4**.

5. Enter the *Output image* filename in the text box provided: **ratiofcc**.

6. Enter in the *Title* text box: **5/7 as blue, 3/1 as green, and 5/4 as red**.

7. Accept all other defaults, and click *OK* to create and display the false color composite (Figure 5.5.4.b).

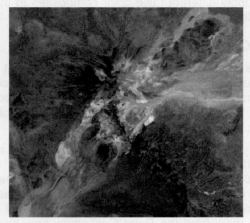

Figure 5.5.4.b   Ratio false color composite. 5/7 as blue, 3/1 as green, and 5/4 as red.

With Figure 5.5.4.b to guide you, you should now be able to draw a sketch map of the main minerals present in the image. For example, the central core of the alteration zone has a blue color, indicating high values in the 5/7 ratio, which in turn indicates the presence of clay minerals. In interpreting all the colors in the image, remember the mixing of red and blue gives cyan (a light, sky blue color), green and red gives yellow, and red and blue gives magenta (purple) (see the color mixtures shown by Figure 5.4.4.b).

Chapter 6　Other Spectral Enhancement Techniques

6.1　Introduction

This chapter is a companion to Chapter 5, on ratios, and is a second chapter on spectral enhancement techniques. We will start by investigating methods for enhancing information in highly correlated bands. In highly correlated data, the colors in the image will not appear very vibrant, and we will explore techniques to address this problem. One of the techniques, principal component analysis, has very widespread use in remote sensing because it is an effective method of dealing with another problem commonly encountered, namely the need to visualize more than three bands at a time. Three bands is the maximum number that can be used in a false color composite.

After the section on highly correlated data, we then look at specialized image enhancement. We will segment an image, separating water from land. We will then apply different false color composites to the water and land features, thus providing an overall optimal image.

6.2　Copy Data for This Chapter

In this chapter we will work with two different image sets, one for the highly correlated data section (6.3) and one for the segmenting and density slice for advanced display (6.4) sections. Therefore, you should now copy the *Chap6* folder from the CD, and paste it as a new subfolder within the *ID Man* folder on your computer.

After you have copied the folder, you should remove the Read-Only attribute from this new folder on your computer. This is done by right-clicking on the *Chap6* folder name, selecting *Properties* from the pop-up menu. A dialog box will open, labeled *Chap6 Properties* (if you apply this procedure to the entire *ID Man* directory, then the dialog box will be labeled *ID Man Properties*). Now clear the check mark from the *Read Only* check box, by clicking in the box. You should then click on the button for *Apply*, and in the subsequent *Confirm Attribute Changes* dialog box, accept the default *Apply changes to this folder, subfolder and files*, and click on *OK*. You will need to also click on *OK* in the *Chap6 Properties* dialog box.

Note: Section 1.3.1 provides detailed instructions on how to copy the data from the CD, and also on how to remove the *Read-Only* attribute from the data. Also, the procedure for setting up the *ID Man* folder on your computer is described.

6.3　Enhancing Highly Correlated Data using Data Transformations

6.3.1　Background

The NASA airborne Thermal Infrared Multispectral Scanner (TIMS) instrument collects six bands of long wavelength infrared radiation (Table 6.3.a). The thermal infrared part of the electromagnetic part of the spectrum includes an atmospheric window from 8-12 μm, which is the region where the TIMS bands are located. Thermal wavelengths are characterized by emission of energy from objects that are at approximately room temperature. The measured thermal energy also includes a reflected component, but the magnitude is generally small, and can be ignored.

Table 6.3.a.   Approximate TIMS band passes.

Band	Wavelength (μm)
1	8.15 - 8.5
2	8.6 - 9.0
3	9.0 - 9.3
4	9.6 - 10.2
5	10.3 - 11.1
6	11.3 - 11.6

Each multispectral thermal band is dominated by the temperature of the surface radiating energy. This is because the total radiance is proportional to the fourth power of the temperature of the surface (the Stefan-Boltzman radiation law). Furthermore, the wavelength at which maximum radiance occurs is a function of the inverse of the temperature (Wien's displacement law).   The dominant influence of temperature in multispectral thermal data has the effect of making the bands highly correlated. False color images made from highly correlated data are characterized by gray tones, and very pale colors, with low saturation. In this exercise, we shall investigate three methods of enhancing highly correlated data: principal component analysis (PCA), decorrelation stretch (which is based on PCA), and an intensity-hue-saturation (IHS) stretch. These methods, especially PCA, also have general use in image processing, for example in the analysis of Landsat imagery. Thus, for example, we will also use PCA in Chapter 8, as a change detection method.

The data we will work with is a subscene from a flight line over Mauna Loa, Hawaii, and was collected at 22:03 GMT, September 30, 1989. The image covers an area approximately 2.5 kilometers on a side. The band 3 (9.0 to 9.2 μm) radiance image is shown in Figure 6.3.a. This is a daytime image, and the image is clearly dominated by topographic effects. For example, notice the way temperature differences associated with solar heating cause the cinder cones to stand out. The cinder cones are quite distinctive because they have a conical shape, with a central depression.

Figure 6.3.a   TIMS Band 3 (9.0 - 9.2 μm) image of lava flows on Mauna Loa, Hawaii.

It is apparent from Figure 6.3.a that there are slight temperature differences associated with the different lava flows. These lava flows are all historic flows, and thus the lava flows have long since cooled from their original molten state. Therefore the brightness variations are unrelated to the original molten lava temperatures. Instead, the temperature differences you can see in this image are entirely due to differences in heating, due to slope and aspect effects, as well as differences in the rate at which heat is absorbed, due to variations in surface properties.   As an example of how surface properties can affect local temperature, you might think about the difference in temperatures between dark vehicles, which absorb more heat, than light or shiny vehicles.

The differences in temperature between the different lava flows are relatively small, and mapping the different lava flows from Figure 6.3.a would be quite difficult. In this exercise, we will investigate spectral enhancement methods to make the different lava flows more clear.

6.3.2 Preparation

In Section 6.2 you should have already copied the data from the CD. However, we still need to set the *Project* and *Working Folders* for the TIMS data.

Before starting you should close any dialog boxes or displayed images in the IDRISI workspace.

Create a new project file and specify the working folders with the IDRISI EXPLORER
Menu Location: **File – IDRISI EXPLORER**

1. Start the IDRISI EXPLORER from the main menu or toolbar.
2. In the *IDRISI EXPLORER* window, select the *Projects* tab.
3. Right click within the *Projects* pane, and select the *New Project Ins* option.
4. A *Browse For Folder* window will open. Use this window to navigate to the *ID_Man* folder, which is the folder you created on your computer for the data for this manual. Now navigate to the *Chap6_3* subfolder, within the *ID Man/Chap6* folder.
5. Click *OK* in the *Browse For Folder* window.
6. A new project file *Chap6_3*, will now be listed in the *Project* pane of the IDRISI EXPLORER. The working folder will also be listed in the Editor pane.
7. Close the IDRISI EXPLORER by clicking on the red *x* in the upper right corner of the *IDRISI EXPLORER* window.

Before we begin our enhancements, let's first simply look at the data. We will display two bands as single band images, and thus we will use a GreyScale palette. In addition, we will create a false color composite, using three different bands.

Initial display of images
Menu: **Display – DISPLAY LAUNCHER**

1. Start the DISPLAY LAUNCHER from the main menu or icon bar.
2. In the *DISPLAY LAUNCHER* window, double click in the text box for the file name, and select **TIMSb1**.
3. Select a *GreyScale* palette.

4. Click on *OK* to display the image.

5. Start the DISPLAY LAUNCHER again.

6. In the *DISPLAY LAUNCHER* window, double click in the text box for the file name, and select *TIMSb3*.

7. Select a *GreyScale* palette.

8. Click on *OK* to display the image.

Compare the two images, and note how similar, and thus how highly correlated, the two images appear to be. We will now create the false color composite. Refer to Table 6.3.a for the wavelength regions associated with each band.

Create a color composite image

Menu Location: **Display - COMPOSITE**

1. Start the COMPOSITE program using the main menu or tool bar.

2. In the *COMPOSITE* dialog box, specify the file name for the *Blue image band* **TIMSb1**. Click on *OK* to close the *Pick list*.

3. Specify the *Green image band as* **TIMSb3**.

4. Specify the *Red image band as* **TIMSb5**.

5. Enter the *Output image* filename in the text box provided: **135fcc**.

6. Accept all other defaults, and click *OK* to create and display the false color composite (Figure 6.3.2.a).

Figure 6.3.2.a   TIMS false color composite. Band 1 (8.15 - 8.5 µm) as blue, band 3 (9.0 - 9.3 µm) as green and band 5 (10.3 - 11.1 µm) as red.

The resulting false color composite (Figure 6.3.2.a) shows distinct differences in colors between the different lava flows, suggesting that there are chemical or weathering differences between the various flows. Although the false color composite helps a great deal in separating the different flows, it is still rather difficult to separate the different units because the colors are rather pale.

6.3.3 Principal Component Analysis (PCA)

Principal component analysis (PCA) is a statistical method for generating new, uncorrelated variables, from a data set. If you are not familiar with PCA, you should consult a remote sensing text. Most remote sensing texts, including Lillesand *et al.* 2004, and Jensen 2005, have excellent descriptions of this method. For completeness sake, however, we provide a very short reminder of the purpose and concepts of PCA.

PCA is a rotation and translation of the original band axes to produce an equal number of new bands that are orthogonal (at right angles to each other in the data space) and uncorrelated (Figure 6.3.3.a). The first principal component band, PCA band 1, is oriented to capture the maximum variance. Thus, in the case of Figure 6.3.3.a, PCA1 is oriented along the diagonal of the bispectral plot, along the direction of the main data distribution. Subsequent bands are oriented to capture the maximum remaining variance, and are perpendicular to the earlier bands. PCA produces as many new bands as there were old bands, although it usually assumed that most of the information is present in the first few new bands, which comprise most of the variance.

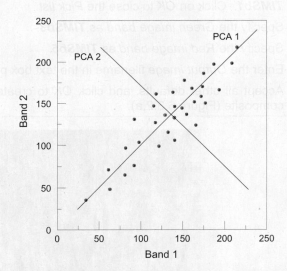

Figure 6.3.3.a   Bispectral plot of two band data showing original band axes and the new axes associated with the principal components.

Apply a principal component analysis with PCA

Menu location: **Image Processing – Transformation – PCA**

1. Start the PCA program using the main menu.

2. In the *PCA* dialog box window, click on the button to *Insert layer group*. In the pick list window, select the *tims* raster group file.

3. Set the *Number of components to be extracted* to **6** (the maximum possible, if there are 6 input files).

4. In the text box next to *Prefix for output files (can include path):*, enter **PCA**.

5. In the *Text output option* section of the *PCA* dialog box, select the radio button for *Complete output*.

6. Accept all other defaults. (See Figure 6.3.3.b for the completed dialog box.)

7. Click on *OK*.

The *Module Results* window will display a text file of the results of the analysis (Table 6.3.3.a).

Figure 6.3.3.b   The *PCA* dialog box with the TIMS data specified.

Table 6.3.3.a   PCA results for TIMS data of Hawaii

VAR/COVAR	timsb1	timsb2	timsb3	timsb4	timsb5	timsb6
timsb1	3049.735087	3167.563987	2896.607208	2814.089180	2408.649538	2117.097105
timsb2	3167.563987	3328.996188	3056.881097	2940.704585	2515.199971	2206.764671
timsb3	2896.607208	3056.881097	2863.842080	2696.184573	2282.163491	1997.237795
timsb4	2814.089180	2940.704585	2696.184573	2685.575131	2347.519245	2055.336047
timsb5	2408.649538	2515.199971	2282.163491	2347.519245	2122.048568	1859.768873
timsb6	2117.097105	2206.764671	1997.237795	2055.336047	1859.768873	1649.966022

COR MATRX	timsb1	timsb2	timsb3	timsb4	timsb5	timsb6
timsb1	1.000000	0.994117	0.980131	0.983305	0.946814	0.943783
timsb2	0.994117	1.000000	0.990028	0.983504	0.946320	0.941590
timsb3	0.980131	0.990028	1.000000	0.972202	0.925752	0.918793
timsb4	0.983305	0.983504	0.972202	1.000000	0.983361	0.976398
timsb5	0.946814	0.946320	0.925752	0.983361	1.000000	0.993903
timsb6	0.943783	0.941590	0.918793	0.976398	0.993903	1.000000

COMPONENT	C 1	C 2	C 3	C 4	C 5	C 6
% var.	97.404921	2.040407	0.335480	0.112832	0.072828	0.033525
eigenval.	15292.732438	320.347217	52.670862	17.714852	11.434155	5.263552
eigvec.1	0.443114	-0.241191	-0.700588	-0.108803	0.408736	-0.275227
eigvec.2	0.463738	-0.310442	-0.146321	0.330072	-0.723611	0.186018
eigvec.3	0.425695	-0.457113	0.676808	0.095475	0.327058	-0.188894
eigvec.4	0.417582	0.164644	0.095411	-0.671154	0.021111	0.581825
eigvec.5	0.362757	0.572312	0.143408	-0.175841	-0.286340	-0.638271
eigvec.6	0.318455	0.530898	-0.005285	0.623483	0.346294	0.328718

LOADING	C 1	C 2	C 3	C 4	C 5	C 6
timsb1	0.992263	-0.078170	-0.092070	-0.008292	0.025027	-0.011434
timsb2	0.993937	-0.096302	-0.018405	0.024078	-0.042408	0.007397
timsb3	0.983709	-0.152883	0.091786	0.007509	0.020666	-0.008098
timsb4	0.996474	0.056864	0.013362	-0.054509	0.001378	0.025758
timsb5	0.973823	0.222364	0.022593	-0.016066	-0.021019	-0.031788
timsb6	0.969512	0.233929	-0.000944	0.064604	0.028828	0.018566

One of the difficulties of using PCA is that the output images can be difficult to interpret. Nevertheless, by carefully examining the output text from the PCA program (Table 6.3.3.a), some interpretation can usually be made. Therefore, these results should be saved, for example by clicking on the *Save to File* button of the bottom of the *Module Results* window.

The *Module Results* includes information on:

- The variance/covariance matrix (i.e. the variability of the bands, and how they relate to one another).

- The correlation matrix (the relationship between the bands).

- The eigenvalues of the principal components (amount of variance explained, or accounted for by each new component).

- The eigenvalues expressed as a proportion of the total ("% var.") in the output.

- The eigenvectors, which give the equation to convert the input data to the output data.

- The Loadings, which provide information on the correlation between the original bands and the new components.

For the discussion below, you should refer to the relevant images, and the *Module Results* (Table 6.3.3.a), to see if you can verify the interpretations suggested.

The files created by the PCA module have names that are generated systematically. Each name starts with *PCA* (the prefix that we specified in the program), and a suffix of *cmp#*, where the # indicates the file number.

Use the IDRISI DISPLAY LAUNCHER to display the 6 output files, each time using a GreyScale Palette, as described below.

Display the PCA images
Menu: **Display – DISPLAY LAUNCHER**
1. Start the DISPLAY LAUNCHER from the main menu or icon bar.
2. In the *DISPLAY LAUNCHER* window, double click in the text box for the file name, and select ***pcacmp1***.
3. Select a *GreyScale* palette.
4. Click on *OK* to display the image.
5. Repeat steps 1-4 above, five times, to display the five files, ***pcacmp2*** through ***pcacmp6***. Rember to use the GreyScale palette each time.

Note that principal component images 3 and 5 are very dark, and therefore you will need to change the contrast stretch for these images.

Change palette and contrast enhancement of an image
1. Make sure the ***pcacmp3*** image is the focus of the IDRISI workspace by clicking in the image.
2. Find the *Composer* window, and select the button for *Layer Properties.*
3. In the *Layer Properties* window, move the slider for *Display Max* until the display has a better contrast. (A good value appears to be about **16**, however the choice is quite subjective.)
4. Now move the *Display Min* slider to improve the contrast further. (A good value appears to be about **-30.0)**

5. Click on the buttons for *Apply*, *Save* and *OK*.

6. Repeat steps 1-5 for **prncmp5**, selecting appropriate *Display Max* and *Display Min* values.

In interpreting the values for the TIMS data (Table 6.3.3.a), we see that the first component (C1 = **PCAcmp1**) comprises a total of over 97.4% of the original variance. This suggests that the majority of the variability in the images is common to all the images. In this case, that common information is the temperature of the rocks. The remaining 5 components represent only 0.6% of the variance in the data. However, it is this 0.6% that is of interest to us. Note how the images appear to get progressively noisier with higher numbers. For example, notice how **PCAcmp2**, **PCAcmp3** and **PCAcmp4** shows the pattern of lava flows well, but **PCAcmp5** and **PCAcmp6** are dominated by noise.

The eigenvectors, as explained before, represent the formula for the calculation of the new principal component bands. Thus, they can help us understand what each output band means. For example, we find that the eigenvectors for C1 are all positive, and similar (0.44 to 0.32). This suggests that C1 (the image **PCAcmp1**) represents an average of all the bands. Indeed, the loadings, the last section of the table, show that C1 is highly correlated with all the input bands (the values vary between 0.97 and 0.99).

Likewise, we can interpret the eigenvectors of each of the remaining principal components, or output bands, in terms of the original input values. For C2, the eigenvectors are negative for the first three bands, and positive for the remaining three. This suggests that **PCAcmp2** can be understood to be the difference between the first three bands and the second three bands. C3, on the other hand, is generated by the difference between the first two bands, and the third band. However, without knowledge of the emittance spectra of the lava flows, interpreting the meaning of the bands is difficult. We can, however, see from the eigenvectors that C1 is an average of the input data, and that C2 – 5 are all enhancing subtle spectral features in the original images. A simple visual inspection of the images tells us that **PCAcmp2**, **PCAcmp3** and **PCAcmp4** have some interesting information, whereas **PCAcmp5** and **PCAcmp6** have relatively little.

As a final step, the PCA components can be visualized as a false color composite, using the program COMPOSITE and principal components 2, 3 and 4 as the input bands, as described below.

Create a color composite image
Menu Location: **Display - COMPOSITE**

1. Start the COMPOSITE program using the main menu or tool bar.

2. In the *COMPOSITE* dialog box, specify the file name for the *Blue image band* **PCAcmp2**. Click on *OK* to close the *Pick list*.

3. Specify the *Green image band* as **PCAcmp3**.

4. Specify the *Red image band* as **PCAcmp4**.

5. Enter the *Output image* filename in the text box provided: **PCAfcc234**.

6. Accept all other defaults, and click *OK* to create and display the false color composite (Figure 6.3.3.c).

Figure 6.3.3.c   False color composite of TIMS data.   Principal components
                   2,3,4 as BGR.

Based on the discussion above, we can understand that by excluding **PCAcmp1**,
we are excluding the majority of the temperature information, which is of less
interest to us. The false color composite without this first principal component
(Figure 6.3.3.b) is remarkably impressive, given that it comprises less than 1% of
the original variance. The lava flows are now very clearly differentiated.

Note, however, that the PCA false color composite does appear rather noisy,
with a distinctive striping. The stripes are from the scan-lines. It is, generally
speaking, inevitable that we will enhance the noise in this type of PCA operation,
since we are boosting a minor part of the signal (the spectral variation) at the
expense of the majority of the signal (the temperature information).

6.3.4   PCA Decorrelation Stretch

PCA is a powerful data transformation technique that has many applications and
variations. One variation on PCA is the decorrelation stretch. In a decorrelation
stretch, the image is first transformed with PCA. Selected principal component
bands are then stretched, and a reverse PCA transformation is applied, in which
the data are retransformed back to the original data space. Figure 6.3.4.a
illustrates how the data shown in Figure 6.3.3.a might appear after a
decorrelation stretch. In comparing the two figures, note how the data have been
stretched out in the direction of PC2, thus filling the bispectral plot area to a much
greater degree.

Gillespie *et al.* (1986) point out a very useful attribute of the decorrelation stretch
is that if a false color composite is made of the decorrelated data, the color
saturation will be much stronger compared to that of a false color composite of
the original bands. However, the *hues* should be unchanged, thus making it
possible to interpret the colors in terms of the original spectral bands. (*Hue*
refers to the dominant color, such as red, or green, and *saturation* refers to the
brightness of the color, for example, pink has less saturation than red.

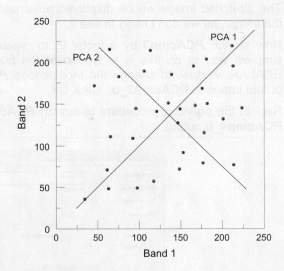

Figure 6.3.4.a   Bispectral plot showing the effects of a decorrelation stretch.
Compare to Figure 6.3.3.a, which shows the data prior to the
stretch.

Further information on these terms is provided in Section 4.2.2, where color
terminology is explained in detail.) Let us investigate whether this improvement
of the colors seems to apply with the Hawaii TIMS data.

In Section 6.3.3 we already calculated the principal components for the Hawaii
data. Therefore, in this exercise we only need to apply a stretch to the selected
bands, and then re-transform the principal components back to the original
bands. The IDRISI PCA program, which we used in Section 6.3.3, has an option
to do the reverse transformation.

We will specifically only stretch principal components 2, 3 and 4, as these
components appear to carry most of the spectral information.   Principal
component 1 is mostly temperature and will be used in the retransformation back
to the original space, but it is not stretched. Principal components 4 and 5 are
mainly noise, and will be excluded entirely.

The stretching is applied with the IDRISI program SCALAR, a program for
applying simple arithmetic (scalar) operations to an image, including
multiplication, addition, division exponentiation, and subtraction.

Multiplying an image by a number with SCALAR
Menu Location: **GIS Analysis – Mathematical Operations - SCALAR**
1. Start the SCALAR program using the main menu. 2. In the *SCALAR* dialog box, use the *pick list button* (…) to specify the name of the *Input image* as **PCAcmp2**. Click on *OK* to close the *Pick list.* 3. In the text box labeled *Output image*, type **PCAcmp2_b**. 4. In the text box labeled *Scalar value*, type *2.* 5. In the *Operation* section of the window, select the radio button for *Multiply* (Figure 6.3.4.b). 6. Click *OK*.

7. The stretched image will be displayed automatically; however you can close the image, as we don't need to see it.

8. Now stretch **PCAcmp3** by a factor 2, to create **PCAcmp3_b** output. The simplest way to do this is to type over the number **2** in text boxes in the SCALAR window, to change the Input image **PCAcmp2** to **PCAcmp3**, and output image to **PCAcmp3_b**. Click *OK*.

9. Repeat the previous procedure to stretch **PCAcmp4** by a factor of 2, create **PCAcmp4_b** output.

Figure 6.3.4.b   The *SCALAR* dialog box, with the *Multiply* option selected.

Now that we have stretched the data, we have two minor steps to complete before we can run the inverse PCA program. First, we have to create a raster group file. A raster group file is a file that tells IDRISI that a group of files belongs together as a single group. Raster group files were introduced in Section 1.3.7, and if you have trouble with this section, you may want to review that material.

Create a raster goup file collection with the IDRISI EXPLORER

Menu Location: **File – IDRISI EXPLORER**

1. If the *IDRISI EXPLORER* window is not already open, open it again using the main menu or the icon toolbar.

2. Click on the tab for *Files*.

3. If the files are not listed in the *Files* pane, double click on the directory name to display the files.

4. If need be, slide the divider for the *Metadata* pane down, so you can see all the files we need to work with: **PCAcmp1.rst** through **PCAcmp6.rst**, as well as the three new files **PCAcmp2_b.rst, PCAcmp3_b.rst** and **PCA.cmp4_b.rst**.

5. Click on **PCAcmp1.rst**, so the file is highlighted.

6. Keeping the keyboard Ctrl button pressed, now click on the following files in the order listed:
PCAcmp2_b.rst
PCAcmp3_b.rst
PCAcmp4_b.rst
PCAcmp5.rst
PCAcmp6.rst

7. You should now have 6 files highlighted.

8. Right click in the *Files* pane. Select the menu option for *Create – Raster Group* (Figure 6.3.4.c). This will create a file **Raster group.rgf.**

9. Click on the file **Raster group.rgf** in the *Files* pane. In the *Metadata* pane, below the *Files* pane, enter a new name in the right hand cell of the first row, typing over the default name of *Raster Group*. Use **PCA2** for the new name.

10. Click on the *save* (floppy disk) icon, at the bottom left hand corner of the *Metadata* pane. The name of the Raster Group File will immediately be updated in the *Files* pane.

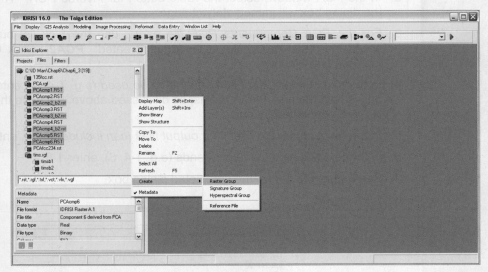

Figure 6.3.4.c   Selecting the raster files to combine into a Raster Group File.

The next step is to rename the eigenvector file, associated with our original PCA raster group file, so that it matches the new raster group file name. You can use the Windows Explorer to do this, or follow the directions below to use the IDRISI EXPLORER.

Rename a file with the IDRISI EXPLORER
Menu Location: **File – IDRISI EXPLORER**

1. The *IDRISI EXPLORER* window should still be open from the last step. If you have closed it, open it again using the main menu or the icon toolbar.

8. In the *IDRISI EXPLORER* window, click on the tab for *Files*.

9. If the files are not listed in the *Files* pane, double click on the directory name to display the files.

2. The unlabeled text box at the bottom of the *Files* pane is a listing of file formats to be shown. The default is **.rst,*.rgf,*.ts,*.vct,*.vlx,*.vgf.* Use the down arrow on the right hand side of the text box to select the option for this text box of *All files (*.*).*

3. Find the file **PCA.eig**, and click on it to highlight it.

4. With the mouse over the highlighted text, right-click, and select *Rename* from the pop-up menu.

5. Edit the name of the file, so it reads **PCA2.eig.**

6. Close the IDRISI Explorer.

We are ready now for the final step for retransforming the data.

Perform an inverse principal component analysis with PCA

Menu location: **Image Processing – Transformation – PCA**

---

1. Start the PCA program using the main menu.

2. In the *PCA* window, select the radio button for *Inverse PCA*. The options in the dialog box will immediately change.

3. For the *PCA Components RGF file name*, use the *pick list* button (...) to select the raster group file we have just created: **PCA2**. Click *OK* to close the *Pick List* window.

4. In the text box for *List of components to be used (e.g. 1-4, 6)*, enter **1-4**. (We only select the first 4 PCA bands, as discussed above, because the remaining two are dominated by noise).

5. In the text box next to *Prefix for output files (can include path):*, enter **Decor**.

6. In the text box next to Output bands (e.g. 1-4, 6), enter **1-6**.

7. See Figure 6.3.4.d for the completed dialog box.

8. Click on *OK*.

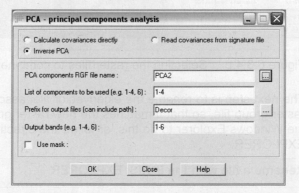

Figure 6.3.4.d   Inverse PCA transformation in the *PCA* dialog box.

We can now create the false color composite, and see whether we have indeed improved the colors of the lava flows.

Create a color composite image

Menu Location: **Display - COMPOSITE**

---

1. Start the COMPOSITE program using the main menu or tool bar.

2. In the *COMPOSITE* dialog box, specify the file name for the *Blue image band* **Decor1**. Click on *OK* to close the *Pick list*.

3. Specify the *Green image band as* **Decor3**.

4. Specify the *Red image band as* **Decor5**.

5. Enter the *Output image* filename in the text box provided: **135decor**.

6. Accept all other defaults, and click *OK* to create and display the false color composite (Figure 6.3.4.e).

Figure 6.3.4.e   Decorrelation stretch of TIMS bands 1,3,5 as BGR.

You should compare this decorrelation stretch to the original false color composite, **135fcc**, created in Section 6.3.2 (Figure 6.3.2.a). You should notice that the colors are indeed much brighter. In particular, the details of the lava flow on the left hand side should now be much clearer.

6.3.5 HLS Stretch

In section 4.2.2, we introduced the concept of color transformations. We provide only the briefest summary here. If you need to be refreshed regarding color space concepts, you should review Section 4.2.2, and possibly also refer to a text such as Jensen (2005).

We saw in Section 4.2.2 that colors on a computer monitor are normally specified in terms of red, green and blue (RGB values), and therefore this a convenient system for addressing many remote sensing problems. However, in some instances, it is useful to work in the alternative hue, lightness, and saturation (HLS) color system. The term *hue* is relatively intuitive and refers to the characteristic tint. *Lightness* refers to the brightness, which extends from black to white. *Saturation* refers to the purity of the color, so that low saturation colors tend to gray, and have a typically pastel quality, whereas high saturation colors are the purest colors.

It is important to understand that HLS and RGB are equivalent ways of specifying color, and thus it is possible to move back and forth between systems. In this exercise, we will transform an image between RGB and HLS space. This will allow us to increase the saturation of the image, making the colors much purer. Since we don't alter the hue, the tints of the colors should not change at all. This will help discriminate the different lava flows in the image, but because we don't change the hues, the color tints will still be useful for interpreting the different colors in the image.

Convert three image bands from RGB to HLS space

Menu location: **Image Processing – Transformation – COLSPACE**

1. Start the COLSPACE program from the menu.

2. In the *COLSPACE* window, select the radio button for *RGB to HLS.*

3. In the section for *Input files*, note that it is a little bit confusing that IDRISI specifies the input files here in the reverse order of that used for the COMPOSITE program, namely as *Red, Green*, and then *Blue*.

4. Use the pick list button (…) next to the text box for *Red image band*, to select the original band 5 TIMS image, **timsb5**. Click *OK* to close the *Pick List* window.

5. Repeat the previous step, to select **timsb3** for the *Green image band.*

6. Repeat the previous step, to select **timsb1** for the *Blue image band.*

7. In the section for *Output files*, type the filename in the textbox for *Hue image band*: **hue**.

8. In the textbox next to *Lightness image band*, type **lightness**.

9. In the textbox next to *Saturation image band*, type **saturation**.

10. Compare your completion of the text box options to Figure 6.3.5.a.

11. Click *OK*. Unlike most other IDRISI programs, an image is not displayed on completing the program.

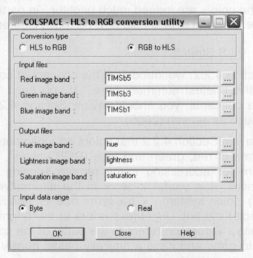

Figure 6.3.5.a.   The *COLSPACE* dialog box for RGB to HLS transformation.

Use the IDRISI DISPLAY LAUNCHER to view the *saturation* image created by the COLSPACE program, as described below

Initial display of images

Menu: **Display – DISPLAY LAUNCHER**

1. Start the DISPLAY LAUNCHER from the main menu or icon bar.

2. In the *DISPLAY LAUNCHER* window, double click in the text box for the file name, and select **saturation**. Click *OK* in the *Pick List* window.

3. Select a *GreyScale* palette.

4. Click on *OK* to display the image (Figure 6.3.5.b).

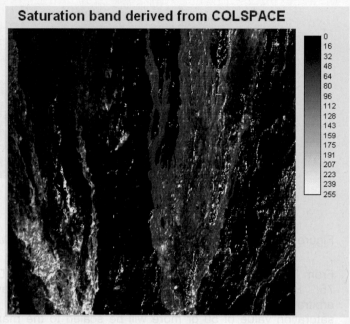

Saturation band derived from COLSPACE

Figure 6.3.5.b   Saturation image of the TIMS data.

As shown by Figure 6.3.5.b, the saturation image is very dark, and although the image is scaled over the range 0-255, most of the image values are in the lower half of the DN range, as indicated by the radiometric scale bar. This image therefore confirms what we had observed visually, namely that the saturation of this image is very low. We can improve the image by stretching the saturation, and then transforming the hue, stretched saturation, and lightness (HLS) bands back to RGB. However, first we need to decide how much to stretch the saturation, and we will do that by looking at the image histogram.

Display the image data distribution with HISTO

Menu Location: **Display - HISTO**

1. Start the HISTO program from the main menu or the toolbar.

2. In the *HISTO* dialog box, click on the browse button (…) next to the text box for the *Input file name* to select **saturation**. Click on *OK* to close the *Pick List* window.

3. Set the class width to **1**.

4. Leave the remaining parameters set at their default values.

5. Click on *OK*.

6. The histogram will appear in a new HISTOGRAM window. In this new window, in the section labeled *Mode*, click on the option for *Cumulative*. The graph will automatically update (Figure 6.3.5.c).

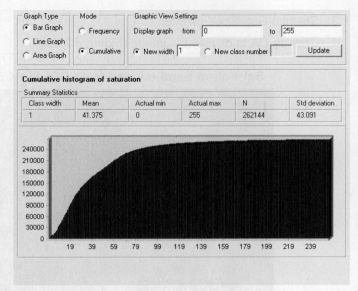

Figure 6.3.5.c   Histogram of the **saturation** image, in *Cumulative* mode.

From Figure 6.3.5.c, we can see that the majority of the DN values are less than 75. However, to increase the saturation to give an even clearer image, we arbitrarily select 50 as the maximum for the scaling. This means that any saturation value of 50 or more will be scaled to the maximum, 255. From the graph we can see this will still leave about 75% of the image with saturation values less than the maximum of 255.

There are a variety of ways to do the rescaling of the saturation values. One simple way is through the program STRETCH. The concept of a stretch operation should be familiar to you, as a stretch operation is typically used in displaying data. This is done so that the image brightness levels are shown in an optimal manner on the screen (Chapter 2). The type of stretch applied in displaying an image is normally temporary, and does change the original file values. For this exercise, however, we need to create a new file with the stretch applied permanently.

Rescaling the DN values of an image with STRETCH

Menu location: **Image Processing – Enhancement – STRETCH**

1. Use the main menu to start the STRETCH program.

2. In the *STRETCH* window, click on the pick list button (…) next to the *Input image* text box to select the image **saturation**. Click *OK* to close the *Pick List* window.

3. In the text box next to *Output image*, enter **sat_str**.

4. Check the box for *Specify an upper bound other than maximum*.

5. In the text box that will open to the right of the *Specify an upper bound other than maximum*, enter **50**.

6. Accept the remaining defaults (Figure 6.3.5.d), and Press OK.

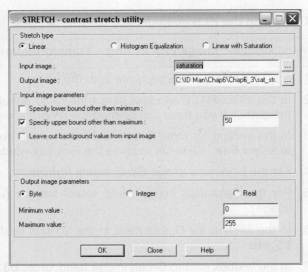

Figure 6.3.5.d   The *STRETCH* dialog box.

We can now confirm that the data have indeed been stretched by running the HISTO program once again, using *sat_str* as the input file.   See if you can complete this without instructions.   If you do have problems, return to the HISTO instructions earlier in this Section.   Figure 6.3.5.e shows the output you should obtain.

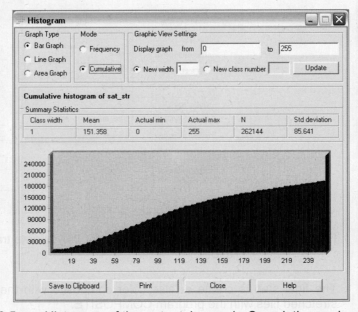

Figure 6.3.5.e   Histogram of the *sat_str* image, in *Cumulative* mode.

In comparing the two histograms shown in Figures 6.3.5.c and 6.3.5.e, you should note that in the latter figure only a small portion of the image has low DN values, and approximately 25% of the image has the maximum DN value.   This confirms that the DN values in the *sat_str* image are now much higher with the stretch applied.

Therefore, we are now ready to transform the HLS data back to RGB space.

Transform the HLS images back to RGB images

Menu location: **Image Processing – Transformation – COLSPACE**

1. Start the COLSPACE program from the menu.

2. In the *COLSPACE* window, select the radio button for *HLS to RGB.* (This is the default if you have just opened the program window.)

3. In the section for *Input files,* double click in the text box for *Hue Image Band,* to select **hue**. Click *OK* to close the *Pick List* window.

4. For the *Lightness Image Band,* select **lightness**.

5. For the *Saturation Image Band* select **sat_str** (i.e. the stretched saturation image).

6. In the section for *Output files,* in the textbox next to *Red image band,* enter **b5_str**.

7. In the textbox next to *Green image band,* enter **b3_str**.

8. In the textbox next to *Blue image band,* enter **b1_str**.

9. Compare your completion of the text box options to Figure 6.3.5.f.

10. Press *OK*. As before, the program will not automatically display the output file.

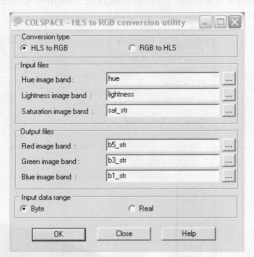

Figure 6.3.5.f   *COLSPACE* dialog box for the reverse transformation of HLS to RGB.

The final step is create a false color composite with the three new saturation-stretched files with the program COMPOSITE.

Create a color composite image

Menu Location: **Display - COMPOSITE**

1. Start the COMPOSITE program using the main menu or tool bar.

2. In the *COMPOSITE* dialog box, specify the file name for the *Blue image band* **b1_str**. Click on *OK* to close the *Pick list*.

3. Specify the *Green image band* as **b3_str**.

4. Specify the *Red image band* as **b5_str.**

5. Enter the *Output image* filename in the text box provided: **135sat_str**.

6. Accept all other defaults, and click *OK* to create and display the false color composite (Figure 6.3.5.g).

Figure 6.3.5.g   TIMS false color composite of saturation-stretched data. Band 1 as blue, band 3 as green and band 5 as red.

Compare the false color composite with the stretched saturation, **135_satstr** (Figure 6.3.5.g) with the false color composite made from the original data, **135fcc** (Figure 6.3.2.a), by redisplaying the latter image if necessary. In comparing the two images, evaluate whether the hues are indeed unchanged in the saturation stretched image. You should also compare these two images to the decorrelation image, **135decorr** (Figure 6.3.4.e). Of the three images, which is the best for interpreting the lava flows?

In doing this exercise, you may have noted that in applying the stretch to the saturation image, we selected an arbitrary cut-off of 50 DN. You may want to experiment with values of 10 (an extreme stretch) and 100 (a rather mild stretch), to see whether a different value might give you better results.

6.4 Segmenting and Density Slicing Images for Advanced Display

For some applications it is useful to be able to use non-standard display options. In this section we will therefore explore some alternative ways of displaying an image, including masking of features not of interest, and density slicing.

6.4.1 Preparation

In Section 6.2 you should have already copied the data from the CD. Specifically, we will work with the data in the folder **Chap6\Chap6_4**, which like the folder for Chapters 1-4, contains ETM+ Hong Kong. However, the area we will be studying in this section is focused on the Pearl River Estuary.

In order to create a more manageable data size, the original image, with its 30 meter pixels, has been degraded by pixel averaging to produce 90 meter pixels.

If you would prefer to work with the original 30 meter pixel data, the original 30 meter data are available in the folder **Chap6\Chap6_4alt**. If you do use this alternative data set, in the instructions that follow, set the subfolder to this alternative location. When prompted to use files that have names such as hk_etm_b1, substitute the name of the files in the new directory, e.g. hk_etm_large_b1, etc.

Before starting you should close any dialog boxes or displayed images in the IDRISI workspace. Now, set the *Project* and *Working Folders* for this new data, as described below.

Create a new project file and specify the working folders with the IDRISI EXPLORER
Menu Location: **File – IDRISI EXPLORER**

1. Start the IDRISI EXPLORER from the main menu or toolbar.

2. In the *IDRISI EXPLORER* window, select the *Projects* tab.

3. Right click within the *Projects* pane, and select the *New Project Ins* option.

4. A *Browse For Folder* window will open. Use this window to navigate to the *ID_Man* folder, which is the folder you created on your computer for the data for this manual. Now navigate to the *Chap6_4* subfolder, within the *ID Man/Chap6* folder. (If you decide to work with the full resolution data set, simply navigate to the *Chap6_4alt* subfolder.)

5. Click *OK* in the *Browse For Folder* window.

6. A new project file *Chap6_4*, will now be listed in the *Project* pane of the IDRISI EXPLORER. The working folder will also be listed in the Editor pane.

7. Close the IDRISI EXPLORER by clicking on the red *x* in the upper right corner of the *IDRISI EXPLORER* window.

On starting a new project, it is always good to look at the data. We will therefore create a standard color composite, with simulated natural colors. We will increase the percent that is saturated to the extremes of the brightness range, in order to increase the image contrast.

Create a color composite image
Menu Location: **Display - COMPOSITE**

1. Start the COMPOSITE program using the main menu or tool bar.

2. In the *COMPOSITE* dialog box, double click in the text box for the *Blue image band*. The *Pick List* will open automatically. Double click on **hk_etm_b1** to select the blue band (band 1).

3. Repeat this selection process to specify the *Green image band* as **hk_etm_b2**.

4. Specify the *Red image band* as **hk_etm_b3**.

5. Enter the *Output image* filename in the text box provided: **hk123**.

6. Change the value of the *Percent to be saturated from each end of the grey scale* from *1.0* to **7.5**.

7. Accept all other defaults, and click *OK* to create and display the false color composite.

Notice how the pattern of sediment in the Pearl River Estuary is apparent in this image (Figure 6.4.1.a).

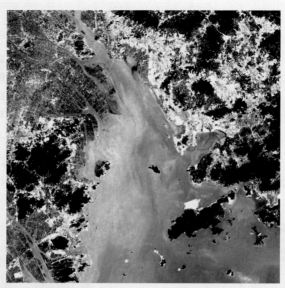

Figure 6.4.1.a   Simulated natural color composite of the Pearl River Delta, using TM bands 1, 2 and 3 as blue, green and red.

6.4.2 Developing a Land Mask

In order to explore further the patterns in the water, it would be useful to develop a mask, so that we can ignore the land. A straightforward method of developing this mask is to use a threshold value in ETM+ Band 5 (1.55-1.75 µm). Water absorbs strongly in the mid infrared, and therefore we will assume that all dark pixels in the mid infrared band are water. The only difficult step is to choose the value of the threshold between water and land. In a tidal area, the boundary is obviously a zone, not an absolute line. In addition, water logged soils will tend to have similar spectral characteristics to water.

In the next step we will modify the image palette file, in order to display the image DN values around the potential threshold very clearly. Specifically, we want a clear idea of the area that would be included in the mask, for each potential threshold value.

Displaying an image with an alternative palette file

Menu Location: **Display – DISPLAY LAUNCHER**

1. Start the DISPLAY LAUNCHER from the main menu or icon bar.

2. In the *DISPLAY LAUNCHER* window, double click in the text box for the file name, and double click on ***hk_etm_b5*** in the *Pick List* window that opens automatically.

3. Click on the tab for *Advanced Palette/Symbol Selection*. This will open up additional options in the dialog box.

4. Click on the brightly colored color ramp in the bottom right column (Figure 6.4.2.a). The palette file's name, RADAR, will be displayed in the data entry line labeled *Current Selection*.

5. Accept all the remaining default options.

6. Click on *OK* to display the image (Figure 6.4.2.b).

Figure 6.4.2.a.   The *DISPLAY LAUNCHER*, with the *Advanced Palette/Symbol Selection* tab and the *RADAR* palette indicated by the arrows.

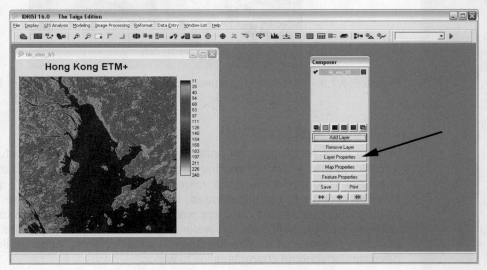

Figure 6.4.2.b   ETM+ Band 5 image with the *RADAR* palette file. The *Layer properties* button in the *Composer* window is indicated by the arrow.

Note that in this rendition of the Band 5 image (Figure 6.4.2.b), the water is generally shown in cool colors, such as blue. We will now adjust the range of DN values over which the color ramp is applied, in order to select a precise threshold that discriminates between land and water.

Adjusting the thresholds for color ramp display in the *Composer* Window

1. Find the *Composer* window, which is automatically opened whenever an image is displayed.

2. In the *Composer* window, select *Layer Properties* (see Figure 6.4.2.b). The *Layer Properties* dialog box will open.

3. Slowly adjust the *Display max* slider to successively lower positions. Observe how, when you slide the pointer to lower values, more and more of the land area of the image is displayed as white. Stop moving the slider when you reach a DN value of between 18 and 22.

4. Now use the legend and the colors in the image to help you choose an optimum DN threshold that differentiates between the water and land. Specifically, we want a value **below** which most pixels are water. (For example, 18 might seem a good value.)

5. Make a note of the value you selected for the threshold.

Now that we have selected the threshold, we need a mechanism to apply the threshold so as to assign all pixels that have a value below the threshold as water, and all those above the threshold as land. There are at least two ways to do this in IDRISI. One way is to use the program RECLASS, which is available from the main menu from GIS Analysis – Database Query – RECLASS, and which we used in Section 5.4.5. However, we will use an alternative method, using the IMAGE CALCULATOR, a particularly powerful tool with broad application to image analysis.

Creating a land mask with the IMAGE CALCULATOR

Menu location: **GIS Analysis – Mathematical Operators – IMAGE CALCULATOR**

1. Use the main menu or the icon tool bar to open the IMAGE CALCULATOR.

2. In the *IMAGE CALCULATOR* window, click on the radio button for *Operation Type: Logical Expression*.

Before continuing, we will stop and take a moment to familiarize ourselves with the IMAGE CALCULATOR (Figure 6.4.2.c). The interface for this program is based on the concept of a hand calculator. However, unlike a hand calculator, the IMAGE CALCULATOR can operate on images.

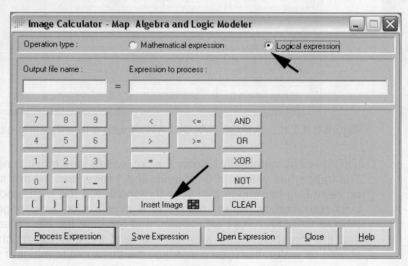

Figure 6.4.2.c   *IMAGE CALCULATOR* window.

The top part of the *IMAGE CALCULATOR* window has radio buttons for specifying whether you wish to create a *Mathematical expression* or a *Logical expression.* (The latter option, *Logical expression*, is indicated by the upper arrow in Figure 6.4.2.c.) Below the radio buttons are two text boxes, on the left for the *Output file name*, and the right for the *Expression to process*. Developing an expression, or formula, is easy using the buttons in the large, main area below the two text boxes. In particular, the *Insert image* button (indicated by the lower arrow in Figure 6.4.2.c) is used to place an entire image in the expression. There are additional buttons for logical operations. At the bottom of the window are some basic commands for processing, saving, and opening expressions.

Creating a land mask with the IMAGE CALCULATOR (cont.)

3. In the *Output file name* text box, enter the file name **landmask**

4. Click on the button for *Insert Image*.

5. A *Pick List* will open. Double click on *hk_etm_b5*.

6. The *Expression to Process* text box will now contain the image name in square brackets: **[hk_etm_b5]**.

7. Click on the button for the less than sign ("<"), and then enter the threshold you determined in the previous step. Your equation should now look something like the following: **[hk_etm_b5]<18**.

8. Figure 6.4.2.d shows the resulting IMAGE CALCULATOR expression.

9. Click on the *Process Expression* button.

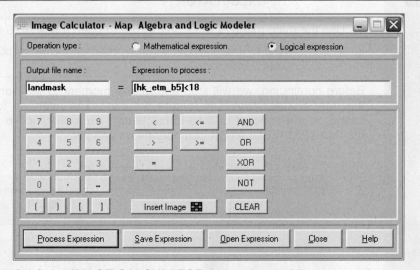

Figure 6.4.2.d   IMAGE CALCULATOR with a thresholding expression.

IDRISI will automatically display the processed land mask image (Figure 6.4.2.e). The image has values of 0 for land, and 1 for water. At this stage, if you decide on reviewing the image that your threshold was too high, and there is too much land classified as water, then it is a simple step to change the value in the IMAGE CALCULATOR expression, and recreate the file. Likewise, if you decide that the threshold value was too low, and there is too much land where there should be water, then you can adjust the threshold to a higher number.

Figure 6.4.2.e   The land mask image.

6.4.3 Displaying Patterns in Water

In this section we will use our mask to suppress all land area pixels, leaving only the water pixels for an image of water patterns. We will then apply a look up table (palette file) that highlights patterns of sediment in the water in the Pearl River Estuary, and the surrounding lakes.

The land mask, created in the previous section, has values of 1 in the areas interpreted to be water, and 0 elsewhere. We therefore can apply the mask simply by multiplying the land mask by a selected image band.

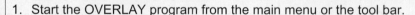

Applying the land mask with OVERLAY

Menu location: **GIS Analysis – Mathematical Operators – OVERLAY**

1. Start the OVERLAY program from the main menu or the tool bar.

2. In the *OVERLAY* dialog box, double click in the text box for the *First Image*, and then in the automatically opened *Pick List*, double click on **hk_etm_b3**.

3. Double click in text box for the *Second Image*, and select the land mask image, **landmask**.

4. In the window for the *Output image*, enter **b3_landmask**.

5. In the Overlay option section of the dialog box, select the radio button for the option for *First * Second* (i.e. first times second images).

6. Click on *OK* to process the overlay operation, and also display the image.

The masked image, with a color ramp applied by IDRISI automatically (Figure 6.4.3.a), shows the complex sediment patterns in the bay very clearly. Higher DN values, shown in oranges and reds, indicate more sediment-laden water, or shallower water. Lower values, indicated by greens, indicate clearer, deeper water.

The ETM+ thermal band also shows interesting patterns in the water. We can follow the same procedure as with the red band to mask the thermal band. Try doing this on your own using the OVERLAY program. If you have trouble, follow the instructions below.

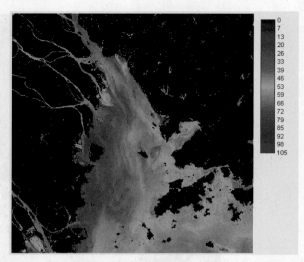

Figure 6.4.3.a   ETM+ band 3 (red), with land masked out and color ramp applied.

Applying the land mask with OVERLAY
Menu location: **GIS Analysis – Mathematical Operators – OVERLAY**

1. Start the OVERLAY program from the main menu or the tool bar.

2. In the *OVERLAY* dialog box, double click in the text box for the *First Image*, and then in the automatically opened *Pick List*, double click on **hk_etm_b6**.

3. Double click in text box for the *Second Image*, and select the land mask image, **landmask**.

4. In the window for the *Output image*, enter **b6_landmask**.

5. In the Overlay option section of the dialog box, select the radio button for the option for *First * Second* (i.e. first times second images).

6. Click on *OK* to process the overlay operation, and also display the image (Figure 6.4.3.b).

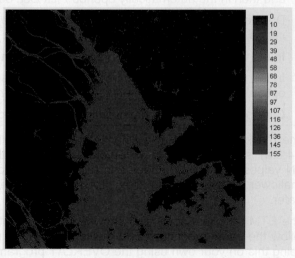

Figure 6.4.3.b   ETM+ band 6 (thermal) with land masked out.

The image that is created (Figure 6.4.3.b) this time appears to be dominated by just one color value in the water, namely red. You might therefore think that there is no thermal variation in the water. However, you may notice from the legend, that the color ramp has been applied from 0, and that red encompasses a range of values. Therefore, if we select a higher value than 0 for the lower end of the color ramp, we may well see differentiation in the water. (Note that actually a similar issue applied to the red band data, processed earlier. In that case, however, the issue wasn't as noticeable, since the maximum value was so much lower.)

We will therefore adjust the thresholds for the display, just as we did in Section 6.4.2.

Adjusting the thresholds for color ramp display in the *Composer* Window

1. Find the *Composer* window, which is automatically opened whenever an image is displayed.

2. In the *Composer* window, select *Layer Properties*. The *Layer Properties* dialog box will open.

3. Slowly adjust the *Display min* slider to successively higher positions. Observe how patterns in the water appear and vary as you move the slider.

4. Slowly adjust the *Display max* slider to successively lower positions.

5. The optimal values for *Display Min* and *Display Max* are somewhat arbitrary. However, one set of values that gives a good visual representation of the patterns is **121** and **150**, respectively (Figure 6.4.3.c). You can manually enter these values in the relevant text boxes, and click on *Apply*.

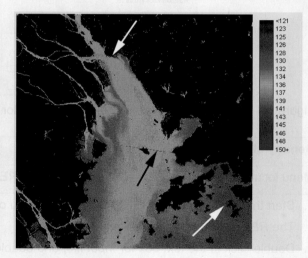

Figure 6.4.3.c   ETM+ band 6 (thermal) with land masked out and modified color ramp. White arrows point to thermal pollution sources, black arrow to noise in the data.

The masked thermal image with the adjusted display range (Figure 6.4.3.c), looks very different compared to the original display of the masked data (Figure 6.4.3.b). This reminds us that the nature of the display stretch can be very important in interpreting an image.

The thermal image also has a number of interesting features, and shows patterns not evident in the red band image (Figure 4.3.a). A major source of thermal pollution is evident as a dark red (high DN value) plume extending from the island in the bottom right corner of the image (indicated by a white arrow in Figure 6.4.3.c). This source for this warm water is the discharge from a power station. A second major plume, also indicated by a white arrow, is evident where the main channel of the Pearl River becomes much narrower, at the top of the image. With careful examination, additional, smaller plumes can be made out at other locations along the coastline.

Note also that there is some noise in the data, as shown by the narrow line of warm temperatures that crosses the bay. This feature is indicated by a black arrow in Figure 6.4.3.c.

6.4.4 Density Slicing Landsat Band 3

Sometimes it may be useful to summarize the complexity of the multiple DN values into just a few discrete classes, a process termed *Density slicing*. Density slicing can be conceptualized as a simple type of classification, using just one band of data.

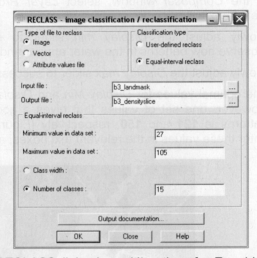

Figure 6.4.4.a   *RECLASS* dialog box with options for *Equal-interval reclass*.

Density slicing an image with RECLASS

Menu location: **GIS Analysis – Database Query - RECLASS**

1. Start the RECLASS program from the main menu or toolbar.

2. The *RECLASS* dialog box will open.

3. Double click in the text box for *Input file*, and double click on **b3_landmask** to select that file.

4. Enter a name for the *Output file*: **b3_densityslice**.

5. In the *Classification type* section of the RECLASS dialog box, click on the radio button for *Equal-interval reclass*. The controls in the dialog box will be changed automatically to reflect this option.

6. Change the *Minimum value in data set* to **27**.

7. Leave the *Maximum value in the data set* at the default (*105* in this case).

8. Click on the *Number of classes* radio button, and enter **15** in the text box that opens to the right.

9. Figure 6.4.4.a shows the dialog box, with the parameters specified.
10. Click on *OK*.

In the above instructions, you were given a minimum value of 27 to enter, rather than the default of 0. You can verify that this is a good choice by examining the **b3_landmask** histogram, available with the program HISTO.

Once the RECLASS program has completed, the image will be displayed automatically (Figure 6.4.4.b). In comparing this image to the original masked band 3 data (**b3_landmask**, shown in Figure 6.4.3.a), you should note that the range of the color ramps are different.   In addition, the density slicing has resulted in discrete steps in the colors, instead of the appearance of a smooth surface.

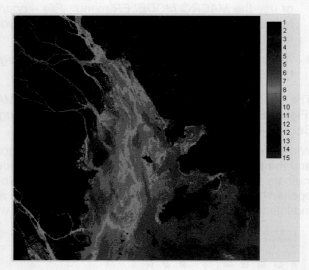

Figure 6.4.4.b   Density-sliced and land-masked ETM+ band 3 data.

6.4.5 Combination False Color Composite for Land and Water

Occasionally it may be useful to create a false color composite that uses a different band combination for different parts of the image. For example, a band combination that is good for the land is not always good for water, which has very different spectral properties. Therefore, for an effective display, it may be useful to use one band combination for the water, and another for the land. Water quality patterns are most apparent in the visible wavelengths, because water's peak transmissivity is in the green part of the electromagnetic spectrum. However, land cover materials, especially vegetation, benefit from a combination of visible, near and shortwave infrared wavelengths. Therefore, for this exercise we will create a combination of Landsat bands 1, 2 and 3 (i.e. visible wavelengths) for water areas, and bands 3, 4 and 5 (i.e. red, near infrared and shortwave infrared) for the land.

It is important to note that combination false color composites such as the one we are creating here should be used with caution. A combination false color composite may be misleading to users who are not aware of the processing history of the image. In addition, unless the user has a reference image that shows the band assignments for each part of the image, even an experienced user might be misled by such a product.

The steps involved in this exercise are fairly numerous. Therefore, we will take advantage of a very powerful tool in IDRISI: the MACRO MODELER. The

MACRO MODELER has already been explained in some detail in Section 4.2, and if this section seems confusing to you, you should review that material.

For this exercise we will see an example of the use of the Macro Modeler as a way to employ "canned" programs, which have been prepared previously.

Adapting and running a previously created MACRO MODELER model
Menu location: **Modeling – MACRO MODELER**
1. Start the MACRO MODELER from the main menu or main icon bar. 2. The *MACRO MODELER* graphical interface will open. 3. In the *MACRO MODELER* window, click on the *Open* icon (second from left), or use the *MACRO MODELER* menu: *File – open*. (Note that if the MACRO MODELER window is highlighted, and you put your cursor over an icon, the icon name is shown.) 4. A *Pick List* window will open. Double click on **segment_composite** to select this file.

The model will be shown automatically in the *MACRO MODELER* window (Figure 6.5.4.a) as a series of linked icons. Although discussed extensively in Section 4.2, we provide a short review here.

Within the MACRO MODELER window, the blue squares represent data layers, and the pink parallelograms are IDRISI program modules. The dark blue arrows indicate the input and output for the processes. Note that the model we have opened is missing one input data layer, as well as a composite generation module and a final output data layer, all of which we will provide.

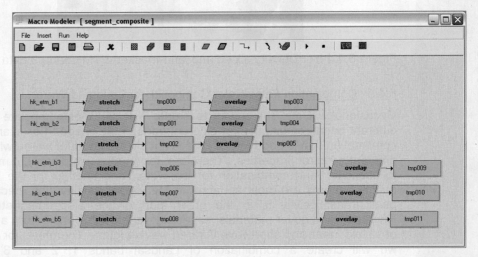

Figure 6.4.5.a   MACRO MODELER, showing the model when first opened.

Models with multiple inputs, outputs and modules, such as the **segment_composite** model, are a bit daunting to try to interpret. However, this model is actually quite simple. The input files are all on the left, and comprise five of the seven Landsat bands. In the model, the five bands are each stretched. The first three are then each processed through an overlay operation. This is followed by a second set of overlay operations.

Note that ETM+ band 3 is linked as input for two different stretch modules. This demonstrates that it is possible for one file to serve as input for multiple modules.

Adapting and running a previously created model (cont.)

5. In the *MACRO MODELER* window, click on the *Raster Layer* icon.

6. The *Pick List* window will open. Select **LANDMASK**, a file created in Section 6.4.2. (This image has DN values of 1 for the water areas, and 0 for land areas.)

7. A new raster layer, indicated by a blue rectangle and labeled **LANDMASK**, will appear in your model.

8. Use the mouse to drag the **landmask** raster layer to a position above the second column of input files (i.e. above raster layer *tmp000*).

9. Click on the *Connect* icon (a blue bent arrow). Now click on the **landmask**, raster layer, and, keeping the mouse button depressed, move the mouse to the top of the first *Overlay* module. Remove your finger from the mouse button. This will connect **landmask** to the *Overlay* function (Figure 6.4.5.b).

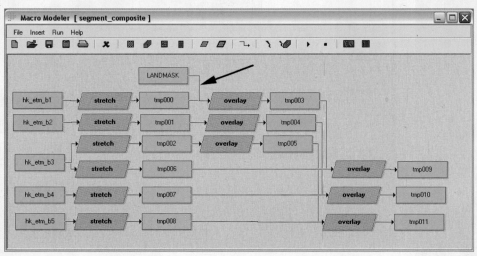

Figure 6.4.5.b   MACRO MODELER with the *Landmask* raster layer added. Arrow points to the new link to the *Overlay* function.

Adapting and running a previously created model (cont.)

10. Repeat the previous step two more times, connecting the **landmask** raster layer to the two *Overlay* modules below the first one. The result will be that the land mask will be connected to all three *Overlay* modules.

11. The connection procedure described above automatically enters the land mask as the second layer in each of the *Overlay* module functions. To confirm that this has indeed taken place, do the following: Place the mouse over the first *Overlay* module (the one used in step 9, above). Right click. A *Parameters: Overlay* window will open (Figure 6.4.5.c), which is essentially a table showing the processing parameters for *Overlay*. Confirm that the *Second input image* is specified as **landmask**. You should also confirm that in the bottom line of the window the overlay *Operation* parameter is specified as *Multiply*.

12. Click on *OK* to close the *Parameters: Overlay* window.

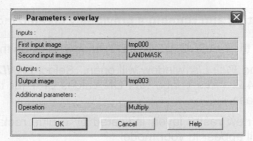

Figure 6.4.5.c   *Parameters: Overlay* window showing *Landmask* as the second input image.

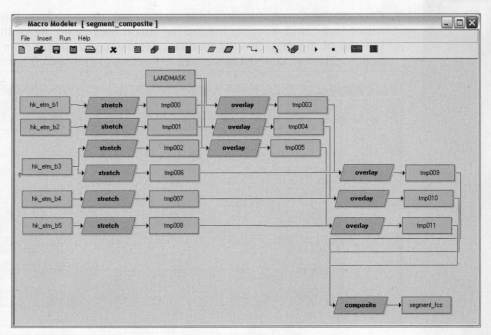

Figure 6.4.5.d   MACRO MODELER with final model.

Adapting and running a previously created model (cont.)

13. Make the MACRO MODELER window a little larger, by dragging the lower frame down a short way.

14. Now add a new module to the model, by clicking on the *Module* icon.

15. A *Pick List* window will open. Double click on *Composite*.

16. A new module, labeled *Composite*, will appear in the model.

17. Use the mouse to drag the *Composite* module and its output raster layer to the bottom right corner of the *MACRO MODELER* window.

18. Click on the *Connect* icon. Click on raster layer ***tmp009***, and keeping the mouse button depressed, move the mouse until you are over the *Composite* module. Remove your finger from the mouse button. The ***tmp009*** raster layer should now be connected as one of the three inputs for the Composite Module.

19. Repeat the previous step to connect ***tmp010*** as the second input to the Composite module.

20. Repeat again to connect **_tmp011_** as the third input to the Composite module.

21. Change the <u>output</u> filename of the *Composite* module from the default name (which will begin with *temp*, and is followed by 3 numbers) by *right-clicking* with the mouse on that raster layer icon.

22. *A Change Layer Name* window will open.   Enter the new file name: **segment_fcc**.

23. The resulting module is shown in Figure 6.4.5.d.

24. Save the model by clicking on the *Save* icon.

25. Run the model by clicking on the *Run* icon.

26. When prompted *"The layer tmp007 will be overwritten if it exists. Continue?,"* click on *Yes to All*.

27. As the model runs, you can track its progress by observing which module is highlighted in green.

When the program is complete, the image will be displayed automatically (Figure 6.4.5.e). The image only has meaning within the context of the land mask image, **landmask** (Figure 6.4.2.e). You should compare the image to a regular false color composite, such as **hk123**, to decide if you feel this combination false color composite image does indeed provide more information.

Figure 6.4.5.e   Combination false color composite. Water: bands 3,2,1 (R,G,B).
Land: 5,4,3 (R,G,B).

Chapter 7   Introduction to Classifying Multispectral Images

In this section you will learn how to classify a scene based on the spectral properties of a pixel, a procedure that is analogous to classification using just the colors of objects. Thus, multispectral classification is quite different compared to our human vision system, which is mainly based on spatial patterns and context. Humans have no trouble identifying objects in black and white images, but the multispectral classification programs we are using do very poorly on such data.

Multispectral classification usually requires some knowledge of the scene. This differentiates multispectral classification from hyperspectral classification, where, at least in theory, it may be possible to identify classes entirely automatically, using generic spectral reflectance libraries. The information about the scene may come from personal knowledge of the area, field trips, and aerial photography. In addition, this information is usually supplemented by image interpretation by the analyst.

Classification is a grouping or generalization of the data. Thus it involves a simplification. Consider for a moment a hypothetical three-band, 8 bit data set. The potential number of unique combinations of DN values is 255^3, or 16.6 million. The number of unique combinations grows exponentially with the number of bands. Nevertheless, the number of useful classes that can be identified reliably in a typical multispectral image is usually quite small, perhaps ten or so. This is partly because usually only a small number of the potential DN combinations are actually found in real data, and partly because there is considerable variation within each class. Thus, the process of multispectral classification involves not just identifying the average DN values of each class, but also the variability of each class.

In classification it is also important to differentiate between **spectral classes** and **informational classes**. The spectral classes are the groups in the data; informational classes are the map classes, the groups the analyst would like to identify. There may be a 1:1 relationship between spectral and informational classes, but in general it is unlikely to be so. For example, an analyst may wish to identify the class Water. However, this class might consist of two relatively distinct spectral classes such as deep, clear water, and shallow, muddy water.

7.1 Introduction to Multispectral Classification Methods

There are many classification methods. To characterize the differences between these many methods, a number of terms are defined:

- Supervised versus unsupervised classification
- Soft versus hard classification
- Relative versus absolute classification

Understanding these terms helps illuminate some of the important characteristics of classifiers that are dealt with in this section.

7.1.1 Supervised Versus Unsupervised Classification

The difference between supervised and unsupervised classification relates to when the analyst uses knowledge of the scene to guide the classification. Unsupervised classification uses an algorithm to identify the spectral classes, and the analyst subsequently assigns informational class names to the algorithm-identified spectral classes. With supervised classification, the analyst identifies regions in the image, known as training areas, to represent the typical spectral classes that make up the informational classes. The classification algorithm then classifies each pixel in the rest of the image based on comparisons with training data, or more commonly, summary properties of the training data.

In the abstract, unsupervised classification sounds like a more reliable and less subjective process. In reality, both supervised and unsupervised classification require considerable subjective judgment and skill.

7.1.2 Soft Versus Hard Classification

The cartographic tradition is that of maps comprising discrete areas, with sharp boundaries, and distinct, contrasting characteristics. This tradition has been transferred to remote sensing classification, where the aim is usually to assign each pixel to only one of a number of classes. The real world is not necessarily so simple: classes are likely to grade into one another, and a location may have characteristics of two or more classes. For example, the classes Clean Water and Muddy Water may represent a continuum, and Muddy Water in turn may grade through Wetlands into Dry Land. In addition, a pixel that falls on a boundary between two or more classes would be expected to have attributes of both classes.

In fuzzy classification, a type of soft classification, a degree of membership in each class is generated for each pixel location, rather than just a value representing the class number, as is the case with hard classifiers. (Note that the IDRISI documentation makes the argument that soft classification is preferable to fuzzy classification as a generic term.)

7.1.3 Relative Versus Absolute Classifiers

It is relatively difficult to determine if two objects are the same, since then one is forced to define how much variation is acceptable in the quality of "sameness." It is generally much easier to invert the process and find differences. Thus, most classifiers are relative classifiers, assigning an unknown pixel to a class only after comparing the unknown with each class, and choosing the one to which it is most similar (or, the least different). In contrast, an absolute classifier usually stops comparing an unknown pixel to the training classes once a match has been met. Relative classifiers require the user to identify training data for all the spectral classes, whereas absolute classifiers only need training data for the class or classes of interest. However, one disadvantage with absolute classifiers is that they are poor generalizers, and often leave many pixels unclassified.

7.2 Copy Data for This Chapter

In this chapter we will work with different image sets for each section. Therefore, you should now copy the *Chap7* folder from the CD, and paste it as a new subfolder within the *ID Man* folder on your computer.

After you have copied the folder, you should remove the Read-Only attribute from this new folder on your computer. This is done by right-clicking on the *Chap7* folder name, selecting *Properties* from the pop-up menu. A dialog box will open, labeled *Chap7 Properties* (if you apply this procedure to the entire *ID Man* directory, then the dialog box will be labeled *ID Man Properties*). Now clear the check mark from the *Read Only* check box, by clicking in the box. You should then click on the button for *Apply*, and in the subsequent *Confirm Attribute Changes* dialog box, accept the default *Apply changes to this folder, subfolder and files*, and click on *OK*. You will need to also click on *OK* in the *Chap7 Properties* dialog box.

<u>Note</u>: Section 1.3.1 provides detailed instructions on how to copy the data from the CD, and also on how to remove the *Read-Only* attribute from the data. Also, the procedure for setting up the *ID Man* folder on your computer is described.

7.3 Unsupervised classification

7.3.1 <u>Overview</u>

The sequence of operations in unsupervised classification is summarized in Figure 7.3.1.a.

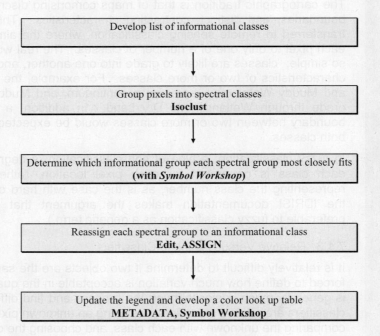

Figure 7.3.1.a   Overview of unsupervised classification.

The first step is to identify the list of informational classes based on knowledge of the area and usually an examination of the image to determine the likely classes that might be discriminated.

The next step is to cluster the image to produce the spectral classes, typically many more than the expected number of final informational classes. The analyst then views each spectral class, and develops a list of the original spectral class numbers and the informational class number to which each spectral class is assigned. Developing this list can be difficult, because often the spectral class consists of more than one informational class. In other words, when you try to decide on the informational class to assign the spectral class to, you find that there are two or even more informational classes that seem appropriate. There are four options when this happens:

1. Label the pixel according to the dominant informational class.

2. Create informational classes that are mixtures.

3. Start again from the beginning choosing clustering parameters that will give you even more classes.

4. Follow a "cluster-buster" procedure, where mixed classes are subjected to a second round of clustering, in the hope that this will split these classes into classes that are more pure.

In this exercise, we will follow option (1) from above, and try to identify the dominant class for each cluster.

After the relationship between each spectral and informational class is established, the image classes are recoded to produce a new image with only informational classes.

7.3.2 Preparation

In Section 7.2 you should have already copied the data from the CD. However, we still need to set the *Project* and *Working Folders* for this section.

Before starting you should close any dialog boxes or displayed images in the IDRISI workspace.

Create a new project file and specify the working folders with the IDRISI EXPLORER
Menu Location: **File – IDRISI EXPLORER**

1. Start the IDRISI EXPLORER from the main menu or toolbar.

2. In the *IDRISI EXPLORER* window, select the *Projects* tab.

3. Right click within the *Projects* pane, and select the *New Project Ins* option.

4. A *Browse For Folder* window will open. Use this window to navigate to the *ID_Man* folder, which is the folder you created on your computer for the data for this manual. Now navigate to the *Chap7* subfolder.

5. Click *OK* in the *Browse For Folder* window.

6. A new project file *Chap7* will now be listed in the *Project* pane of the IDRISI EXPLORER. The working folder will also be listed in the Editor pane.

7. Close the IDRISI EXPLORER by clicking on the red *x* in the upper right corner of the *IDRISI EXPLORER* window.

For this exercise we will investigate multispectral classification using Landsat Thematic Mapper data of the area around Morgantown, West Virginia, USA. Begin by creating a false color composite, in which TM bands 3, 4, and 5 are assigned blue, green and red, as described below.

Create a color composite image
Menu Location: **Display - COMPOSITE**

1. Start the COMPOSITE program using the main menu or tool bar.

2. In the *COMPOSITE* dialog box, specify the file name for the *Blue image band* **tm3**. Click on *OK* to close the *Pick list*.

3. Specify the *Green image band* as **tm4**.

4. Specify the *Red image band* as **tm5.**

5. Enter the *Output image* filename in the text box provided: **tm345fcc**.

6. Accept all other defaults, and click *OK* to create and display the false color composite.

Figure 7.3.2.a shows the results of the image, which will be displayed automatically. The image has been annotated with the major land use types.

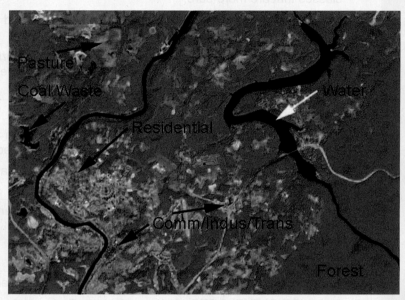

Figure 7.3.2.a   False color composite of Morgantown, WV (Bands 3, 4, 5 as B, G, R). Major land use types are indicated.

The false color composite image we have just created (Figure 7.3.2.a) will be used for interpretation of the land cover types.

Before we go on to run the ISOCLUST unsupervised classification program, we need to generate a *Raster Group File* for the input data. This format is useful, as it means we can specify just one file name (the group), instead of the multitude of individual bands. The procedure to create a raster group file is described below briefly. If you want additional discussion on creating *Raster Group Files*, you may wish to review the material in Section 1.3.7.

Creating a file collection with the IDRISI EXPLORER

Menu Location: **File – IDRISI EXPLORER**

1. Open the *IDRISI EXPLORER* window from the menu or the main icon toolbar.

2. Click on the tab for *Files*. If the files in the directory are not listed, double click on the directory name (e.g. *C:\ID Man\Chap7*), as listed in the *Files* pane.

3. Click on **tm1.rst**. The file name will then be highlighted.

4. Press, and holding the *CTRL* key down, click on the **tm2.rst, tm3.rst, tm4.rst, tm5.rst, and tm7.tst.**

5. You should now have 6 TM files highlighted. Remove your finger from the *CTRL* button. Press the right mouse button.

6. A pop-up menu will appear. Within this menu, scroll down to *Create*, and then select *Raster Group File*.

7. A new file should be listed in the Files pane, **Raster Group.rgf**. Select that file by clicking on it.

8. In the *Metadata* pane of the *IDRISI EXPLORER*, delete the text in the *Name* text box (**Raster Group**), and type: **Tm_all**.

9. Press *Enter* on the computer keyboard, and then click on the *Save* icon in the bottom left hand corner of the *Metadata* pane.

7.3.3 Develop the List of Land Cover Types

Table 7.3.3.a lists five major land cover types, which will form the basis of the informational classes for the unsupervised classification. The information in the table should be compared against the false color composite you have generated to see if you can identify all the classes present (Figure 7.3.2.a). The numbers given in the left hand column will be used to represent the classes in the final classification. Note that the table **does not include the Coal Waste class** shown in Figure 7.3.2.a. The reason for this is that this class is difficult to differentiate with unsupervised classification, and for the moment we will not try to separate it. Instead, for this exercise, you should include the Coal Waste as part of the Commercial/Industrial/Transportation class. For the supervised classification, we will separate out this class.

Table 7.3.3.a. Table of land cover classes for unsupervised classification.

Class Number	Name	Color in 345 false color composite	Texture
1	Water	Black	Smooth
2	Forest	Green	Moderate
3	Pasture/Grass	Pink to light green/yellow	Moderate
4	Commercial / Industrial / Transportation	Blue/Grey	Rough
5	Residential	Bright blue	Rough

7.3.4 Group Pixels into Spectral Classes: ISOCLUST

The ISOCLUST program has a number of parameters that you, as the analyst, have to specify. These parameters all affect the classification output. While the range of options can be daunting, IDRISI does have excellent help documentation, as already described earlier (Section 1.3.3). You should get into the habit of checking the on-line help to find out more about how programs work, or to understand the implications of each of the options offered, when you are faced with options or parameters that you are unsure how to deal with.

Clustering an image with ISOCLUST
Menu location: **Image processing – Hard classifiers - ISOCLUST**

1. Start the ISOCLUST program from the menu.

2. In the *ISOCLUST* dialog box, click on the *Insert layer group* button.

3. A *Pick list* window will open. Double click on **Tm_all**.

4. The six tm bands (***tm1, tm2,....tm5, tm7***) should all be listed now in the *ISOCLUST* dialog box, in the *Bands to processed- Filename* text box (Figure 7.3.4.a).

5. Click on *Next*.

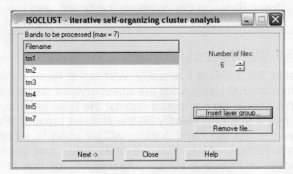

Figure 7.3.4.a   *ISOCLUST* dialog box with the raster group file bands specified.

The program will then generate an analysis of the potential classes and the comparative number of pixels that fall into these classes. This information is reported in a *HISTOGRAM* window (Figure 7.3.4.b). A new *ISOCLUST* window (with a new set of control parameters) will also open.

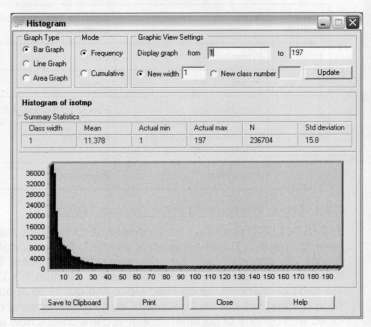

Figure 7.3.4.b   Histogram of potential classes.

The purpose of the histogram is to assist in the process of deciding on the number of spectral classes to generate through the ISOCLUST program. In examining Figure 7.3.4.b, it is apparent that most of the data fall in a small number of classes, each with many pixels. The remainder of the pixels falls in a large number of classes, each with very few pixels. Thus there is a diminishing return as higher numbers of classes are selected. The IDRISI on-line help suggests looking for a break in the histogram curve to decide on a logical value. The number of spectral classes we choose should be much larger than the number of informational classes. Since we are interested in 5 classes, and the histogram seems to flatten out around 20, we shall select 20 spectral classes. This choice of 20 is somewhat arbitrary, however, and the reader might like to experiment with different values, after completing the initial guided exercise.

Clustering an image with ISOCLUST (cont.)

6. In the *ISOCLUST* dialog box, specify the *Number of clusters desired* as **20**.

7. Specify the *Output image* filename as **Isoclust20**

8. Figure 7.3.4.c shows the dialog box with the parameters specified.

9. Click on *OK*.

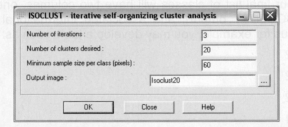

Figure 7.3.4.c   *ISOCLUST* dialog box with clustering parameters.

The classification will take a while to process the image. You can watch the Status bar and progress indicators in the outer IDRISI frame for messages on progress.   When the program is finished it will automatically display the classification (Figure 7.3.4.d).

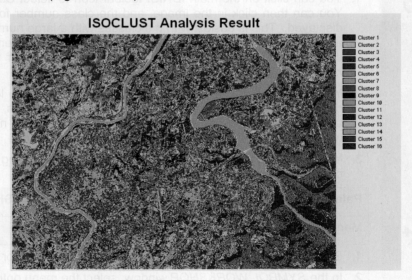

Figure 7.3.4.d   Results of ISOCLUST program, with 20 classes.

Note that, if necessary, you can always redisplay the image you have just created, if you need to stop temporarily at this stage and close IDRISI. However, if you redisplay the image, bear in mind that this is no longer a raw image of radiance values, but a classified image. Therefore, you should use the IDRISI Default Qualitative palette, and also display the legend.

7.3.5 Determine the Informational Class

Even though we now have a classification, we unfortunately have only just begun our work. The next stage is to build a table of values listing the spectral classes from 1-20 (the number of spectral classes we specified in the ISOCLUST program), and the associated informational class number for each of those spectral classes. We will use a visual interpretation of the false color composite of Bands 3, 4, and 5 (*tm345fcc*, Figure 7.3.2.a) to determine the appropriate informational class. This part of the exercise is a somewhat tedious process!

Note that you should expect at least some informational class to have many informational classes. Unfortunately the reverse relationship is not allowed, and you cannot assign one spectral class to two informational classes.

Your final list of classes will have two columns, one each for the spectral class (ISOCLUST output), and associated informational class (final class number). Thus for example, you may develop a table such as:

1 2

2 2

3 2

4 4

...

20 3

There are three ways to decide on the informational class for a spectral class. You may wish to use a combination of the methods.

1. You can click on the main IDRISI toolbar icon to select *Curser inquiry mode.* You can then click in the image, and the class number for that pixel will be displayed. This is easiest with the classes with a large number of pixels, such as sinuous tan cluster (Cluster 7). (This cluster can be identified as Water, by comparing it to the false color composite.) To turn off the *Curser inquiry mode,* simply click again on the icon.

2. You can left-click with the mouse on the color chip in the legend for the map display, and switch between a display with just that class, shown in red, and all other pixels in black. (Unfortunately, this option does not always seem to work reliably, and so we do not recommend it.)

3. You can systematically work through the classes by setting them to distinctive colors. This procedure is described in more detail below.

Palette file interactive modification with SYMBOL WORKSHOP
Menu location: **Display – SYMBOL WORKSHOP**

1. Start the SYMBOL WORKSHOP from the main icon bar, or the main menu.

2. In the *SYMBOL WORKSHOP* window, select the menu option for *File – New*.

3. In the resulting *New Symbol File* dialog box, select *Palette* as the choice for *Symbol File Type*.

4. Enter the *File name* in the text box provided: **iso20**.

5. Click on *OK* to close the *New Symbol File* dialog box.

6. The *SYMBOL WORKSHOP* window will immediately change from a grid of circles, to a uniform red grid (Figure 7.3.5.a).

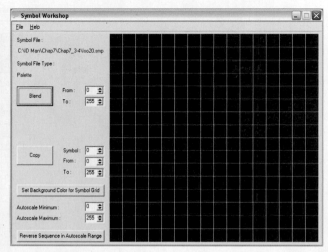

Figure 7.3.5.a   *SYMBOL WORKSHOP* window, after specifying a new palette file.

We will now set up a gray scale range from 0 to 20, the maximum class number. We will specify 0 as black, and 20 as white. The values between 0 and 20 will be progressive shades of gray between those two extremes.

Palette file interactive modification with SYMBOL WORKSHOP (cont.)

7. Run your cursor over the red cells. Note how a small yellow rectangle appears next to the cursor. The number in this rectangle indicates the image DN number associated with that cell.

8. Select the upper left cell, cell 0, by clicking on it.

9. A *Color* dialog box will appear.

10. In the *Color* dialog box, click on the color chip for black (the bottom left color chip in the *Basic colors* section) (Figure 7.3.5.b).

11. Click on *OK*.

12. The *SYMBOL WORKSHOP* window should now have cell zero set to black (Figure 7.3.5.c).

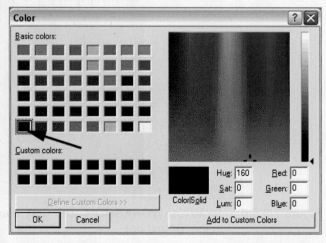

Figure 7.3.5.b   *COLOR* dialog box, with Black chip indicated by the arrow.

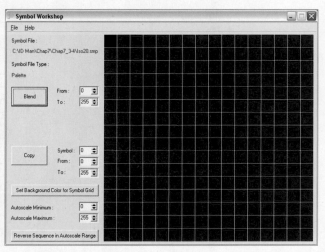

Figure 7.3.5.c   *SYMBOL WORKSHOP* with cell 0 set to black.

Palette file interactive modification with SYMBOL WORKSHOP (cont.)

13. Now select cell *20* (run the cursor over the cells, to identify which cell is 20).

14. The *COLOR* dialog box will open. Select the chip for white (bottom right color chip, in the *Basic colors* section).

15. Click *OK* to close the *COLOR* dialog box, and return to the *SYMBOL WORKSHOP* window.

16. There should now be two cells that are not red: cell 0, which is black, and cell 20, which is white.

17. In the text box labeled *To*, which is situated next to the *Blend* button, enter **20**.

18. Click on the *Blend* button.

19. The result should be a gray scale color ramp from black to white for the first 20 cells (Figure 7.3.5.d).

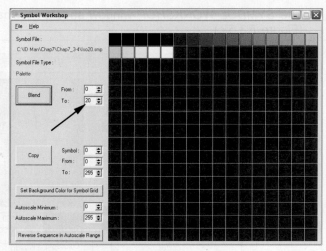

Figure 7.3.5.d   *SYMBOL WORKSHOP*, with gray blend applied. Arrow points to the *To* text box.

Having now established a palette file that goes from black to white for image values that go from 0 to 20, we can now modify a few select values to other colors. In this way, when we apply this palette file to the ISOCLUST image, we will be able to see the general pattern of the classes in gray tones, but just focus on a few classes at a time in the distinctive colors. Note that we start at cell 1, and not 0, since IDRISI has assigned the first class to 1, not 0.

Palette file interactive modification with SYMBOL WORKSHOP (cont.)

20. In the *SYMBOL WORKSHOP* window, select cell 1, and this time set this cell to blue. (The specific blue color chip is not important; we simply want any bright and distinctive color.)

21. Select cell 2, and set it to green.

22. Select cell 3, and set it to red.

23. Use the menu in the *SYMBOL WORKSHOP* window, to save the palette file: *File – Save*.

Figure 7.3.5.e shows the SYMBOL WORKSHOP window, with the gray scale ramp, and three cells set to distinctive colors.

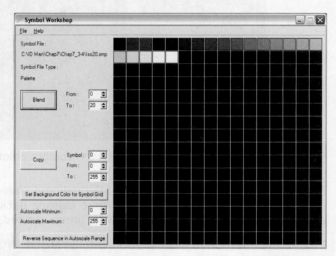

Figure 7.3.5.e   *SYMBOL WORKSHOP* with 3 cells set to distinctive colors.

The next step is to apply the palette file to the image produced by the ISOCLUST program. Therefore, find the *DISPLAY* window, with the **Iso20** image already displayed. If you have closed the window, redisplay the image.

Palette file interactive modification with SYMBOL WORKSHOP (cont.)

24. Click on window that displays **Iso20**. This is to bring the image to the front of your screen.

25. Now find the *Composer* window. This window is automatically opened whenever a *DISPLAY* window is opened.

26. In the *Composer* window, click on *Layer Properties*.

27. The *Layer properties* window will open.

28. In the *Layer Properties* window, select the *Display parameters* tab.

29. Click on the file selection icon (…) next to the *Palette file* text box, and in the *Pick list* that will open, double click on the name of the palette file you have just created: **Iso20**.

30. The image should now be displayed in black and white, except for the selected classes we have set to blue, green and red, respectively (Figure 7.3.5.f).

31. Compare the patterns in the classified image to the false color composite (**tm345fcc**), which should be redisplayed if necessary.

32. Note the informational class numbers for each spectral class. (Hint: Classes 1, 2 and 3 all appear to be Forest. Forest is new class number 2 – see Table 7.3.3.a).

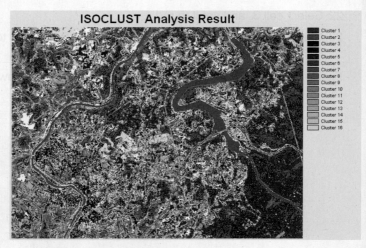

Figure 7.3.5.f   ISOCLUST image with the custom palette applied.

Now that you have decided on the informational class numbers for the first 3 classes, we will now modify the first three classes back to the gray scale ramp, and assign DN values 4, 5, and 6 to blue, green and red, respectively.

Palette file interactive modification with SYMBOL WORKSHOP (cont.)

33. Find the *SYMBOL WORKSHOP* window.

34. Click on the button for *Blend*. This should remove the colors that were applied to cells 1, 2 and 3, and the color ramp should once again be from black to white without additional colors in between.

35. Click on cell 4, and select the blue color chip.

36. Click on cell 5, and select the green color chip.

37. Click on cell 6, and select the red color chip.

38. Save the file, by using the *SYMBOL WORKSHOP* window menu for *File - Save*.

39. Find the *DISPLAY* window, with the **Iso20** image. Click in that window.

40. In the *Composer* window, click on *Layer properties*.

41. In the Layer properties window, click on *Apply* to update the palette file used for displaying the image.

42. Determine which informational class each spectral cluster belongs to.

At this stage you should have a list of the spectral class numbers and the associated informational class numbers for the first 6 of the 20 classes. Repeat this procedure for the remaining 14 classes, so that you have a complete table of values.

7.3.6 Reassign Each Spectral Class to an Informational Class

This part of the procedure has two steps. First we use the IDRISI program EDIT to enter the list of spectral and informational classes in a table, then we use that table in the program ASSIGN. The advantage of developing a table is that we have a record of the assignment we made, and it is easy to reapply the recoding operation if we want to change a few values.

Enter the recode values table with EDIT

Menu location: **Data Entry – EDIT**.

1. Open the program EDIT from the main menu or the main icon bar.

2. The *IDRISI TEXT EDITOR* window will open.

3. In the blank window enter the spectral class number, leave a space, and then enter the informational class number. Enter each spectral class and the associated informational class on a new line. Start with spectral class 1 and end with 20. (For example, if you want to assign spectral class 1 to informational class 3, your first line would be: 1 3). See Figure 7.3.6.a for an example of how the completed list might look.

4. Use the *IDRISI TEXT EDITOR* menu to save the file: **File – Save As.**

5. A *SAVE AS* dialog box will open. In the Save as type text field, click on the pull-down list, and select *Attribute Values File*. This automatically gives the file you create an AVL extension.

6. Enter the file name **reclass1**.

7. Click *SAVE*.

8. A *Values File Information* dialog box will open. Take the default *Integer* option, and click on *OK*.

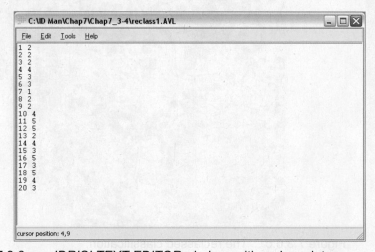

Figure 7.3.6.a   *IDRISI TEXT EDITOR* window, with reclass data.

Now, use the *Attribute Values* file you have just created to create a new image, with DN values recoded according to the scheme specified in the text file.

Create a new image with informational class numbers, using ASSIGN

Menu location: **Data Entry – ASSIGN**

1. Use the IDRISI main menu to start the ASSIGN program.

2. In the *ASSIGN* window, use the pick list button (…) to specify the *Feature definition image* as the output of the ISOCLUST program, *Isoclust20*.

3. The *Output image* is the new classified map with informational classes. Therefore type the new file name: **Isoclus20_reclass**.

4. The *Attribute values file* is the text file ***reclass1***.

5. Enter an Output title, such as: **Unsupervised ISOCLUSTER classification**.

6. Figure 7.3.6.b shows the dialog box with the parameters specified.

7. Click on *OK*.

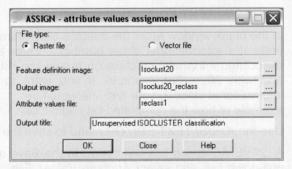

Figure 7.3.6.b   *ASSIGN* dialog box with parameters specified.

The program will automatically display the reclassed image when processing is complete (Figure 7.3.6.c.).

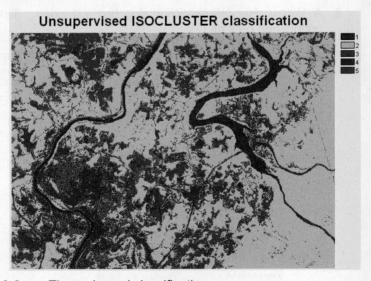

Figure 7.3.6.c   The reclassed classification.

If you are satisfied with the output, you are ready to proceed to the next section (7.3.7). However, if you decide that you'd prefer to change one or more class assignments, it is very easy to do so, especially if all the dialog boxes are still open. Simply edit the values you want to change in the *IDRISI TEXT EDITOR* window, and click on Save. Then find the ASSIGN window, and click on OK. You will be asked if you want to over-write the original file. Click on Yes. A new image will automatically be displayed.

7.3.7 Update the Legend and Create a Custom Image Palette File

The final output is almost created. However, we need to enter the informational class names and choose colors for each class.

Update the classified image with the IDRISI EXPLORER
Menu location: **File – IDRISI EXPLORER**

1. Start the IDRISI EXPLORER from the main menu, or the main icon bar.

10. In the *IDRISI EXPLORER* window, click on the tab for *Files*.

11. If the files are not listed in the *Files* pane, double click on the directory name to display the files.

2. In the *Files* pane, click on the ***Isoclus20_reclass.rst*** classified image file.

3. In the Metadata pane below the Files pane, scroll down, and find the blank cell next to the label *Categories* (Figure 7.3.7.a).

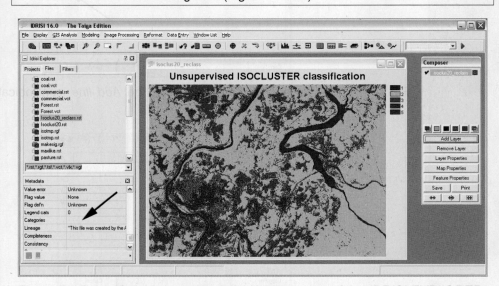

Figure 7.3.7.a   *Categories* cell in the *Metadata* pane of the *IDRISI EXPLORER*

Update the classified image with the IDRISI EXPLORER (cont.)

4. Click in the blank *Categories* cell. The cell will turn white, and a *Pick list* button (…) will appear. Click on that button.

5. A *Categories* dialog box will open.

6. In the first cell below *Code*, enter **1**.

7. In the cell below *Category*, enter **Water**.

8. Find the *Add line* icon on the right of the *Categories* dialog box (Figure 7.3.7.b). Click on this icon.

9. In the new line enter the *Code* **2** and the *Category* **Forest**.

10. Repeat the previous two steps in order to enter the remaining classes on three additional rows:
    3 Pasture
    4 Comm/Ind/Trans
    5 Residential

11. Figure 7.3.7.c shows the *Categories* dialog box with the legend specified.

12. Click on *OK* to close the *Categories* dialog box.

13. The *IDRISI EXPLORER Metadata* pane should now have the number **5** in the cell next to *Legend cats*, indicating we have specified category names for 5 classes.

14. Click on the icon for *Save*, in the bottom left corner of the *Metadata* pane. After the file is saved, the icon will go blank.

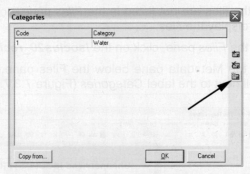

Figure 7.3.7.b   *Categories* dialog box with the *Add line* icon indicated by the arrow.

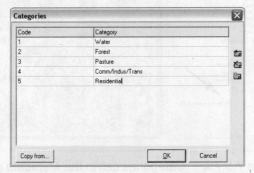

Figure 7.3.7.c   *Categories* dialog box with the 5 legend categories specified.

The final step is to update the classified image palette file (color scheme) with the *SYMBOL WORKSHOP*. You can refer back to earlier in this exercise (Section 7.3.5) for more details, if the instructions below are too brief.

Create a color look up table for the final map with SYMBOL WORKSHOP

Menu location: **Display – SYMBOL WORKSHOP**.

1. Start the SYMBOL WORKSHOP from the main menu or the main icon bar.

2. Once the *SYMBOL WORKSHOP* dialog box and window has opened, use the window menu for *File – New*.

3. In the *New Symbol File* dialog box, click in the radio button for *Palette*.

4. Enter a file name: **Iso_lookup**.

5. Click on *OK* to close the *New Symbol File* dialog box.

6. The *SYMBOL WORKSHOP* window will now change to red squares.

7. Place the cursor over the second cell from the top left. Confirm from the label that will be shown that this is cell 1. Click in this cell.

8. Since class 1 is Water, click on a dark blue color chip in the *Color* dialog box that will open.

9. Click on *OK* to close the *Color* dialog box.

10. Repeat steps 8 and 9 above to specify 2 (Forest) as a dark green, 3 (Pasture) as light green, 4 (Com/Indus/Trans) as light blue, and 5 (Residential) as pink.

11. When you have completed specifying the five colors, save the palette file through the *SYMBOL WORKSHOP* window menu *File – Save*.

Finally, redisplay your image, as described below. The displayed image should now have the updated palette file and legend applied.

Displaying an image with a custom palette file using the DISPLAY LAUNCHER

Menu Location: **Display – DISPLAY LAUNCHER**

1. Start the DISPLAY LAUNCHER program from the main menu, or the tool bar.

2. In the *DISPLAY LAUNCHER* dialog box, click on the option to browse for a file by selecting the *Pick list* button (…) in the center left column.

3. A file *Pick List* window will open. Double click on the **Isoclus20_reclass** raster file.

4. In the *Palette File* section of the DISPLAY LAUNCHER window, click on the *Pick list* button (…).

5. Select the **Iso_lookup** file by double clicking on it.

6. Click on *OK* to display the image (Figure 7.3.7.d).

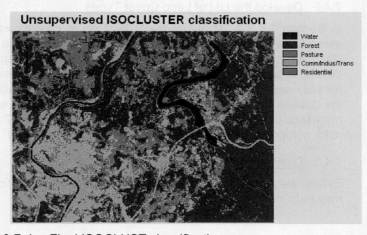

Figure 7.3.7.d   Final ISOCLUST classification map.

7.4 *Supervised Classification*

Figure 7.4.a illustrates the steps involved in supervised classification. First we identify small areas for which we know the land cover. These areas are called *training sites*. The image DN values within the training sites are generalized to represent the typical spectral properties of the training classes. Finally, the rest of the image is compared on a pixel by pixel basis to the generalized data of the training classes, to determine which class each pixel belongs to.

The first step is to define the training sites. Each known land cover type will be assigned an integer identifier, and one or more training sites will be identified for each integer.

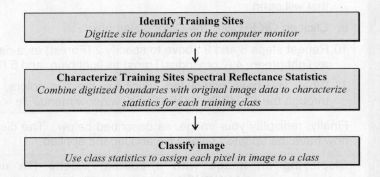

Figure 7.4.a   Overview of the Supervised Classification Process.

7.4.1 Preparatory

It is recommended that you do this exercise only after completing the unsupervised classification of Section 7.3. If you choose to do this section first, or have not saved your results from Section 7.3, you will need to complete Section 7.2 (copy the data from the CD) and 7.3.2 (set project space, create a false color composite, and a raster group file) before continuing with this exercise.

Open the IDRISI EXPLORER from the main menu or the main icon bar, click on the *Projects* tab, and check that the radio button for the **Chap7** has been selected.

7.4.2 Develop the List of Land Cover Types

In Section 7.3.3 a list of five major land cover classes was developed. In this exercise, we will add a sixth class, Coal Waste. We did not separate out this class in the unsupervised classification (Section 7.3) because coal waste was not clearly separable in that exercise. You will see, however, that it is at least partially separable through supervised classification. Table 7.4.2.a lists the full six classes for this exercise. The numbers in the table will be the DN used to represent the classes in the final classification. Figure 7.3.2.a shows the false color composite with the examples of each class indicated.

7.4.3 Digitize Training Classes

Before we begin digitizing, a general background and tips regarding digitizing may help improve the effectiveness of your work.

Table 7.4.2.a   Supervised classification classes.

Class Number	Name	Color in 345 false color composite	Texture
1	Water	Black	Smooth
2	Forest	Green	Moderate
3	Pasture/Grass	Pink to light green/yellow	Moderate
4	Commercial / Industrial / Transportation	Blue/Grey	Rough
5	Residential	Bright blue	Rough
6	Coal Waste	Dark purple/Black	Smooth

- **Select typical areas**. The training polygons are supposed to represent the typical properties of the class. Thus it is important that your training sites should be as *homogeneous* as possible (i.e. they should contain only that land cover type, and typically only one dominant color on the monitor). However, the training sites should also cover the *range of typical values* for that cover-type.

- **Digitize efficiently**. Do not spend hours digitizing each class - it is important to be able to outline a "typical" area rapidly. You probably should zoom in (i.e. expand the image on the screen), to make digitizing easier. However, it is not worthwhile to zoom in so much that you are digitizing individual pixels. In most cases you should be able to digitize a polygon quite rapidly.

- **Digitize a reasonable number of pixels.** Your training sites should contain an adequate sample of pixels for statistical characterization. A general rule of thumb is that the number of pixels in each training set (i.e. the total over all sites for a single land cover class) should not be less that 10 times the number of bands. Therefore, since we will use 6 bands of TM data, we should aim to have no less than 60 pixels per signature. It is not necessary to count the number of pixels when you are digitizing the polygon, as you will be warned later if the polygons are too small. However, if you think a polygon is too small, or you don't think the polygon encapsulates the range of values in the class, you can always digitize several polygons, all with the same number, and that will automatically be combined later into one large spectral class.

- **Bear in mind the difference between spectral classes and informational classes**. For example, assume you have two water bodies, one with clean and deep water, and one with shallow, muddy water. This might give rise to two very different spectral classes (*Clean Water and Muddy Water*), even though we would regard them as one informational class (*Water*). Multiple training sites can be grouped into one informational class by simply assigning the polygons the same value (DN value). Alternatively, you might want to have different numbers for each training sites. With this latter approach, once you are finished with the entire classification you would then go back and reclass the different spectral classes as one informational class (by using the IDRISI programs

RECLASS or ASSIGN). In this exercise, however, we will take the simpler approach of assigning multiple spectral classes to one DN value.

- **Keep careful track of the class name you are digitizing**. *The most common problem in this exercise is losing track of the class you are digitizing.* Always make a conscious effort to keep track of which class you are digitizing. This will help avoid confusion.

We now need to display an image, to digitize on. Therefore, as described below, open the false color composite, created earlier, in Section 7.3.2.

Displaying a previously created false color composite using the DISPLAY LAUNCHER

Menu Location: **Display – DISPLAY LAUNCHER**

1. Start the DISPLAY LAUNCHER program from the main menu, or the tool bar.

2. In the *DISPLAY LAUNCHER* dialog box, click on the option to browse for a file by selecting the *Pick list* button (…) in the center left column.

3. A *Pick List* window will open. Double click on the **tm345fcc** raster file to insert this file name into the *DISPLAY LAUNCHER* dialog box.

4. In the *DISPLAY LAUNCHER* dialog box, click on *OK* to display the image.

The next step is to digitize the training polygons, at least one for each informational class, on the image we have just we have just opened.

Digitizing polygons

Menu location: Main tool bar icons only (Note that the icons are grayed out if an image is not yet displayed.)

1. An image should already be open in the IDRISI workspace.

2. Click on the *Full extent maximized* icon from the main tool bar to enlarge the image display to the maximum possible within the constraints of your monitor.

3. Zoom in to a region with a large area of water. To do this, first select the *Zoom Window* icon from the main tool bar.

4. Now, use the left mouse button to click in the image, and, with your left finger still depressed, stretch the screen box to delineate the area you want to zoom into. Release the left mouse button, and the display should only show the zoomed area, much enlarged.

5. Click on the *Digitize* icon. A dialog box labeled *Digitize* will open.

6. Enter the file name **Water** in the text box labeled *Name of layer to be created*. Leave all other values at their defaults.

7. Click on *OK* to close the *Digitize* window.

8. Move the cursor over the image. Note how when the cursor is over the image, it takes on a form similar to the *Digitize* icon, instead of the normal arrow.

9. Move the cursor over the water feature. Digitize the first vertex of the polygon that will represent Water, by pressing the *left* mouse button. Continue clicking in the image to specify the outer boundaries of the polygon you wish to digitize.

10. Close the polygon by pressing the *right* mouse button. Note that the program automatically closes the polygon by duplicating the first point; so you do not need to attempt to close the polygon by digitizing the first point again.

11. Figure 7.4.3.a shows an example of what the Water digitized polygon might look like.

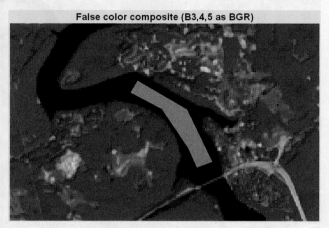

False color composite (B3,4,5 as BGR)

Figure 7.4.3.a   Digitized Water training polygon.

Correcting a mistake is relatively easy. You can delete an entire polygon, after it has been closed, by following the procedure below. The first step, perhaps somewhat counter-intuitively, is to save the polygon.

Digitizing polygons (cont.): Deleting a polygon

12. Click on the *Save digitized data* icon in the main IDRISI toolbar.

13. In the *Save Prompt* window, click on *Yes*.

14. Click on the *Delete Feature* icon in the main IDRISI toolbar.

15. After clicking on the icon, the cursor becomes a pointing hand.

16. Click on the polygon you wish to delete, and it will be highlighted.

17. Now press the delete key on the computer keyboard.

18. A *Delete feature* dialog box will open.

19. Select *Yes*, if you wish to confirm deleting the polygon, otherwise click *No*.

The polygon we have just digitized is in an area of deep water. To the south (i.e. bottom of the image), that same body of water is quite shallow, and the spectral properties differ from the area we have just digitized. Additionally, the river to the east (left) is also a little different spectrally. Therefore, we should add two more polygons to this vector layer. However, because they are just part of the same water class, and are not separate spectral classes, we will use the same number to represent all three polygons.

For this additional digitizing for this class, and for the subsequent digitizing of additional classes, it will be helpful to get a general idea of the size and distribution of the training classes from Figure 7.4.3.b. Note that each class has been coded a different color in this figure for ease of interpretation, unlike on your screen, where the classes should all have the same color.

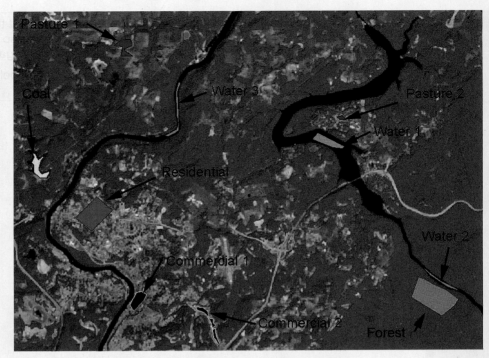

Figure 7.4.3.b   Training classes for supervised classification.

Digitizing polygons (cont.): Adding additional polygons to a class

20. Return the view to the original full image, by clicking on the *Full extent normal* icon in the main IDRISI tool bar.

21. Then click on the *Full extent maximized* icon.

22. Use the *Zoom window* icon to zoom in on the bottom right hand corner of the image, where the river channel is very narrow. As the river is narrow, and it will be harder to digitize here, you should zoom in a great deal. If necessary, you can repeat the zoom function to zoom in multiple times.

23. Click on the *Digitize* icon.

24. A dialog box labeled *Digitize* will open.

25. Accept the default to *Add features to the currently active vector layer*, and click on *OK*.

26. The *Digitize* dialog box will now show the digitizing parameters. It is very important that we change the number in the *ID or Value* text box to the value of the previous polygon, since we want to add it to that class, and not have a new class. Therefore, *ID or Value* text box which currently should show the number 2, should be changed to **1**.

27. Click on *OK*.

28. Now digitize the river channel. Be sure not to include any pixels from the forested river banks.

29. Close the polygon by clicking with the right mouse button. If you feel the polygon is not quite what you want, review the material above for deleting a polygon, and try again.

30. Now digitize a third polygon for the Water class, this time for the river on the west (left) side of the image. Remember to set the *ID or Value* to **1** in the *Digitize* dialog box.

31. If you are satisfied with this second polygon, save the polygon file by clicking on the *Save digitized data* icon.

32. A *Save prompt* dialog box will open. Click on *Yes*.

We will now add the Forest class. In order to make our work simpler, each time we add a new class, we will digitize it in a separate file. An alternative approach is to digitize all the classes in the same file. However, digitizing in one file can get confusing.

Digitizing polygons (cont.): Digitizing a second class

33. Return the view to the original full image, by first clicking on the *Full extent normal icon* in the main IDRISI tool bar.

34. Then click on the *Full extent maximized* icon.

35. Use the *Zoom window* icon to zoom in on the bottom right hand corner of the image, which is dominated by Forest. Include both the poorly illuminated (darker color) steep canyon slopes and brightly illuminated (brighter color) ridge top.

36. Click on the *Digitize* icon.

37. A dialog box labeled *Digitize* will open.

38. Click on the radio button to *Create a new layer for the features to be digitized.*

39. Click on *OK*.

40. The *Digitize* dialog box will now provide a text box for the *Name of the layer to be created*. Enter the new class name: **Forest**.

41. Digitize a polygon that includes both poorly illuminated forest areas and brightly illuminated areas. Close with a right click.

42. Save the file by clicking on the on the *Save digitized data* icon.

43. A *Save prompt* dialog box will open. Click on *Yes*.

44. Repeat the steps 30 to 39 for the next class, **Pasture**. Note that the pasture and grass class comprises mostly agricultural pasture, which has a distinctive pink to brown color (Pasture 1 in Figure 7.4.3.b). However, the class also includes golf courses, which are irrigated, and therefore have a different color, yellow (Pasture 2 in Figure 7.4.3.b). Therefore, it will be necessary to digitize two polygons for this class, as we did for Water. Follow the procedure outlined in 18 to 29, being sure to remember to set the *ID or Value* text box to **1** when you digitize the second polygon in the *Pasture* file.

45. Repeat steps 30 to 38 for **Residential**. The Residential class is a difficult class because it is characterized more by a rough texture, than a distinct color.

46. Now digitize the class **Commercial**. The Commercial class has a distinctive dark blue color, and also has a rough texture.

47. Because the area of the region digitized for the first Commercial polygon is quite small (indicated by the polygon labeled Commercial 1 in Figure 7.4.3.b), we will need to add a second polygon for this class (indicated by Commercial 2 in Figure 7.4.3.b). Follow the procedure outlined in 18 to 29, being sure to remember to set the *ID or Value* text box to **1**.

48. Now digitize the class **Coal**. The region shown in Figure 7.4.3.b for the class Coal consists of a large settling pond, where coal is cleaned to remove waste.

49. Close the image before proceeding to the next step. If there are any unsaved polygons, you will be prompted whether you wish to save them. Click on *Yes* in the *Save Prompt* dialog box to save the polygons.

7.4.4   Generate Class Signatures with MAKESIG

Once you are satisfied that your training sites were digitized satisfactorily, you can create signature files for each cover class. These files have statistical information about the reflectance values for each band for each site, derived from the polygons we have just digitized.

Create signature files using MAKESIG
Menu location: **Image Processing - Signature development – MAKESIG**

1.   Start the MAKESIG program from the main menu.

2.   In the *MAKESIG* dialog box, click on the Pick list button (…) to the right of the text box of *Vector file defining training sites.*

3.   In the Pick list window, double click on the **Water** file.

4.   In the *MAKESIG* dialog box, click on the button *Enter signature filenames.*

5.   An *Enter signature filenames* dialog box will open. In the blank cell to the right of 1, type **Water**.

6.   Uncheck the box labeled *Create signature group file* (Figure 7.4.4.a).

7.   Click on *OK* to close the *Enter signature filenames* dialog box.

8.   In the *MAKESIG* dialog box, click on the button for *Insert layer group.*

9.   From the *Pick list,* double click on **Tm_all**.

10. The *MAKESIG* dialog box should now show the six bands of the TM data (Figure 7.4.4.b).

11. Note in *MAKESIG* dialog box the text box for the minimum sample size has been set automatically to 60 (10 pixels x the number of bands).

12. Click *OK*.

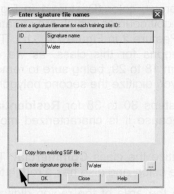

Figure 7.4.4.a   *Enter Signature file names* dialog box.

Figure 7.4.4.b   *MAKESIG* dialog box with parameters set.

After the program has completed, the *MAKESIG* dialog box will remain open, because of IDRISI's persistent windows.

If you have sufficient pixels in each class, the program should execute normally, and you will see a brief indication that the program is running in the status bar of the IDRISI workspace.

However, if you do not have enough pixels, you will receive a warning message. You will then need to either (a) increase the number of pixels in the class, or (b) reduce the threshold of number of pixels required. Adding additional pixels is relatively straightforward, and is described below. However, if the program did end normally, then you can skip these instructions below.

Digitizing additional polygons in an existing vector file

Menu location: Main tool bar icons only

1. An image should already be open in the IDRISI workspace, with the training polygons overlaid. If not, first display the image **tm345fcc**. Then add the vector file you wish to add to by clicking on the *Composer window* button for *Add layer*. Add the vector layer you wish to work on, and then select the radio button for a **Qualitative** *Symbol file.*

2. If the image is still open from the Digitizing exercise, find the *Composer window*, and click on the name of the class you wish to add to. This will highlight the name of the class in *Composer window*. Figure 7.4.4.b shows the Commercial class selected.

3. You can now follow the procedures you are already familiar with to add an additional polygon, as summarized below.

4. Maximize the viewer by clicking on the *Full extent normal* icon in the main IDRISI tool bar.

5. Click on the *Full extent maximized* icon. This enlarges the display window to the largest size possible with the IDRISI window.

6. Zoom in to the area of interest by clicking on the *Zoom window* icon. Draw a rectangle around the area of interest.

7. Click on the *Digitize* icon.

8. When the *Digitize* dialog box opens, take the option to *Add features to the currently active vector layer*, and remember to change the *ID or Value* back to **1**.

9. Digitize with the left mouse button.

10. Close the polygon with the right mouse button.

11. Save the file when you are done.

12. You will then need to rerun the *MAKESIG* program for the class for which you added one or more new polygons.

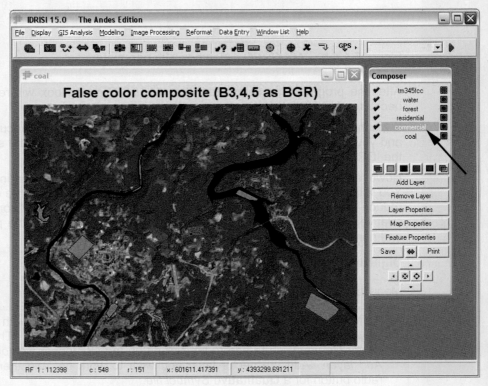

Figure 7.4.4.c   Selecting a vector layer prior to adding additional polygons.

So far we have created only one signature file, for Water. We now need to create the signature files for the remaining classes. Each signature will be in its own separate file.

Create signature files using MAKESIG (cont.): Remaining signatures

1. The *MAKESIG* dialog box should still be open from creating the Water signature. The *Bands to processed* should still list the tm bands 1 through 5 and 7.

2. In the *MAKESIG* dialog box, click on the Pick list button (...) for *Vector file defining training site*.

3. In the *Pick list* window, double click on the **Forest** file.

4. In the *MAKESIG* dialog box, click on the button *Enter signature filenames*.

5. An *Enter signature filenames* dialog box will open. In the cell to the right of 1, type **Forest**.

6. Ensure the check box for *Create signature group file* is not checked.

7. Click on *OK* to close the *Enter signature filenames* dialog box.

8. Click on *OK* in the *MAKESIG* dialog box, to create the Forest signature file.

9. Repeat steps 2 through 8 above to create the signature files for the remaining vector files: **Pasture**, **Commercial** (this class also includes Industrial and Transportation, but we shorten the name to Commercial for simplicity's sake), **Residential** and **Coal** (the Coal Waste class).

If you need to recreate any signature (maybe you are unhappy with the signature, or something didn't work, or maybe at a later stage you decide you did not collect all the cover classes needed) re-display the image using **DISPLAY**, digitize the boundaries of the new polygon, save the file (either with a new name, or use the old name, and thus over-write the file) and then run **MAKESIG** again on the new vector file.

7.4.5 Group the Class Signatures into a Single Signature Collection

We have now created the six signatures, each of which is in a separate file. Although we could now proceed to the classification step, it is convenient to group the signature files into a single collection. This will make repeat handling of the files simpler, in that we will then only need to specify the collection, instead of each file individually. Section 1.3.7 discusses working with collections in some detail, and you may wish to review that section if the instructions below are not sufficient. In addition, in Section 6.3.4, we worked with a raster collection to streamline the PCA decorrelation stretch. In this exercise we work with a signature collection, but the principle is the same.

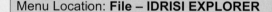

Creating a signature file collection with the IDRISI EXPLORER

Menu Location: **File – IDRISI EXPLORER**

1. Open the IDRISI EXPLORER.

2. In the *IDRISI EXPLORER* window, click on the tab for *Filters*.

3. Uncheck all the boxes that are checked (these are the default files that will be displayed in the *IDRISI EXPLORER* window).

4. Now click on the box to check the option to display *Signature (*.sig, *.spf)* files, and uncheck the boxes for *Raster Group (*.rgf)* and *Raster image (*.rst)* files (Figure 7.4.5.a).

5. Click on the tab for *Files*.

6. If the files are not listed in the *Files* pane, double click on the directory name to display the files.

7. The *Files* pane should list the six signature files you have created. Each signature will be listed twice: once as a *.sig file, and once as a *.spf file. In addition, the vector files (*.vct) files will be listed. We will only work with the *.sig files.

8. Highlight the signature files for the six signatures *__in this order__*: **Water.sig, , Forest.sig, Pasture.sig, Commerical.sig, Residential.sig,** and **Coal.sig.** Select multiple bands by clicking on each file sequentially, while simultaneously pressing the *Ctrl* key on the computer keyboard.

9. Right click in the *Files* pane. Select the menu option for *Create – Signature Group* (Figure 7.4.5.b).

10. Check the *Metadata* pane to see that the six signatures are listed in the same order as in step 7 above, i.e. *Water.sig* as *Group item (1)*, *Forest.sig* as *Group item (2)* etc. If the order is not the same, you should redo steps 7 and 8.

Figure 7.4.5.a   *IDRISI EXPLORER Filters* pane, with *Signature* filter checked.

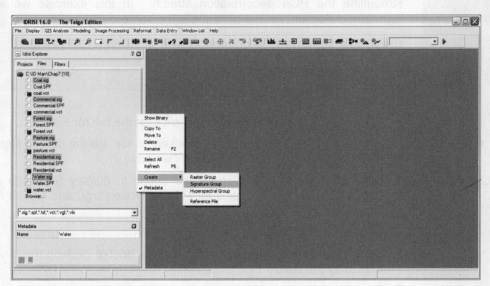

Figure 7.4.5.b   *IDRISI EXPLORER Files* pane, with signatures selected, and pop-up menu for creating a signature group (collection) file.

Creating a signature file dollection with the IDRISI EXPLORER (cont.)

11. Click on the new signature group collection file name (*Signature Group.sgf*), to highlight the file in the *Files* pane.

12. In the *Metadata* pane, enter a new name for the file in the right hand cell of the first row, typing over the default name of *Signature Group*. Since this is the collection of classification training signatures, we will enter **Train**.

13. Press the *Enter* key on your computer keyboard.

14. Click on the save (floppy disk) icon, at the bottom left hand corner of the *Metadata* pane. The name ***Train.sgf*** will immediately be updated in the *Files* window.

7.4.6 Comparing and Summarizing Signatures with SIGCOMP

It can be useful to visualize the statistics of your training signatures both as a check for gross errors, and also to help understand which classes are spectrally similar, and thus potentially poorly classified.

Compare the statistics of the training data with SIGCOMP

Menu location: **Image Processing - Signature development - SIGCOMP**

1. Use the main menu bar to start the SIGCOMP program.

2. In the *SIGCOMP* window, click on the button to *Insert signature group*.

3. A *Pick list* will open. Double click on the ***Train*** file.

4. In the *SIGCOMP* window, select the radio button to compare all signatures based on their *means* (Figure 7.4.6.a).

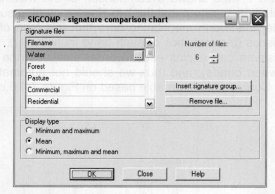

Figure 7.4.6.a   SIGCOMP window.

A graph of the signature means will open automatically in a new window (Figure 7.4.6.b). (Note that your graph should look somewhat similar, but will not be exactly the same, as it is unlikely you have digitized precisely the same pixels.)

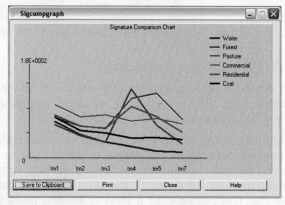

Figure 7.4.6.b   Signature means for the six classes.

The graph in Figure 7.4.6.b tells us a lot about the classes we have identified, especially if we mentally associate the band numbers with their respective wavelengths (Table 5.5.3.a). For example, we note that *Forest* and *Pasture* both have a very distinct pattern of high near infrared (TM4) and low visible (especially TM3) values. This is typical of vegetation and this spectral pattern is exploited in vegetation ratios (Section 5.3.4). We can also see that Residential is somewhat similar to the Forest class, a result of the many trees in residential areas in this city. It is apparent that Coal and Water are similar, with the latter being just slightly darker at all wavelengths. It is this similarity of spectral shape that makes water and coal waste difficult to separate, especially in unsupervised classification (Section 7.3).

You may also want to experiment with the other options in the *SIGCOMP* dialog box. For example, you can select radio buttons to compare the signatures based on their maxima and minima, and then click on the button for *OK* to generate the new graph. A graph of maxima and minima is useful for understanding signature overlap. However, since the maximum and minimum graphs get very confusing with many signatures displayed simultaneously, it is best to select a subset of the signatures – for example, just the Coal and Water signatures. Simply highlight in the *SIGCOM* window a file you would like to exclude, and click on the button for *Remove file*.

Figure 7.4.6.c shows a comparison of the minima and maxima of Water and Coal. It is apparent that the two classes overlap substantially in all bands. As an aside, it is worth mentioning here that this type of graph shows only first order statistics (the statistics of each band individually). Some remote sensing image classifiers can exploit second order statistics (the statistics of the relationships between bands), and thus we should not automatically assume that the Water and Coal are not separable based on Figure 7.4.6.c.

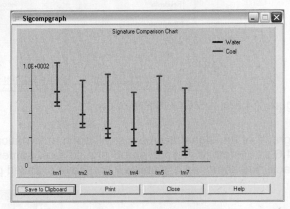

Figure 7.4.6.c   Comparison of minima and maxima of *Water* and *Coal*.

7.4.7 Parallelepiped Classification

We will now run the first of two classifiers which we will use to classify the Landsat data. In this section we do parallelepiped classification, in Section 7.4.8 we will do a maximum likelihood classification.

Parallelepiped is an absolute classifier, which simply checks each unknown pixel to see if it falls within the range of DN values for each band, for each of the training classes. Either an unknown pixel falls within the ranges defined by the training data, or it doesn't. In the latter case, the pixel would remain unclassified. Note that it is possible for a pixel to fall into more than one class. In this case, usually an arbitrary decision is made, for example, based on the order the classes were entered into the classifier. More details on parallelepiped classification can be found in most basic remote sensing texts.

We will run the parallelepiped classification *twice*. Parallelepiped is a relatively simple classifier (and therefore a very quick classifier), and is susceptible to outliers (noise, slight variations) in the training data. The second time we run the classification we will see how using a more conservative definition of the class extents will help the classification. The Z-score option defines the parallelepipeds based on the number of standard deviations for each class. This approach, which assumes each class has a Gaussian distribution, allows the analyst to exclude outliers in a systematic fashion. However, note that by making the class boundaries narrower, a greater percentage of pixels fall outside the range of the training classes.

Classify an image with PIPED

Menu location: **Image processing - Hard classifiers – PIPED**

---

1. Start the PIPED program from the menu.

2. In the *PIPED* dialog box click on the *Insert signature group* button.

3. In the *Pick list* that opens, double click on **Train** to select that signature group file.

4. For the *Output file name*, enter **Piped-min-max**.

5. The PIPED dialog box should now appear as in Figure 7.4.7.a.

6. Click on *OK*.

7. The classification should appear in a new window.

8. In the PIPED window, select the radio button for *Z-Score*.

9. Change the Output file new to **Piped-Z**.

10. Click on *OK*.

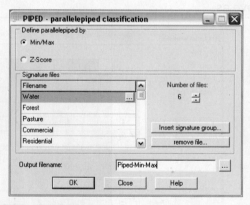

Figure 7.4.7.a   PIPED dialog box.

At this stage you should have produced two classifications. In order to compare this classification to our previous unsupervised classification (Section 7.3) and our future maximum likelihood classification, it will be useful to apply our earlier *Iso_lookup* palette file so that the colors in the map are the same as those we used before. However, we will need to add a color for the *Coal* class. Therefore, before we proceed, we will modify our previous palette file, created in Section 7.3.7.

(Note: If you did not do Section 7.3, or you did not save those files, you will need to follow the instructions in Section 7.3.7 to create a new palette file, and assign colors for DN values 1-5, before following the instructions below.)

Modify an existing look up table with SYMBOL WORKSHOP

Menu location: **Display – SYMBOL WORKSHOP**.

1. Start the SYMBOL WORKSHOP from the main menu or the main icon bar.

2. Once the *SYMBOL WORKSHOP* dialog box and window has opened, use the window menu for *File – Open*.

3. In the *Open Symbol File* dialog box, click in the radio button for *Palette*.

4. Click on the *File name* pick list button (…).

5. In the *Pick list* window, double click on **iso_lookup**.

6. Click on *OK*.

7. The *SYMBOL WORKSHOP* window should now display the palette file that you developed for the unsupervised classification. Specifically, it should have different colors assigned to DN values 1-5, and the remaining values should all be red.

8. Place the cursor over the cell for a DN value of 6 (this should be the first red cell to the right of the cells previously assigned colors). Confirm that the label shown that this is cell 6. Click in this cell.

9. Since class 6 is *Coal*, click on a black color chip in the *Color* dialog box that opens automatically.

10. Click on *OK* to close the *Color* dialog box.

11. Repeat steps 8 and 9 above to specify white for a DN value of 0 (the first cell in the grid).

12. Save the palette file through the *SYMBOL WORKSHOP* window menu *File – Save* as.

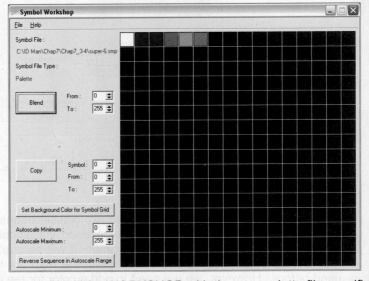

Figure 7.4.7.b   SYMBOL WORKSHOP with the new palette file specified.

13. In the *Save symbol file as* dialog box, enter the new file name: **Super-6**.

14. Click *OK* to close the *Save symbol file as* dialog box.

15. Figure 7.4.7.b shows the SYMBOL WORKSHOP with the two new colors specified.

Now that we have created the modified palette file, we can apply it to each of the two classified images.

Apply a custom palette file to a previously displayed image

1. Click in the display window for the *Piped-min-max* classification to give it focus (bring this window to the front).

2. Find the *Composer* window, which is always opened when an image is displayed. Click on this window to give it focus.

3. In the Composer window, click on the *Layer Properties* button.

4. Click on the tab for *Display parameters*.

5. Click on the *Pick list* button (…) next to the *Palette file* text box.

6. In the Pick list window that will open automatically, double click on the **Super-6** Palette file.

7. In the Layer properties window, click on *Apply*.

8. This should update the color scheme for the Piped-min-max classification. (Figure 7.4.7.c shows the results. Keep in mind that your training classes will be slightly different from those used to produce the figure, therefore your results will not be identical.)

9. Repeat steps 1-8 for the Piped-Z image. (See Figure 7.4.7.d, but bear in mind that your results will also be slightly different for this figure, too.)

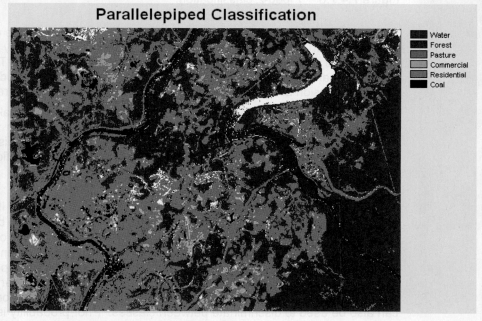

Parallelepiped Classification

■	Water
■	Forest
■	Pasture
■	Commercial
■	Residential
■	Coal

Figure 7.4.7.c   Piped-min-max classification.

It is important to note that the legends besides each classification do not include an important class: 0. The 0 class is the Unclassified. The Unclassified class is a typical characteristic of an absolute classifier, such as the parallelepiped classifier. Since we set a DN of 0 to white, any pixel that is white is unclassified. It is immediately apparent that that the z-scores approach (Figure 7.4.7.c) produces far more unclassified pixels than the min-max approach (Figure 7.4.7.d). Although the latter might seem a better product, close inspection of the original Landsat image suggests that the min-max image has a very low overall

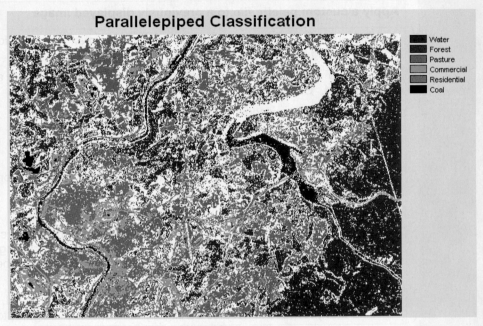

Parallelepiped Classification

Water
Forest
Pasture
Commercial
Residential
Coal

Figure 7.4.7.d   Piped-Z classification.

accuracy. In particular, an excessive number of pixels appear to be classified as Residential. In comparison, though the z-scores image has many unclassified pixels, those that are classified appear to be relatively accurate. The z-scores image appears to have a more reasonable distribution of the Residential class, and the confusion between Water and Coal appears to be much more limited.

The z-score approach defines the class extents based on a statistical distribution. Try running the classification again with a large (e.g. 3), and then with a small number (e.g. 1) to see the tradeoffs associated with changing this parameter. Remember to apply the new palette file to the image after the classification.

7.4.8 Maximum Likelihood Classification

Maximum Likelihood is a powerful classification technique. It draws on differences between the class means, as well as differences between the covariance matrices (i.e. the variability and the degree and type of correlation between bands). The latter parameter, difference between covariance matrices, is difficult to visualize in an image or as graphs, but can be as important, if not more so, than the difference between the class means. This is particularly true as the number of bands increases. An additional parameter, prior probability, can also be used to discriminate between classes. Prior probability is the chance a certain class is like to occur before you even run the classification. For example, assume that based on prior knowledge of an area, you were able to estimate that your scene is likely to be approximately 20% Water, 50% Forest and 30% Pasture. You could then enter values of 0.2, 0.5 and 0.3 as the prior probabilities for those classes. (The values sum to 1.0 by convention). In practice, however, this is difficult to do, and most of the time we just set the prior probabilities as equal values, which is the default in IDRISI. Additional information on maximum likelihood can be found in most introductory remote sensing texts.

Classify an image with MAXLIKE

Menu location: **Image processing - Hard classifiers – MAXLIKE**

1. Start the MAXLIKE program from the menu.

2. In the *MAXLIKE* dialog box, click on the *Insert signature group* button.

3. In the *Pick list*, double click on the *Train* signature group file.

4. In the MAXLIKE dialog box, specify the *Output image* as **maxlike**.

5. Leave the option for prior probabilities as the default (*Use equal prior probabilities for each signature*), as well as the *Proportion to exclude* at the default of *0%*.

6. Figure 7.4.8.a shows the dialog box completed.

7. Click on *OK* to run the classification.

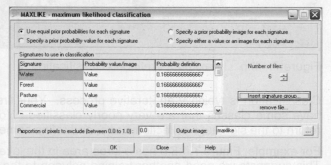

Figure 7.4.8.a   MAXLIKE dialog box.

As a final step, we will now apply the palette file developed in Section 7.4.7 to this image, to aid comparison with the parallelepiped classification.

Apply a custom palette file to a previously displayed image

1. Click in the display window for the *Maxlike* classification to give it focus (bring this window to the front).

2. Find the *Composer* window, which is always opened when an image is displayed. Click on this window to give it focus.

3. In the Composer window, click on the *Layer Properties* button.

4. Click on the tab for *Display parameters*.

5. Click on the *Pick list* button (…) next to the *Palette file* text box.

6. In the Pick list window that will open automatically, double click on the **Super-6** Palette file.

7. In the Layer properties window, click on *Apply*.

8. This should update the color scheme for the *Maxlike* classification. (Figure 7.4.8.b shows the results, however bear in mind that your training classes will be slightly different from this used to produce the figure, therefore your results will not be identical.)

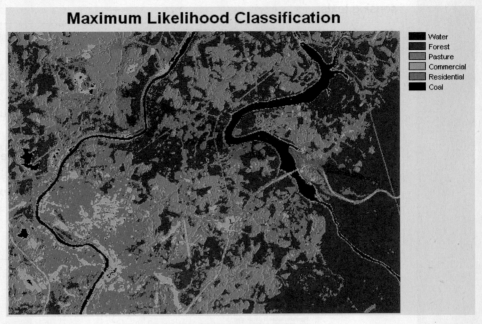

Maximum Likelihood Classification

Water
Forest
Pasture
Commercial
Residential
Coal

Figure 7.4.8.b   Maximum likelihood classification.

Classification is typically an iterative process. Your first classification is likely to have some classes that are very poorly classified. You almost certainly should return to the signature collection stage, and refine some or all of your signatures.

For example, Figure 7.4.8.b has a large area in the lake that is classified as Coal. This suggests we need another training polygon to the existing *Water* vector file, specifically in the area that is incorrectly labeled as *Coal*. To do this, you should follow the instructions for *Digitizing additional polygons in an existing vector file* in Section 7.4.4, except selecting the *Water* vector file for the overlay. You would then need to run the MAKESIG program again for this new Water class. As long as you overwrite the existing *Water.sig* signature file, when you run MAKESIG, you do not need to worry about changing the signature group file. Instead you can run the MAXLIKE program directly, after you have specified a new file name (e.g. **maxlike2**).

Figure 7.4.8.c shows the results of an improved classification, simply by digitizing one extra water polygon, and illustrates how iterative improvements can increase the accuracy of a classification greatly.

Finally, you should take a moment to compare the parallelepiped and maximum likelihood classifications. The latter is a much more powerful classification approach, although it is computationally intensive. Generally, we would expect a much more accurate product from maximum likelihood, and that does indeed appear to be the case for our study area. Just how accurate the classifications are is something we can, and indeed should, quantify. This is the first topic of the next chapter.

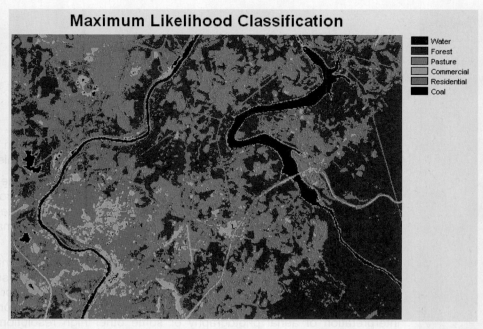

Maximum Likelihood Classification

■	Water
■	Forest
■	Pasture
■	Commercial
■	Residential
■	Coal

Figure 7.4.8.c   Maximum likelihood classification with modified *Water* class statistics applied.

Chapter 8   Advanced Classification Issues

8.1 Introduction

The previous chapter provided an introduction to basic classification methods. It is assumed that you have completed that chapter before you start this chapter.

In this chapter, we focus on two issues related to classification. The first is error analysis. There is a strong tradition in remote sensing classification of always conducting an error analysis. The error analysis provides a statement regarding the reliability of the classification, and is therefore essential information for the map user.

The error should be estimated using an independent source of information to provide a check of selected points. Ideally the independent data source would be based on a field visit. Oftentimes, limited access, expense, or changes in land cover over time, make a field visit impossible. Therefore, a visual interpretation of aerial photography or some other high resolution imagery is often a more practical alternative.

The second major focus of this chapter is on linear pixel unmixing, or fuzzy classification. This is a particularly interesting topic in remote sensing, and is an area of intensive current research. It is notable that IDRISI is very strong in classification techniques in general, including in the area of sophisticated classification approaches, such as fuzzy classification. Even if you never use fuzzy classification in your own work, the theoretical issues associated with this topic are well worth considering, and have ramifications in more traditional methods.

8.2 Copy Data for This Chapter

In this chapter we will work with two different image sets, one for the error analysis (Section 8.3) and one for the fuzzy classification (Section 8.4). Therefore, you should now copy the *Chap8* folder from the CD, and paste it as a new subfolder within the *\ID Man* folder on your computer.

You may wish to use your own classification for the error analysis exercise, rather than the one provided on the CD. If so, you should copy the raster file and associated metadata from your best maximum likelihood classification, e.g. maxlike2.rst and maxlike2.rdc, (note the extensions) from your working directory (e.g. *\ID Man\Chap7*) to the new location *(\ID Man\Chap8\Chap8_3)*.

After you have copied the *Chap8* folder, you should remove the *Read-Only* attribute from this new folder on your computer. This is done by right-clicking on the *Chap8* folder name, selecting *Properties* from the pop-up menu. A dialog box will open, labeled *Chap8 Properties*.   Now clear the check mark from the *Read Only* check box, by clicking in the box. You should then click on the button for *Apply*, and in the subsequent *Confirm Attribute Changes* dialog box, accept the default *Apply changes to this folder, subfolder and files*, and click on *OK*. You will need to also click on *OK* in the *Chap8 Properties* dialog box.

<u>Note</u>: Section 1.3.1 provides detailed instructions on how to copy the data from the CD, and also on how to remove the *Read-Only* attribute from the data. Also, the procedure for setting up the *ID Man* folder on your computer is described.

8.3 Classification error analysis

8.3.1 Overview

Figure 8.3.1.a provides an overview of the error analysis procedure: sample points are selected, the correct land cover class for those points is determined independently, and then those points are used to estimate the overall classification error. The figure also shows the main IDRISI programs we will use to conduct the error analysis.

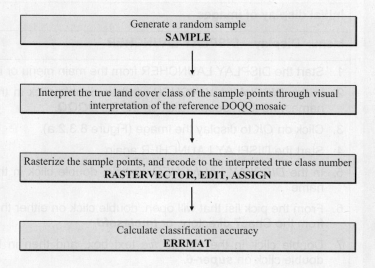

Figure 8.3.1.a   Overview of the classification error analysis procedure.

8.3.2 Preparatory

In Section 8.2 you should have already copied the data from the CD. However, we still need to set the *Project* and *Working Folders* for this section.

Before starting you should close any dialog boxes or displayed images in the IDRISI workspace.

Create a new project file and specify the working folders with the IDRISI EXPLORER

Menu Location: **File – IDRISI EXPLORER**

---

1. Start the IDRISI EXPLORER from the main menu or toolbar.

2. In the *IDRISI EXPLORER* window, select the *Projects* tab.

3. Right click within the *Projects* pane, and select the *New Project Ins* option.

4. A *Browse For Folder* window will open. Use this window to navigate to the *ID_Man* folder, which is the folder you created on your computer for the data for this manual. Now navigate to the *Chap8,* and then the *Chap8_3* subfolder.

5. Click *OK* in the *Browse For Folder* window.

6. A new project file *Chap8_3* will now be listed in the *Project* pane of the IDRISI EXPLORER. The working folder will also be listed in the Editor pane.

7. Close the IDRISI EXPLORER by clicking on the red *x* in the upper right corner of the *IDRISI EXPLORER* window.

Check that the project directory has been set correctly, by displaying the images, as described below. (If IDRISI is not able to find the image, then you have not set the directory correctly.) The **DOQQ.rst** is a false color composite mosaic of USGS digital orthophoto quarter quadrangles (DOQQs) with 1 meter pixels. The **tmclassfd.rst** image is a maximum likelihood classification, produced in Section 7.4.

Initial display of images

Menu: Display – DISPLAY LAUNCHER

1. Start the DISPLAY LAUNCHER from the main menu or icon bar.

2. In the *DISPLAY LAUNCHER* window, double click in the text box for the file name, and then double click on the file **DOQQ**.

3. Click on *OK* to display the image (Figure 8.3.2.a).

4. Start the DISPLAY LAUNCHER again.

5. In the *DISPLAY LAUNCHER* window, double click in the text box for the file name

6. From the pick list that will open, double click on either the file you have copied from the Chap7 directory, or **tmclassfd**.

7. Double click in the *Palette file* text box, and then in the resulting pick list, double click on **super-6.**

8. Click on *OK* to display the image (Figure 7.4.8.c).

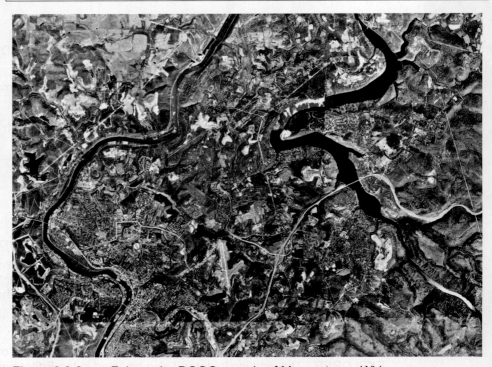

Figure 8.3.2.a   False color DOQQ mosaic of Morgantown, WV.

Compare the two images you have just displayed. The DOQQ is a false color image. IDRISI automatically scales an image so that the entire image can be displayed on your monitor. Therefore, even if you have a very large monitor, you are probably not seeing the full resolution of the data. However, it is easy to zoom in to see more detail in selected areas.

In standard false color images, red typically represents green vegetation. The DOQQ photographs were acquired in the very early spring (April), before the deciduous trees had leafed out. Therefore the deciduous trees are a rather dark red or even magenta to blue, and evergreen vegetation has a very strong red color. Grass typically has a light red color, trending to pink or even white where the grass is sparse.

An interesting feature of Figure 8.3.2.a is the small patches of white, and occasionally red, in the water. The white areas are sun-glint, and not rapids or other features in the water. The red features are related to the sun glint and the mosaicking process, and are therefore also artifacts.

8.3.3 Generate the Random Sample

Generate a random sample of test points with SAMPLE
Menu Location: **Image Processing – Accuracy Assessment – SAMPLE**.
1. Start the SAMPLE program from the main menu. 2. In the *SAMPLE* dialog box, double click in the text box labeled *Reference image*. 3. Double click on the name of the image which will be evaluated for its accuracy (***tmclassfd***, if you are using the image provided on the CD). 4. From the list under the heading *Sampling scheme,* select the option for *Stratified random*.

As you can see from the SAMPLE dialog box, IDRISI provides three sample selection strategies:

1. Random: the points are distributed randomly in no clear pattern throughout the entire image. Some will randomly be close together, some farther away from each other.

2. Systematic: the points are distributed an equal distance apart from each other across the entire image. This is a dangerous option to select if there is any structure to your data. For example, in an agricultural landscape, if the fields are a typical size, systematic sampling may result in over-sampling or under-sampling some cover types.

3. Stratified random: the points are distributed randomly, but an equal number in each strata, or class. IDRISI seems to be rather limited in that the user is not allowed to determine what is used for strata. The on-line help seems to suggest that the strata used are created simply by applying a matrix or grid to the image. Each grid cell is then sampled randomly.

It is important to be aware that classes that are relatively rare (in our classified image, this would include the Water, Commercial and Coal classes) will have fewer samples than classes that are more common. Therefore, other image processing packages have the option for the user to specify the strata using an image.

Generate a random sample of test points with SAMPLE (cont.)

4. Enter the number of points as **30**.

5. Enter the output vector file name: **sample**.

6. Figure 8.3.3.a shows the dialog box with the parameters completed.

7. Click on *OK*. A blank image with 30 points (the random sample) indicated by small black dots will be generated.

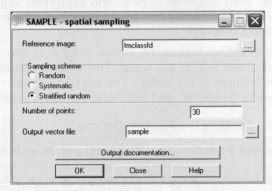

Figure 8.3.3.a   The *SAMPLE* dialog box.

A total of just 30 points is probably much too low for a reliable estimate of the accuracy of the classification. At least 100 points would be a recommended minimum, with a number closer to 300 preferred. However, this exercise with 30 points should at least illustrate the procedures involved, and give an approximate idea of the overall map accuracy. We should be particularly cautious about interpreting the accuracy of the individual classes, however, as some classes will have very few, if any, test samples. This is a consequence of our not being able to stratify by class.

8.3.4 Interpret the True Land Cover Class for Each Sample Point

The next step involves careful image interpretation. You will examine the DOQQ to determine the "true" land cover for each of the 30 random points. Because each random image generation is unique, your selection of 30 points will not be the same as the one used to illustrate this manual. Therefore, in the next section, only the general procedure is described. You will have to use your best judgment in interpreting the DOQQ.

We will record the true land cover class (coded by the DN values of each class) in a simple text file, using the program EDIT. The values will be stored in an Attribute Values File (AVL extension).

The final AVL text file we have the point number (from 1 to 30), followed by the class number. For example, if point 1 was associated with class 3, and point 2 with class 5, then the first two lines of your table will be

1 3

2 5

Note that each point is on a new line and there is a single space between the point number, and the associated class. Since you have 30 points, your file will have 30 lines. At this initial stage we will only list the point numbers; we will add the interpreted class numbers subsequently.

Build the initial values for the recode values table with EDIT
Menu location: **Data Entry – EDIT**.

1. Start the EDIT program from the main menu or the main icon tool bar.

2. The *IDRISI TEXT EDITOR* window will open.

3. In the *IDRISI TEXT EDITOR*, sequentially enter the sample point number, followed by a carriage return ("Enter" on your keyboard), starting with 1, and ending with 30. Thus each point will be on a new line. Start with point 1, and end with point 30.

4. Use the menu in the *IDRISI TEXT EDITOR* window to initiate saving the file: *File – Save As*.

5. In the *Save file* window, select from the *Save as type* pull-down list *Attribute values file*.

6. In the *File name* text box, enter **landcover**. The file will automatically be given an AVL extension.

7. Click on *Save*.

8. A *Values File Information* window will open. In this new window, select the radio button for *Integer*, and click on *OK*.

9. Figure 8.3.4.a shows the **landcover.AVL** file in the *EDIT* window.

10. Do not close the *IDRISI TEXT EDITOR* window, as we will enter our land use interpretations directly in the file.

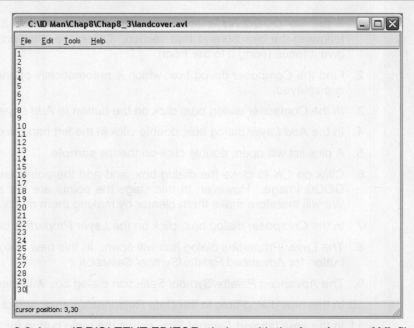

Figure 8.3.4.a   *IDRISI TEXT EDITOR* window with the **Landcover.AVL** file.

We are now ready to start the interpretation. Table 8.3.4.a gives a short description of each class, as well as the associated code (DN value). The DN for each class is the same as the scheme used in the classifications produced in Section 7.4 and thus for the **tmclassfd.rst** image.

Table 8.3.4.a   Maxlike class numbers, to be used in coding the random points generated by the **SAMPLE** program

Class Number	Class Name	Appearance on false color DOQQ
1	Water	Black (also white sun glint and associated red artifacts); smooth texture, sinuous water bodies
2	Forest	Red, magenta, blue in places, characteristically rough texture.
3	Pasture	Red, to pale pink, occasionally white, characteristically smooth texture
4	Commercial / Industrial / Transportation	Blue to black, characteristically geometric shapes of buildings and sinuous and straight linear features for roads
5	Residential	Mixture of colors, red dominates, blue common. Characteristically very rough texture from roads, houses and gardens
6	Coal Waste	Black to dark blue, smooth to rough texture. Found in dammed valleys, and adjacent to river, where it is associated with barge loading.

Display vector file as overlay on DOQQ

1. If the file **DOQQ.rst** is not still displayed from Section 8.3.2, open it now, following the directions in that section. Otherwise, click on DOQQ display, to give it focus (bring it to the front).

2. Find the *Composer* dialog box, which is automatically opened when an image is displayed.

3. In the Composer dialog box, click on the button to *Add Layer*.

4. In the *Add Layer* dialog box, double click in the left hand text box.

5. A pick list will open; double click on the file **sample**.

6. Click on *OK* to close the dialog box, and add the points as an overlay to the DOQQ image. However, at this stage the points are too small to be visible. We will therefore make them clearer by making them much larger.

7. In the *Composer* dialog box, click on *the Layer Properties* button.

8. The *Layer Properties* dialog box will open. In this new dialog box, click on the button for *Advanced Palette/Symbol Selection*.

9. The *Advanced Palette/Symbol Selection* dialog box will open.

10. In this new dialog box, in the *Data Relationship* area, select *Qualitative*.

11. In the area labeled *Symbol Size*, select the radio button for *16*

12. Click on *OK*.

13. The vector points should now be displayed on the DOQQ as very large circles. Figure 8.3.4.b. shows an example of what your display should look like. Note, however, that the specific locations of your sample points will be different, since the selection of locations is supposed to be random.

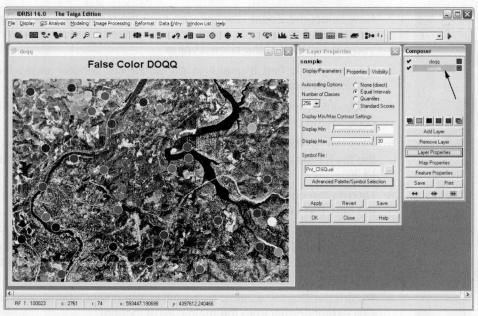

Figure 8.3.4.b   False color DOQQ showing the 30 sample points overlaid. Note the *Composer* and *Layer Properties* dialog boxes. In the *Composer* dialog box, the **sample** layer is highlighted.

Now that we have set up the *IDRISI TEXT EDITOR* window and the display of the DOQQ with the SAMPLE overlay, we are ready to compile the list of land use / land cover interpretations. In many cases determining the correct value to assign the point is very difficult. What if the point falls on the boundary of two classes? Technically, you should estimate the dominant land use class over the 30 meter Landsat pixel centered on the point. Since the DOQQ has 3 meter pixels, this would be a 10 by 10 pixel window. This is actually rather difficult to do, so we usually just take the land use class directly at the point itself.

Though making a decision of the spectral class for each sample point is really hard, it illustrates well why the classification is so complex. For example, you may find a point that falls in a large patch of trees in a residential area. The land use is clearly residential (and this is how you should code the point). Nevertheless, the land cover, which is what is observed by the remote imaging device, is Forest.

If you truly don't know how to label a pixel, you could label it 0, which will effectively delete that point. Use this approach with caution, though, as it will reduce your number of sample points, and potentially bias your results.

Note: If you get RGB values instead of the point number when you try to query a point as described in the next section, make sure that the **sample** vector layer is highlighted in the *Composer* window (Figure 8.3.4.b).

Interpret land use / land cover class for each point

---

1. In the DOQQ image display, select each sample point in turn. For example, start in the bottom left corner. Query the value of the sample point by clicking on the icon for *Cursor Inquiry Mode* in the main tool bar, and then clicking on the circle representing the sample in the image display. Note the value that will be indicated for this point. (It should be a value between 1 and 30.)

2. Now select the *Zoom Window* icon form the main tool bar, and zoom in to an area around the sample point. You may need to zoom in several times until you are satisfied of the correct value.

3. You may also find it useful to maximize the window using the *Full extent maximized* icon.

4. Photo-interpret the land use / land cover class, and identify the correct DN code for the class (Table 8.3.4.a).

5. Find the *IDRISI TEXT EDITOR* window, and scroll down to the correct line in the file for the point you have just worked with (i.e. the sample number, from 1 to 30).

6. Next to the correct sample number, enter a space and then the DN code for the land use / land cover.

7. Figure 8.3.4.b shows sample 1, with the interpreted land cover (Forest, coded as 2), entered in the AVL file. (Note that your sample #1 will not be in the same location, and therefore will not necessarily have the same land use / land cover.

8. Return the Display window to the full image display, by clicking on the icon for *Full extent normal* from the main IDRISI tool bar.

9. Iterate through the process for interpreting each point (steps 1 through 8 above) until you have developed a complete table of the "true" land cover class for each of the 30 samples.

10. Figure 8.3.4.d shows the completed table. (Note that your table will have a different set of land use / land cover classes, because your sample will be different.)

11. Save the text file by using the *IDRISI TEXT EDITOR* main menu: *File – Save*.

12. A *Values File Information* window will open. In this new window, select the radio button for *Integer*, and click on *OK*.

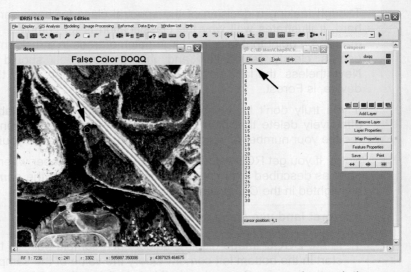

Figure 8.3.4.c   A zoomed in window around a sample, and the associated value for Forest entered in the **landcover.AVL** file. (Note that your sample 1 will not be in the same location as shown.)

Figure 8.3.4.d   Example of completed ***landcover.AVL*** file. Your list will have different land cover class numbers in the second column.

8.3.5 Rasterize the Recode of the Sample Points

Now that we have interpreted what each sample represents, we need to convert our vector file to a raster file. This raster file will have zeros everywhere, except where the samples are located. For the samples, the DN value will initially bee equal to the sample number. We will then use the text ***landcover.AVL*** file to recode the values in this image to the "true" values.

Rasterize the sample vector file with RASTERVECTOR
Menu Location: **Reformat - RASTERVECTOR**
1. Open the RASTERVECTOR program from the main menu.
2. In the *RASTERVECTOR* dialog box, select the radio button for *Vector to Raster*.
3. Select the radio button for *Point to Raster*.
4. Select the radio button for *Change cells to record the identifiers of points*.
5. Click on the file pick list button (…) next to the *Vector point file* text box.
6. In the pick list window that will open, double click on the ***sample*** vector file.
7. In the *Image file to be updated* text box enter **point_locations**.
8. Figure 8.3.5.a shows the *RASTERVECTOR* dialog box completed.
9. Click on *OK*.
10. A dialog box will open with the following message: *Image to be updated (point_location.rst) does not exist. Bring up **INITIAL** to create this image?*
11. Click on *Yes*.
12. The window for the program INITIAL will open. This program creates a blank file, into which the rasterized vector points are subsequently inserted.

13. In the *INITIAL* window, find and double click in the text box for *Image to copy parameters from*.

14. In the *Pick list* that will open, double click on **tmclassfd**.

15. Figure 8.3.5.b shows the *INITIAL* window with the parameters selected.

16. Accept all other defaults, and click on *OK*.

17. The rasterized sample image will open in a new *DISPLAY* viewer (the points themselves are very small, and may be hard to see, and thus the image may appear to be almost entirely black (DN = 0).)

Figure 8.3.5.a   *RASTERVECTOR* window.

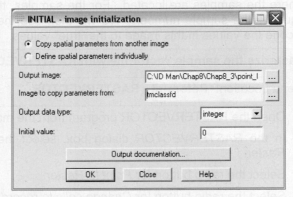

Figure 8.3.5.b   *INITIAL* window.

The rasterized image that you have created will have a DN value equal to the sample number, or zero if there is no sample at that location. For our accuracy assessment we need the DN value the "true" land use / land cover. Therefore, we will now use the *Attribute Values file* to create a new image of the sample points, with values according to the true classes of those points.

Create new image with land cover class values using ASSIGN

Menu location: **Data Entry – ASSIGN**

1. Use the main IDRISI menu to start the ASSIGN program.

2. In the *ASSIGN* window, select the radio button for *Raster file*.

3. Double click in the *Feature definition image* text box, and in the subsequent pick list, double click on **point_locations**.

4. In the textbox for Output image, enter **truth_sample**.

5. Double click in *The Attribute values* file text box, and in the subsequent pick list, double click on **landcover**.

6. In the *Output title* text box, enter **Photo-interpreted land use / land cover**.

7. Figure 8.3.5.c shows the *ASSIGN* text box with parameters selected.

8. Click on *OK*, and the new image of sample points will be displayed automatically. Again, the image may appear to be entirely black, with the points hardly visible.

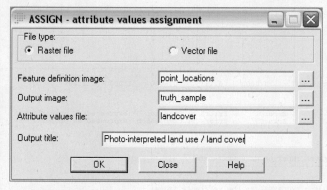

Figure 8.3.5.c   *ASSIGN* window.

8.3.6 Calculate the classification Accuracy using ERRMAT

In the previous steps we created an image that is blank everywhere, except for the 30 pixels for which we determined the "true" land cover from the visual interpretation of the DOQQ mosaic. We can now overlay this image with the classification to determine the overall accuracy of that latter image.

Calculate classification accuracy using ERRMAT
Menu Location: **Image Processing – Accuracy Assessment – ERRMAT.**

1. Use the main IDRISI menu to start the ERRMAT program.

2. In the *ERRMAT* window, double click in the text box next to *Ground truth image*.

3. In the pick list that will open, double click on **truth_sample**.

4. Double click in the *Categorical map image* text box.

5. In the *Pick list* that will open, double click on the name of the file you would like to evaluate the accuracy of. If you are using the classified image from the CD, this will be **tmclassfd**.

6. Figure 8.3.6.a shows the *ERRMAT* window with the files specified.

7. Click on *OK*.

8. The accuracy assessment results will open in a new text window, labeled *Module Results*. Note that you can save the results to a file, or to the clipboard, thus facilitating pasting the results in a text editor.

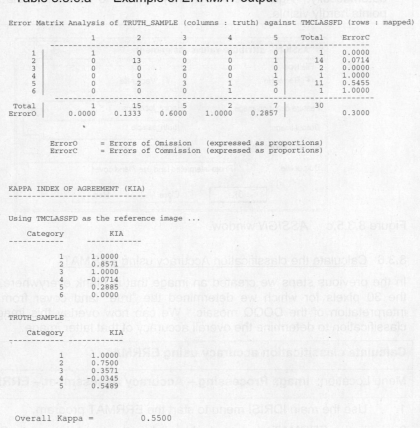

Figure 8.3.6.a   *ERRMAT* window.

Table 8.3.6.a   Example of *ERRMAT* output

```
Error Matrix Analysis of TRUTH_SAMPLE (columns : truth) against TMCLASSFD (rows : mapped)

                    1         2         3         4         5      Total     ErrorC
             -----------------------------------------------------------------------
         1  |       1         0         0         0         0    |     1      0.0000
         2  |       0        13         0         0         1    |    14      0.0714
         3  |       0         0         2         0         0    |     2      0.0000
         4  |       0         0         0         0         1    |     1      1.0000
         5  |       0         2         3         1         5    |    11      0.5455
         6  |       0         0         0         1         0    |     1      1.0000
             -----------------------------------------------------------------------
     Total  |       1        15         5         2         7    |    30
    ErrorO  |  0.0000    0.1333    0.6000    1.0000    0.2857    |            0.3000


         ErrorO    = Errors of Omission   (expressed as proportions)
         ErrorC    = Errors of Commission (expressed as proportions)



KAPPA INDEX OF AGREEMENT (KIA)
------------------------------

Using TMCLASSFD as the reference image ...

     Category        KIA
     -----------     -----------

         1        1.0000
         2        0.8571
         3        1.0000
         4       -0.0714
         5        0.2885
         6        0.0000

TRUTH_SAMPLE

     Category        KIA
     -----------     -----------

         1        1.0000
         2        0.7500
         3        0.3571
         4       -0.0345
         5        0.5489


Overall Kappa =           0.5500
```

The ERRMAT accuracy assessment shows a detailed breakdown of how each of your sample pixels in the "truth" file compares to its assignment in the classified file. Table 8.3.6.a shows an example data set. Remember your results will be different, as your random sample will be different.

If the table is too wide, IDRISI breaks the accuracy table up into pieces to make it fit in a standard format on a piece of paper. If this is the case, you may wish to create a version of the table that is not broken across the page, using a text editor. Table 8.3.6.a is not broken up, however, because no samples were identified in the photo interpretation as the Coal class (DN = 6). Thus, the last column of the table is absent.

In the error matrix, correctly classified pixels are listed down the diagonal. In Table 8.3.6.a the diagonal is a bit difficult to identify because of the missing column 6. An error matrix that indicated a 100% accurate classification would have zeros everywhere, except the diagonal. Errors are the non-zero values that are not on the diagonal.

The error of the overall classification is the proportion of incorrectly classified test pixels. In table 8.3.6.a, the overall error is reported as 0.30 (i.e. 30%) in the bottom right cell in the main table. A 30% error rate is higher than that normally desired for a remote sensing classification.

The Overall Kappa statistic is an attempt to adjust the accuracy for the anticipated chance agreement if you just randomly assigned classes to the image. The Kappa value is thus lower than the overall accuracy. For Table 8.3.6.a, the accuracy would be 0.70 (i.e. 1.0 minus the error, or 1.0 − 0.3 = 0.7). The reported Kappa is only 0.55, 0.15 lower than the accuracy.

When it comes to the pixels off the diagonal, there are two types of errors - errors of commission, and errors of omission. For example, say you classified **all** of Morgantown image as Water. Clearly your *errors of omission* for Water would be *low*, since you would *not omit* a single pixel that should have been Water, because the whole classification is assigned to Water! However, the *errors of commission* would be *high*, since you would *commit* an error in calling the rest of Morgantown Water, when it clearly is not.

For Table 8.3.6.a it is probably best not to pay too much attention to the class errors of commission and omission, since the number of pixels for each class is so small.

As a final step in this exercise, you may want to calculate the accuracy of your parallelepiped classifications, and compare them to your maximum likelihood classifications. Carrying out such a task is quite straightforward, since after copying the *.rst and *.rdc files to your *\ID Man\Chap8\Chap8_3* directory, you can immediately run the ERRMAT program (this Section, 8.3.6), as you do not need to replicate the preparatory steps of generating the random sample, rasterizing it, and recoding it to the correct land use / land cover classes.

8.4 Linear Pixel Unmixing

8.4.1 Overview

As discussed in the Introduction to this chapter, soft classification is an alternative to the relatively simple hard classification methods discussed so far, where each pixel is assigned to one class only. In soft classification methods, a pixel can potentially be associated with more than one class.

There are three main applications for soft classification:

1. **Classification of mixed pixels that arise from integrating discrete areas of different classes.** For example, an individual pixel along a river bank may include both water and land areas. Mixed pixels are a direct result of the spatial integration across the instantaneous field of view (IFOV) of the sensor. The standard way to analyze mixed pixels is linear pixel unmixing, however soft classifiers can also be used to investigate class mixing.

2. **Classification of conceptually fuzzy classes that arise from variability in the underlying classes.** Where classes have transitional, rather than discrete boundaries, pixels from the transitional areas will typically have a spectral radiance that is intermediate between those of the pure classes. For example, river water may vary from deep and clear to shallow and muddy. Thus, the deep and clear water is simply one end of a continuum of classes, and the variability is inherent in the land cover, not the mechanics of imaging the site.

3. **Investigation of the confidence the user has in the classification of each pixel.** For example, how do we know that we haven't ignored an important spectral class in defining our class training areas?

In this exercise we will investigate the use of soft classification for unmixing pixels. In forest cover mapping, the IFOV of the Landsat ETM+ sensor, at approximately 30 meters, is much larger than the typical size of the canopy of a single tree. Thus, we can consider forest spectral radiance as a mixture of the trees within each pixel. Foresters traditionally recognize forest communities as groups of trees. However, the boundaries of those communities may be gradational, and the same species may occur in more than one community. Thus, it would seem that forest applications are ideally suited to a fuzzy approach.

Our study site for this exercise is Chestnut Ridge, West Virginia, a subset of the area on the extreme eastern edge of the area we were examining in the supervised and unsupervised classification exercises in this chapter. (More background on this area can be found in Nellis et al. 2000).

8.4.2 Preparatory

In Section 8.2 you should have already copied the data from the CD. However, we still need to set the *Project* and *Working Folders* for this section.

Before starting you should close any dialog boxes or displayed images in the IDRISI workspace.

Create a new project file and specify the working folders with the IDRISI EXPLORER
Menu Location: **File – IDRISI EXPLORER**

1. Start the IDRISI EXPLORER from the main menu or toolbar.

2. In the *IDRISI EXPLORER* window, select the *Projects* tab.

3. Right click within the *Projects* pane, and select the *New Project Ins* option.

4. A *Browse For Folder* window will open. Use this window to navigate to the *ID_Man* folder, which is the folder you created on your computer for the data for this manual. Now navigate to the *Chap8,* and then the *Chap8_4* subfolder.

5. Click *OK* in the *Browse For Folder* window.

6. A new project file *Chap8_4* will now be listed in the *Project* pane of the IDRISI EXPLORER. The working folder will also be listed in the Editor pane.

7. Close the IDRISI EXPLORER by clicking on the red *x* in the upper right corner of the *IDRISI EXPLORER* window.

The data for this section consists of Enhanced Thematic Mapper Plus imagery from October 30, 2000. The bands are labeled ***tm30oct1*** to ***tm30oct7***, where the last digit is the band number. (Note that the sixth band is not provided, as this is the thermal band, and is not needed for this exercise).

It is always useful to become familiar with the data at the start of the project. Therefore, we will now create a simulated natural color composite. By now you should be familiar with the process of creating color composites. To create a simulated natural color composite you need to match the colors that a band is displayed to the approximate wavelengths of the sensor (Table 5.5.3.a). Thus, for a simulated natural color image, the blue image display band should be TM band 1, and the green band should be TM band 2 and the red band TM band 3.

Create a color composite image
Menu Location: **Display - COMPOSITE**
1. Start the COMPOSITE program using the main menu or tool bar.
2. In the *COMPOSITE* dialog box, double click in the *Blue image band* text box, and then double click on the file ***tm30oct1*** in the subsequent *Pick list*.
3. Double click in the *Green image band* text box, and then double click on ***tm30oct2***.
4. Double click in the *Red image band* text box, and then double click on ***tm30oct3***.
5. Enter the *Output image* filename in the text box provided: **tm123**.
6. In the *Title* text box enter **Simulated natural color composite**.
7. Accept all other defaults, and click *OK* to create and display the false color composite.
8. Once the image has been displayed, you can close the *COMPOSITE* window.

Figure 8.4.2.a shows the results of the image, which will be displayed automatically. The sinuous band of blue in the lower left of the image is a river (the Cheat River), and the sinuous band of white is a major highway (Interstate 68). A faint diagonal linear feature can be observed; this indicates the zone of cleared vegetation associated with an electricity power line.

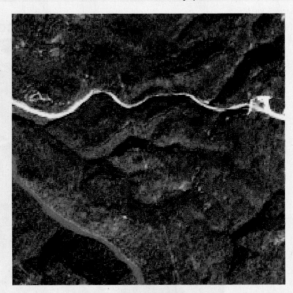

Figure 8.4.2.a   Simulated natural color ETM+ image of Chestnut Ridge.

It is apparent from Figure 8.4.2.a that this is a very rugged area. The average elevation of the upland areas is over 700 meters; in the river below, it is approximately 270 meters. Note the presence of steep slopes in the image, and the associated shadows. Since this is a northern hemisphere image, and the image was acquired in the morning at approximately 10 a.m., the shadows are on the northwest facing slopes.

The forest here is dominantly deciduous. Since this is an autumn image, the colors in the image are much more varied than would be found with, for example, a summer image. Unlike in the September image we were classifying earlier, in this autumn image, two main forest communities are evident. Oaks (*Quercus spp.*) tend to have a red to brown color in this image, and yellow poplar (which we will refer to as "poplar") (*Liriodendron tuliperifera*) have a yellow to green color.

8.4.3 Digitize Training Class Data

Linear pixel unmixing is a type of supervised classification. Therefore, we will begin by digitizing training areas. Because of the variation inherent in the autumn forest colors, we will need to digitize multiple training areas for each of the two forest classes. We will also digitize a third class, shade, to account for some forest areas that are shaded by the steep topography (Figure 8.4.3.a). Figure 8.4.3.a gives an overview of the recommended number and distribution of training polygons that should be digitized. Note that when you digitize your polygons, they will all have the same color, unlike in Figure 8.4.3.a.

Table 8.4.3.a   Training classes for linear pixel unmixing.

#	Class	Color in simulated natural color image
1	Oaks	Red to brown
2	Poplar	Yellow to green
3	Shadow	Black

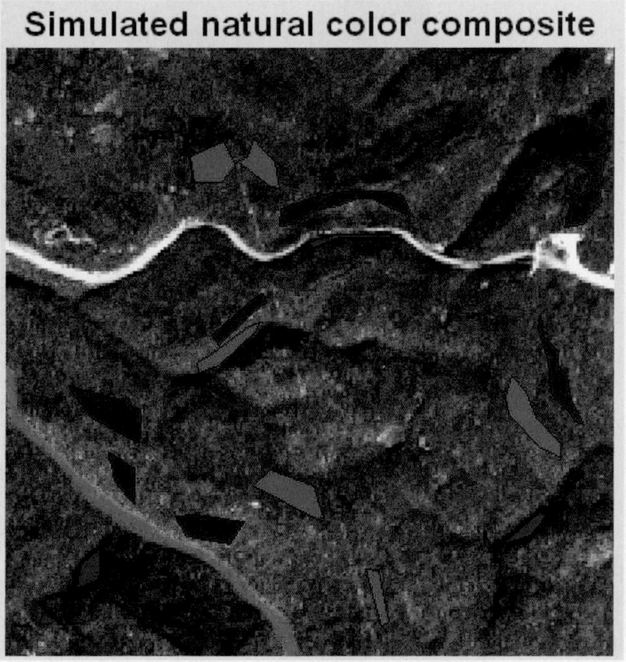

Figure 8.4.3.a   Training classes for the linear pixel unmixing. (Red = Oak, Yellow = Poplar, and Blue = shadow.)

Since you should be familiar with digitizing from Section 7.4.3, a relatively brief description of digitization will be provided below. If this description is not sufficiently clear, please review Section 7.4.3 before proceeding. Note that Section 7.4.3 also includes a description of how to correct mistakes by deleting polygons.

Digitizing training polygons
Menu location: Main tool bar icons only (Note that the icons are grayed out if an image is not yet displayed.)

1. The simulated natural color image *tm123* should already be displayed in a Viewer.

2. Click on the *Full extent normal* icon from the main tool bar, to display the entire image, if not already at the default zoom.

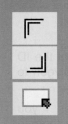

3. Click on *Full extent maximized*, to maximize the size of the display window.

4. If necessary, click on the *Zoom window* icon, to zoom in on area of oak trees (Table 8.4.3.a and Figure 8.4.3.a). (If you have a large monitor, the full extent maximized display may be at a sufficiently high resolution not to require additional zooming in.)

5. Click on the *Digitize* icon. A dialog box labeled *DIGITIZE* will open.

6. Enter the file name **Oaks** in the text box labeled *Name of layer to be created*. Leave all other values at their defaults.

7. Click on *OK* to close the *DIGITIZE* window.

8. Move the cursor over the image. Note how when the cursor is over the image, it takes on a form similar to the *Digitize* icon, instead of the normal arrow.

9. Digitize the first vertex of the first oak polygon by pressing the *left* mouse button. Continue clicking in the image to specify the outer boundaries of the polygon you wish to digitize.

10. Close the polygon by pressing the *right* mouse button. Note that the program automatically closes the polygon by duplicating the first point; so you do not need to attempt to close the polygon by digitizing the first point again.

11. If you have zoomed in on the image, repeat the process to return the image to full extent, and zoom in on another oak area.

12. Now start digitizing the second polygon by clicking on the *Digitize* icon again.

13. The *DIGITIZE* dialog box will open again.

14. Confirm that the radio button for A*dd features to the currently active vector layer* is selected.

15. Click *OK*.

16. The ID for the polygon will be incremented automatically. *Be sure to set it back to 1, as all the oak polygons should be digitized as part of the general Oak class.*

17. Digitize the next polygon.

18. Repeat the process of adding polygons to the Oak class until you have created all five oak training areas.

19. Save the polygon file by clicking on the *Save digitized data icon*.

20. A *Save prompt* dialog box will open. Click on *Yes*.

21. Now start digitizing the second class by clicking on the *Digitize* icon again.

22. The *DIGITIZE* dialog box will open again.

23. Select the radio button for *Create a new layer for the features to be digitized*.

24. Click *OK*.

25. In the text box labeled *Name of layer to be created*, enter **Poplar**.

26. Leave all other values at their defaults, and click on *OK*.

27. Digitize the poplar polygons. *Remember always to set the ID value back to 1 each time you start the process of adding a new polygon to the file.*

28. Save the polygon file by clicking on the *Save digitized data icon*.

29. A *Save prompt* dialog box will open. Click on *Yes*.

30. Repeat steps 21 to 29 for the **shade** class. Remember always to set the ID value back to 1 each time you start the process of adding a new polygon to the file, and remember to save the file.

31. When you are finished digitizing all the training areas, close the viewer. If you have any unsaved vector files you will be given an opportunity to save them.

8.4.4   Create Signature Files of Training Data

The process of creating signature files is described in detail in Section 7.4.4. Here we provide a brief overview of the process.

Create signature files using MAKESIG

Menu location: **Image Processing - Signature development – MAKESIG**

1. Start the MAKESIG program from the main menu.

2. In the *MAKESIG* dialog box, click on the Pick list button (…) to the right of the text box of *Vector file defining training sites*.

3. In the Pick list window, double click on the *Oak* file.

4. In the *MAKESIG* dialog box, click on the button *Enter signature filenames*.

5. An *Enter signature filenames* dialog box will open. In the blank cell to the right of 1, type **Oak**.

6. Uncheck the box labeled *Create signature group file*.

7. Click on *OK* to close the *Enter signature filenames* dialog box.

8. In the *MAKESIG* dialog box, click on the button for *Insert layer group*.

9. From the *Pick list,* double click on *tm30oct_all*.

10. The *MAKESIG* dialog box should now show the six bands of the TM data.

11. Click *OK*.

12. When the program has finished running (it should be very quick), double click in the *Vector file defining training sites* text box and in the subsequent pick list double click on *Poplar*.

13. Click on the button *Enter signature filenames*.

14. An *Enter signature filenames* dialog box will open. In the cell to the right of 1, type **Poplar**.

15. Click on *OK* to close the *Enter signature filenames* dialog box.
16. Click *OK*.
17. Repeat steps 12 to 16 for the class **Shadow**.

8.4.5 Group the Signature Files into a Signature Group File

Now that we have the signatures, we need to group them into a collection of signatures, or a *signature group file*. This procedure was also explained in more detail in Section 7.4.5.

Creating a signature file collection with the IDRISI EXPLORER

Menu Location: **File – IDRISI EXPLORER**

1. Open the IDRISI EXPLORER.

2. In the *IDRISI EXPLORER* window, click on the tab for *Filters*.

3. Uncheck all the boxes that are checked (these are the default files that will be displayed in the *IDRISI EXPLORER* window).

4. Now click on the box to check the option to display *Signature (*.sig, *.spf)* files.

5. Click on the tab for *Files*.

6. If the files are not listed in the *Files* pane, double click on the directory name to display the files.

7. The *Files* pane should list the three signature files you have created. Each signature will be listed twice: once as a *.sig file, and once as a *.spf file. We will only work with the *.sig files.

8. Highlight the signature files for the three signatures <u>*in this order*</u>: **Oak.sig, Poplar.sig,** and **Shadow.sig.** Select multiple bands by clicking on each file sequentially, while simultaneously pressing the *Ctrl* key on the computer keyboard.

9. Right click in the *Files* pane. Select the menu option for *Create – Signature Group*.

10. Check the *Metadata* pane, to see that the six signatures are listed in the same order as in step 7 above, i.e. *Water.sig* as *Group item (1)*, *Forest.sig* as *Group item (2)* etc. If the order is not the same, you should redo steps 7 and 8.

11. Make sure the **Signature Group.sgf** file name is highlighted in the *Files* pane.

12. In the *Metadata* pane, enter a new name in the right hand cell of the first row, typing over the default name of *Signature Group:* **Sig_all**.

13. Press the *Enter* key on your computer keyboard.

14. Click on the save (floppy disk) icon, at the bottom left hand corner of the *Metadata* pane. The name **Sig_all.sgf** will immediately be updated in the *Files* window.

8.4.6 Use UNMIX to Perform Linear Unmixing

Linear spectral unmixing assumes that each pixel can be modeled as a linear function of the input classes. Thus, this approach assumes that the spectral value of a pixel that comprises 50% of each of two different classes should lie half way between the two classes in the feature space (the spectral dimension of the data). Pixels that lie outside the bounding envelope of the training classes in the feature space would have to be modeled as having negative proportions of the training classes, which has no physical meaning, and is normally not allowed.

Unmix an image

Menu location: **Image Processing - Soft Classifiers - UNMIX**

1. Start the UNMIX program from the main IDRISI menu.

2. In the *UNMIX* dialog box, select the option for *Linear spectral unmixing*.

3. Double click in the text box labeled *Signature group file*.

4. In the subsequent pick list, double click on *Sig_all*.

5. In the *Output prefix* text box, type **Unmixed**.

6. Figure 8.4.6.a shows the UNMIX dialog box, with files specified.

7. Click on *OK*.

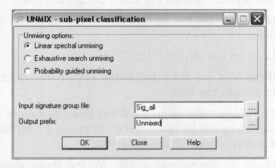

Figure 8.4.6.a   The *UMIX* dialog box.

IDRISI automatically displays the unmixing residual image, with a Quantitative look up table (Figure 8.4.6.b). (Note that your image will be slightly different from that in the figure, because your training classes will not be identical. However, the overall pattern should be similar.)

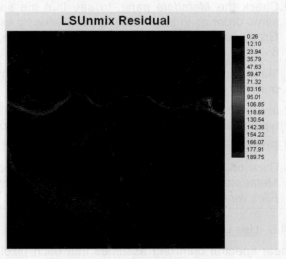

Figure 8.4.6.b   Linear spectral unmixing residuals.

The unmixing residual gives an estimate of how well the training data can produce the original pixels: yellow and red indicate a poor match; black and dark purple indicate a good match. In our case, since we did not collect training data for the water or road classes, these areas have high residuals. It is also interesting to note that the hillside on the northeast side of the river does not appear to be well represented by the training classes, suggesting that perhaps this area is covered by a third forest community.

Now examine the three images that represent the proportion of each class for each pixel. These images have the prefix **Unmixed**, and the rest of the name is the original class signature name. For example, **UnmixedOak** is the proportion of Oak in each pixel (Figure 8.4.6.c). You will need to use the IDRISI DISPLAY module to display each of the images, as they are not automatically shown. When you display the images, use all default options.

The three images showing the proportions of each class in each pixel show that although there are some areas that are very likely one forest class or the other, most areas are a combination of proportions of the two forest classes.

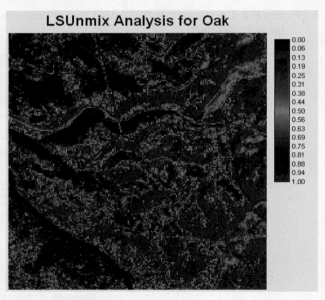

Figure 8.4.6.c   Proportion of oaks in each pixel.

8.4.7 Summarize the Output of the Forest Classification

The images of the proportion of the Oak and Poplar communities might be regarded as an endpoint to the analysis. However, these data are difficult to visualize in their entirety, because the information is present in multiple images, and due to the complexity of the output. Therefore, many soft classification exercises end by returning to a modified version of the traditional approach, where each pixel is summarized by the class with the highest mixture proportion. IDRISI includes the module HARDEN to produce hard classifications from the soft classifiers in an automated fashion.

In this exercise, we will take a slightly different approach in order to preserve the fuzzy information in the forest communities, despite simplifying the classification. We will do this by manually recoding the image to an output that includes mixture classes.

Recode linear unmixing images with RECLASS

Menu Location: **GIS Analysis – Database Query – RECLASS**

1. Open the RECLASS program from the main icon bar or the main menu.

2. In the *RECLASS* window, enter the *Input file* name by double clicking in the text box, and selecting **UnmixedOak**.

3. Enter the *Output file* as **Reclass_UnmixedOak**.

4. In the *Reclass Parameters* sections of the *RECLASS* window, enter the values to compete the table as indicated below:

Assign a new value of	To all values from	To just less than
1	0.0	0.25
2	0.25	0.75
3	0.75	1.1

5. Figure 8.4.7.a shows the RECLASS dialog box with the files specified and the table completed.

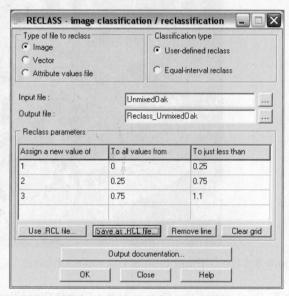

Figure 8.4.7.a   RECLASS dialog box.

Note that the maximum value of **1.1** in the table is well above the limit of 1.0, which is the maximum proportion theoretically possible. We use 1.1, rather than 1.0, because the test is "*to just **less** than*" and not "*to **all values** of*."

In the table, 1 represents a low proportion of oak in the pixel, 2 a moderate proportion, and 3 a dominant proportion.

Recode linear unmixing images with RECLASS (cont.)

5. Click on *Save as .RCL file* button.

6. In the *Recode as* window, enter the Filename as **Recode_table**.

7. Click on *Save* to close the *Recode as* window.

8. In the *RECLASS* window, click on the *OK* button.

9. A dialog box will open with the question: *Warning: The input data contains real values. Would you like to change the output file to integer?* This question is prompted by IDRISI having recognized that you are converting the image from a continuous variable (numbers with decimals) to an integer (whole numbers). Accept the default, and click on *Yes.*

10. The reclassed image will be displayed automatically.

11. We will now reclass the second file. In the *RECLASS* window text box for Input file, double click in the *Input file* text box. In the pick list, double click on **UnmixedPoplar**.

12. Change the Output file name to **Reclass_UnmixedPoplar**.

13. Click on *OK*.

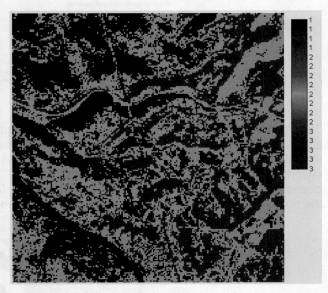

Figure 8.4.7.b   Unmixed Oak image reclassed in the 3 classes.

So far we have produced two 3-class images, one for each species. In the next steps we will combine the two reclassed images into a single image. This will be done in two steps. First we will run the program CROSSTAB, to combine the two images. Finally we will run yet another RECLASS to produce a single summary image.

Combine the two 3-class images with CROSSTAB

Menu Location: **GIS Analysis – Database Query – CROSSTAB**

1. Start the CROSSTAB program from the main menu.

2. In the *CROSSTAB* window, double click in the *First image (column)* text box, and in the subsequent pick list, double click on **Reclass_UnmixedOak**.

3. Double click in the *Second image (row)* text box, and in the subsequent pick list, double click on **Reclass_UnmixedPoplar**.

4. Enter the *Output image* file name as: **Crosstab_oak_poplar**.

5. Accept the default for the *Type of analysis* (*Hard classification*) and *Output type* (*Cross-classification image*).

6. Figure 8.4.7.c shows the *CROSSTAB* window with the files specified.
7. Click on *OK*.

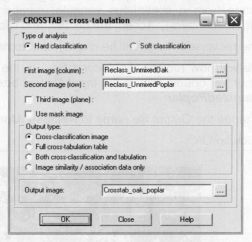

Figure 8.4.7.c   *CROSSTAB* window.

The resulting image is displayed automatically (Figure 8.4.7.d).   The image shows the 6 possible combinations of the two input files. The first number in the legend represents the DN value in the first image (Oaks, in our exercise), and the second the DN value in the second image (Poplar).   Table 8.4.7.a lists these classes and the underlying composition of class. The final column in the table is the number we will use for the final classes in the second RECLASS operation.

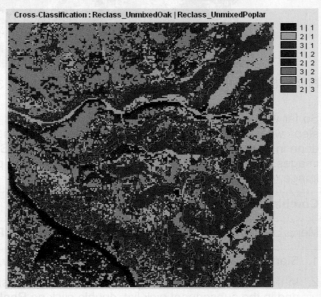

Figure 8.4.7.d   Cross tabulation image of forest classes.

Table 8.4.7.a   CROSSTAB output classes.

DN Value	Class	Oaks	Poplar	Interpretation	Reclass to
1	1 | 1	Low	Low	Non-veg, or shade	1
2	2 | 1	Middle	Low	Oak community	2
3	3 | 1	High	Low	Oak community	2
4	1 | 2	Low	Middle	Yellow poplar community	3
5.	2 | 2	Middle	Middle	Mixed Oak and Yellow poplar	4
6.	3 | 2	High	Middle	Mixed Oak and Yellow poplar	4
7	1 | 3	Low	High	Yellow poplar community	3
8	2 | 3	Middle	High	Mixed Oak and Yellow poplar	4

An interesting case is where we have the class "2 | 3" or "3 | 2". These are not really supposed to happen, because these combinations imply a greater than 100% total for the mixture. However, if you look at the image carefully you will see these pixels are actually quite rare, and are simply a result of rounding errors. They are likely also members of the mixed class.

As a final step in our analysis, we will now reclass the output of the CROSSTAB program to just 4 classes, using the program RECLASS.

Recode the results of the cross tabulation output with RECLASS

Menu Location: **GIS Analysis – Database Query – RECLASS**.

1. Start the RECLASS program from the main menu or the main icon tool bar.

2. In the *RECLASS* window, enter the *Input file* name by double clicking in the text box, and selecting **Crosstab_Oak_Poplar**.

3. Enter the *Output file* as **Reclass_Crosstab_Oak_Poplar**.

4. In the *Reclass Parameters* sections of the *RECLASS* window, enter the values to compete the table as indicated below:

Assign a new value of	To all values from	To just less than
1	1	2
2	2	4
3	4	5
4	5	7
3	7	8
4	8	9

Make sure you understand why these values were chosen by comparing each of these classes to Table 8.4.7.a. Also, double check that you have entered the values correctly in the table.

5. Click on *Save as .RCL file* button.

6. In the *Recode as* window, enter the Filename as **Recode_table2**.

7. Click on *Save* to close the *Recode as* window.

8. In the *RECLASS* window, click on the *OK* button.

9. The reclassed image will be displayed automatically (Figure 8.4.7.e).

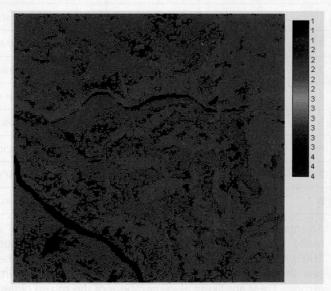

Figure 8.4.7.e   Automatic display of the RECLASS program.

Finally, add a descriptive legend using IDRISI explorer. Additional details of this procedure are described in Section 7.3.7.

Update the classified image with the IDRISI EXPLORER

Menu location: **File – IDRISI EXPLORER**

1. Start the IDRISI EXPLORER from the main menu, or the main icon bar.

2. In the *IDRISI EXPLORER* window, click on the tab for *Files*.

3. If the files are not listed in the *Files* pane, double click on the directory name to display the files.

4. In the *Files* pane, click on the ***Reclass_Crosstab_Oak_Poplar*** file.

5. In the *Metadata* pane below the *Files* pane, scroll down, and find the blank cell next to the label *Categories*.

6. Double click in the blank *Categories* cell.

7. A *Categories* dialog box will open.

8. In the first cell below *Code*, enter **1**.

9. In the cell below *Category*, enter **Non-vegetation or shade**.

10. Find the *Add line* icon on the right of the *Categories* dialog box (it is the third icon on the right side of the dialog box). Click on this icon.

11. In the new line enter the *Code* **2** and the *Category* **Oaks**.

12. Repeat the previous two steps in order to enter the remaining classes on two additional rows:

    3 Yellow Poplar

    4 Mixed Oak and Yellow Poplar

13. Click on *OK* to close the *Categories* dialog box.

14. The *IDRISI EXPLORER Metadata* pane should now have the number *4* in the cell next to *Legend cats*, indicating we have specified category names for 4 classes.

15. Click on the icon for *Save*, in the bottom left corner of the *Metadata* pane. After the file is saved, the icon will go blank.

Finally, redisplay the classification, to show the new legend.

Displaying a previously created false color composite using the DISPLAY LAUNCHER

Menu Location: **Display – DISPLAY LAUNCHER**

1. Start the DISPLAY LAUNCHER program from the main menu, or the tool bar.

2. In the *DISPLAY LAUNCHER* dialog box, double click in the text box in the left side of the window.

3. A *Pick List* window will open. Double click on **Reclass_Crosstab_Oak_Poplar**.

4. Click on *OK* to display the image (Figure 8.4.7.f).

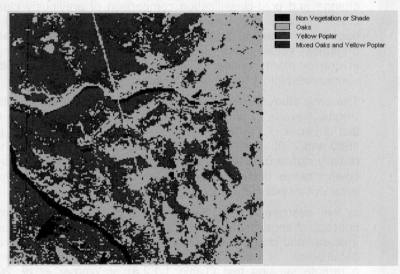

Figure 8.4.7.f   Final mixture image, with updated legend.

The final image (Figure 8.4.7.f) lends strong support for the notion that the forest communities are mixtures. Although some areas are relatively pure, almost one quarter of the scene appears to be a mixture of Oak and Yellow Poplar. It is noteworthy that in Figure 8.4.7.f we have produced a map that shows the relatively pure and mixed classes, although our training areas were exclusively based on pure classes. It is only through the linear unmixing that the mixed classes were identified.

Chapter 9   Image Change Analysis

Change detection is one of the principal applications of remote sensing. Reasons for this include:

- Archived images are often the only available record of past conditions.
- Remote sensing can be very effective and accurate for identifying change.
- There is growing interest in monitoring change from local to global scales.

In principal, change detection is very simple: changes in image brightness values are assumed to represent change in ground conditions.

Broadly speaking, there are two types of change: change in degree, and change in class. Change in degree is a change in some continuous variable, such as biomass, whereas change in class implies a change from one material to another, such as from a forest to a road.

Change Detection methods can be grouped in two classes: spectral analysis of change and post-classification comparison of previously classified data. Post-classification is the simplest to understand, and is based on a GIS overlay operation. Spectral analysis of change involves a comparison of the image brightness values of the two dates. Spectral analysis of change generally results in one or more continuous variables of change, though often the results are summarized into a few change classes.

The case study for this exercise is Multispectral Scanner (MSS) imagery of Las Vegas, Nevada. Las Vegas was the fastest growing city in the U.S. during the last decades of the twentieth century, more than tripling in population between 1980 and 2000, from 460,000 to 1.6 million. The growth of the city is dominantly radially outwards. Most new construction, and consequently most of the land cover change, occurs on the fringes of the city. The arid climate also makes for excellent visibility for remote sensing.

In this exercise, we will investigate post classification comparison and three spectral change analysis techniques: image subtraction, principal component analysis, and change vector analysis. These four methods are described in more detail below. However, as with the other chapters, the reader is urged to consult a remote sensing text (Table 1.1.2.a) or Warner *et al.* 2009b for additional information, as the material below is only a very brief summary of these topics.

9.1 Introduction

9.1.1 Change Detection Methods

9.1.1.1 Image Subtraction

Image subtraction involves the direct comparison of the DN values of the two images. IDRISI offers four different outputs:

1. The raw differenced values

2. The differenced values as a percentage of the original value of the pixel

3. Change values expressed as z-scores, where the change value is expressed in terms of the number of standard deviations it is from the mean.

4. Change value z-scores grouped into 6 classes of change.

9.1.1.2 Principal Component Analysis (PCA)

Principal component analysis (PCA) was originally introduced in Section 6.3.3 as a spectral enhancement technique. As explained in that section, PCA is a rotation and translation of the band axes. The new bands are orthogonal and uncorrelated. The first band is oriented to capture the maximum variance. Subsequent bands are oriented to capture the maximum remaining variance. PCA produces as many new bands as there were old bands, although it is usually assumed that most of the information is present in the first few new bands, which have most of the variance.

PCA can also be used for change detection. Instead of applying the PCA technique to the image of one date, as is done for regular image enhancement, the method is applied to two or more images simultaneously. For change detection, it is assumed that the first PCA band of the multi-date set is likely to be an average image, and therefore is likely to be of less interest. Change is usually isolated in the second and subsequent bands.

9.1.1.3 Change Vector Analysis

Change vector analysis separates change into two components: magnitude and direction.

The magnitude component is the simpler component: it is a measure of how far in the spectral space (also known as feature space) the pixel DN values have changed. It is thus a multiple-band variation of the image subtraction method. Therefore, the magnitude component provides a measure of the amount of change that has taken place, integrated over all wavelengths.

The direction component is a measure of the type of change. Normally the direction is based on just two bands, or derived bands, such as Brightness and Greenness in a Tasseled Cap Transformation. However, a multiband extension to direction changes has been found to be effective, too (Warner, 2005).

9.1.1.4 Post Classification Comparison

In post classification, two independently produced classifications are overlaid, and new classes showing the change from one date to the next are generated. It is important that the two dates are classified to produce the same classes, in the same order (i.e. the relationship between DN values and classes is the same for both images).

9.1.2 Required Preprocessing.

9.1.2.1 Geometric Co-Registration

It is obvious that the quality of co-registration in all change analysis studies must be excellent (less than 1 pixel); otherwise artifacts will be introduced into the analysis. With nadir-viewing satellite imagery such as Landsat, high quality co-registration can usually be achieved. In rugged terrain, orthorectification is usually required for imagery from off-nadir viewing sensors such as SPOT. For aerial imagery, high quality orthorectification is essential.

9.1.2.2 Radiometric Normalization

Radiometric normalization is a process by which the image DN values are adjusted so that the specific values of each date can be compared directly.

Radiometric normalization is an attempt to reduce the effect of variations in illumination and variations in atmospheric transmission and scattering properties.

Unlike co-registration, radiometric normalization is not always needed. Post classification comparison does not require that the images be radiometrically normalized, but doing so can be useful, because then the same class signatures can be applied to both images. Radiometric normalization is also not required for PCA. Radiometric normalization is required for image subtraction and CVA.

Before discussing normalization methods, it is useful to first briefly review some terminology and background. The concentration of the sun's energy is dependent on the angle of incidence of the energy, in other words on the sun's elevation in the sky. Furthermore, sun's energy has to travel through the atmosphere, which absorbs and scatters the energy. At the molecular level, atmospheric gases cause Rayleigh scattering that progressively affects shorter wavelengths (causing, for example, the sky to appear blue). Also, specific atmospheric components, such as ozone and water vapor, cause absorption of energy at selected wavelengths. Furthermore, aerosol particulates, the primary determinant of haze, create Mie scattering, a largely non-selective (i.e., affecting all wavelength equally) effect. In visible wavelengths, moisture vapor has a major effect on atmospheric properties.

The problem of atmospheric normalization has received considerable attention from researchers in remote sensing, and two broad classes of image radiometric normalization have been developed. The first method is to convert image DN values to exoatmospheric radiance, which is in turn, usually converted to estimated reflectance, using physical or empirical models of radiative transfer. Radiance refers to the flux of energy per solid angle in a given direction. While radiance corresponds to brightness in a given direction, it is sometimes confused with reflectance, which is the ratio of reflected and irradiant energy (illumination). Radiance is the energy measured at the sensor and is dependent on the reflectance of the surface being observed, the irradiant energy, and the interaction of the energy with the atmospheric.

Conversion to radiance or reflectance is the best approach in theory, but is often impossible to implement because of a lack of information about atmospheric transmissivity and scattering, or lack of knowledge of the conversion factors from DN values to radiance.

The second class of image radiometric normalization is an empirical regression of one date on the other. This approach is relatively easy to implement, but does require clearly identifiable regions where the image is assumed not to have changed. In some environments, change may be so pervasive, or so complex, that it may not be possible to use this method.

Because radiometric normalization is so important for some change detection methods, and can also be so difficult to implement, both methods will be illustrated. We will first convert the red band from the 1972 and 1992 images to radiance. The next step would be to convert these images to apparent reflectance, but because they were acquired on near anniversary dates (September 10 1972 and September 13 1992), the difference in solar illumination should be small. Furthermore, the IDRISI reflectance conversion program, ATMOSC, is quite complex, and requires data that is often difficult to obtain.

9.2 Copy Data for this Chapter

In this chapter we will work with different image sets for each section. Therefore, you should now copy the *Chap9* folder from the CD, and paste it as a new subfolder within the *\ID Man* folder on your computer.

After you have copied the folder, you should remove the Read-Only attribute from this new folder on your computer. This is done by right-clicking on the *Chap9* folder name, selecting *Properties* from the pop-up menu. A dialog box will open, labeled *Chap9 Properties* (if you apply this procedure to the entire *ID Man* directory, then the dialog box will be labeled *ID Man Properties*). Now clear the check mark from the *Read Only* check box, by clicking in the box. You should then click on the button for *Apply*, and in the subsequent *Confirm Attribute Changes* dialog box, accept the default *Apply changes to this folder, subfolder and files*, and click on *OK*. You will need to also click on *OK* in the *Chap9 Properties* dialog box.

Note: Section 1.3.1 provides detailed instructions on how to copy the data from the CD, and also on how to remove the *Read-Only* attribute from the data. Also, the procedure for setting up the *ID Man* folder on your computer is described.

9.3 Preparatory

In the previous section (Section 9.2) you should have already copied the data from the CD. However, we still need to set the *Project* and *Working Folders* for this section.

Before starting you should close any dialog boxes or displayed images in the IDRISI workspace.

Create a new project file and specify the working folders with the IDRISI EXPLORER
Menu Location: **File – IDRISI EXPLORER**

1. Start the IDRISI EXPLORER from the main menu or toolbar.
2. In the *IDRISI EXPLORER* window, select the *Projects* tab.
3. Right click within the *Projects* pane, and select the *New Project Ins* option.
4. A *Browse For Folder* window will open. Use this window to navigate to the *ID_Man* folder, which is the folder you created on your computer for the data for this manual. Now navigate to the *Chap9.*
5. Click *OK* in the *Browse For Folder* window.
6. A new project file *Chap9* will now be listed in the *Project* pane of the IDRISI EXPLORER. The working folder will also be listed in the Editor pane.
7. Close the IDRISI EXPLORER by clicking on the red *x* in the upper right corner of the *IDRISI EXPLORER* window.

You will find two sets of MSS images in this directory (Table 9.3.a), acquired by Landsat 1, on September 13 1972, and by Landsat 5, on September 10 1992. Note that the band number designation of MSS data changed after 1982, but for convenience the 1972 and 1992 images have been labeled with consistent band numbers, and these are the numbers that will be used in this exercise. Thus, for example the green bands of the two images have been labeled **mss72_1.rst** and **mss92_1.rst**, respectively, and in both cases, will be referred to as *band 1*. Nevertheless, as you will see, there are times when you will need to refer back to the old band numbers for the 1972 images.

Table 9.3.a   MSS imagery of Las Vegas

1972 imagery file names	Original band designation	1992 imagery file names	Original band designation	Wavelength interval (µm)	Wavelength region
mss72_1.rst	4	mss92_1.rst	1	0.5-0.6	green
mss72_2.rst	5	mss92_2.rst	2	0.6-0.7	red
mss72_3.rst	6	mss92_3.rst	3	0.7-0.8	infrared
mss72_4.rst	7	mss92_4.rst	4	0.8-1.1	infrared

The MSS images used in this section are from the National American Landscape Characterization (NALC) Project. These images have been resampled to a 60 meter UTM grid, although the original instantaneous field of view (IFOV) of the MSS sensor was approximately 56 by 80 meters. You can find out more about the NALC project, as well as the preprocessing used to produce the images at: http://eros.usgs.gov/products/satellite/nalc.php

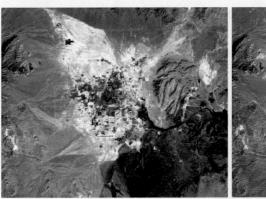

Figure 9.3.a   MSS false color composites of Las Vegas, Nevada.   Left: September 13 1972. Right: September 10 1992.

Create a color composite image

Menu Location: **Display - COMPOSITE**

1. Start the COMPOSITE program using the main menu or tool bar.

2. In the *COMPOSITE* dialog box, double click in the *Blue image band* text box. The *Pick list* window will open.

3. In the *Pick list* window, double click on the file ***mss72_1***. If necessary, click on the plus symbol to display the files.

4. Double click in the *Green image band* text box, and then double click on ***mss72_2***.

5. Double click in the *Red image band* text box, and then double click on ***mss72_4***.

6. Enter the *Output image* filename in the text box provided: **mss72_fcc**.

7. Click *OK* to create and display the false color composite.

8. Repeat steps 2-7, using *mss92_1*, *mss92_2, and mss92_4* to create the image **mss92_fcc**.

9. Once the images have been displayed, you can close the *COMPOSITE* window.

The two false color composite images provide a dramatic demonstration of how rapidly the city of Las Vegas has grown over 20 years (Figure 9.3.a).

For this study, we will use data that have already been co-registered. Co-registration and georeferencing is dealt with in more detail in Chapter 3, especially Section 3.2.

9.4 Change Detection Pre-Processing: Radiometric Normalization through Conversion to Radiance

Note that this section is an alternative method to the regression normalization method discussed in the next section. Of the change detection methods presented in this manual, radiometric normalization is only required as a preprocessing step for *image differencing* and *change vector analysis.*

9.4.1 Convert Raw Image DN Values to Radiance Values

The program RADIANCE converts Landsat 1-5 MSS and 4-5 TM raw satellite DN values calibrated radiance values, using published conversion factors. The program has optional input for specifying the conversion factors manually, so that data from other satellites may also be converted with this program.

Conversion of Landsat image DN values to radiance
Menu Location: **Image Processing - Restoration – RADIANCE**

1. Start the RADIANCE program from the main menu.

2. First, we will convert the 1972 data to radiance. In the *RADIANCE* window, use the pull-down menu to select *Landsat -1 MSS*.

3. Double click in the *Input image* text box. In the subsequent pick list window, double click on *mss72_2*.

4. Enter the *Output image* name: **mss72_2_rad**.

5. In the *Band number* text box, enter **5**.

   (Note that the program will give you an error if you specify the band number according to the new numbering system, i.e. 2. Refer to Table 7.2.1.a for the original band designations for Landsat 1 MSS.)

6. Figure 9.4.1.a shows the *RADIANCE* window, with the parameters specified.

7. Click on *OK*.

8. Once the program has completed processing the first image, it will be displayed automatically (9.4.1.b).

9. Now convert the 1992 data to radiance. Use the pull-down menu to select *Landsat - 5 MSS (On or after Nov 9, 1984)*.

10. Change the *Input image* to **mss92_2**.

11. Enter the new *Output image* name as **mss92_2_rad**.

12. Change the *Band number* to **2**.

(Note that the 1992 image is a Landsat 5 image, and therefore **mss92_2** has a different band designation from the Landsat 1 data, even though it has the same approximate wavelength sensitivity as the **mss72_2** image.)

13. Click on *OK*.

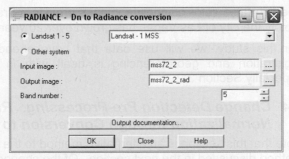

Figure 9.4.1.a   *RADIANCE* window.

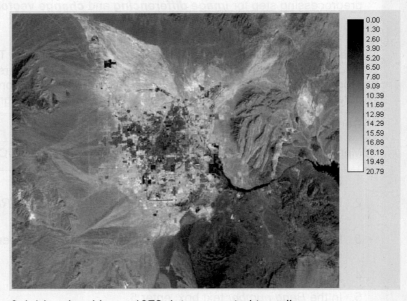

Figure 9.4.1.b   Las Vegas 1972 data converted to radiance.

Figure 9.4.1.b shows the 1972 data converted to radiance. Because the image has an automated contrast stretch applied, it looks no different to the same single-band image prior to radiance conversion. However, in this case, the scale indicated on the right side of the image is in physical units of radiance, mW cm^{-1} sr^{-1} μm^{-1}.

Before continuing on to the next step, we will also radiometrically normalize the near infrared bands of the two dates, as described below.

Conversion of Landsat image DN values to radiance (cont.)

14. In the *RADIANCE* window, use the pull-down menu to select *Landsat -1 MSS*.

15. Double click in the *Input image* text box. In the subsequent pick list window, double click on **mss72_4**.

16. Enter the *Output image* name: **mss72_4_rad**.

17. In the Band number text box, enter **7**.

(Reminder – 7 was the original band number of the fourth band on the MSS instrument.)

18. Click on *OK*.

19. Once the program has completed processing the image, start the process to convert the 1992 data to radiance. Use the pull-down menu to select *Landsat - 5 MSS (On or after Nov 9, 1984)*.

20. Change the *Input image* to **mss92_4**.

21. Enter the new *Output image* name as **mss92_4_rad**.

22. Change the band number to **4**.

23. Click on *OK*.

9.4.2   Preliminary Image Differencing

The two images have now been converted to radiance values, instead of arbitrary image DN values. The simplest way to test the success of this operation, and to illustrate the application to conversion to radiance, is to run a preliminary image differencing operation. The topic of image differencing will be dealt with in more detail later in this chapter.

Preliminary image differencing as a test for image normalization

Menu Location: **GIS Analysis – Mathematical Operators – OVERLAY**

1. Open the OVERLAY program through the main menu or the main toolbar.

2. In the *OVERLAY* window, double click in the text box for *First image*. In the resulting pick list, double click on **mss92_2_rad**.

3. Double click in the text box for *Second image*. In the resulting pick list, double click on **mss72_2_rad**.

4. In the text box for *Output image*, enter **mss92-72_b2_rad**.

5. Select from the list of *Overlay options* the radio button for *First – Second*.

6. Figure 9.4.2.a shows the OVERLAY window with processing parameters specified.

7. Click on *OK*.

Figure 9.4.2.a   *OVERLAY* window.

The difference image should have been displayed automatically (Figure 9.4.2.b). From the legend, note the color associated with a value closest to 0. These should be areas of no change. Although the city shows extensive change (principally a reduction in red brightness values, as shown by the green colors in the image), most of the surrounding desert shows little change, as would be expected.

To end this section, close all open windows.

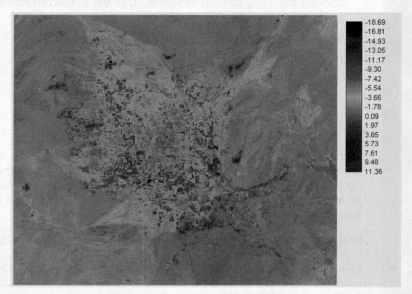

-18.69
-16.81
-14.93
-13.05
-11.17
-9.30
-7.42
-5.54
-3.66
-1.78
0.09
1.97
3.85
5.73
7.61
9.48
11.36

Figure 9.4.2.b   Preliminary change detection of Las Vegas, Nevada, MSS red bands, 1992-1972.

9.5 Change Detection Pre-Processing: Image Normalization through Regression

Sections 9.4 and 9.5 (this section) provide alternative radiometric normalization methods. In the last section, we used the packaged conversion to radiance method provided by IDRISI. In this section, we investigate an alternative method, based on developing a regression relationship between the two images.

The procedure for regression-based radiometric normalization requires the identification of areas of no change, and developing empirical models to convert the one date to have values equivalent to those of the second date. One can select small areas of no change, and use a spreadsheet, or other statistical package to calculate the regression parameters. Our approach, however, will be the opposite: we will first develop a mask to indicate broad regions of change, and then use the remaining pixels to develop the regression.

9.5.1 Create Multitemporal Display

The change mask is digitized manually on a multitemporal false color composite. In the following sections, the preparation of the multitemporal false color composite is first described, then the digitization of the mask.

Preparing a multitemporal false color composite
Menu location: **Display – DISPLAY LAUNCHER**
1. Start the DISPLAY LAUNCHER from the main menu or icon bar.

2. In the *DISPLAY LAUNCHER* window, double click in the text box for the file name, and then double click on the file **mss72_2**.

3. Click on *OK* to display the image, accepting all the other defaults.

4. Find the *Composer* dialog box, which is automatically opened when an image is displayed.

5. In the *Composer* dialog box, click on the **red** button (see arrowed button in Figure 9.5.1.a). (If you place your cursor over the red button the screen tip will show: *Set selected layer as red component of RGB composite or anaglyph.*)

6. The image should now be displayed in tones of red (Figure 9.5.1.a).

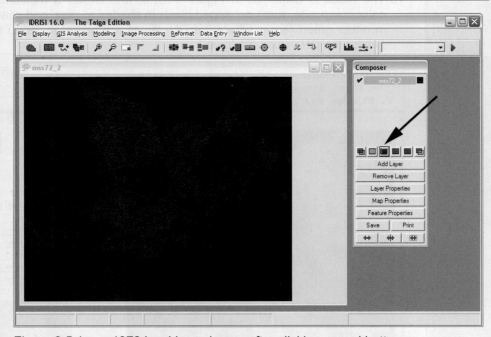

Figure 9.5.1.a   1972 Las Vegas image after clicking on red button.

Preparing a multitemporal false color composite (cont.)

7. In the *Composer* dialog box, click on *Add Layer*.

8. The *Add Layer* dialog box will open.

9. Click on the radio button to change the *File Type* to *Raster Layer*.

10. Double click in the (unlabeled) file name window. In the resulting pick list, double click on **mss92_2**.

11. Click on *OK*.

12. The image will now be displayed in the same viewer as the **mss72_2** image, with the second image, **mss92_2,** opaquely covering the first. The *Composer* dialog box will therefore now show name of both the **mss72_2** and **mss92_2** images.

13. In the *Composer* dialog box, click on the button for the **green** layer. The image should now be dominated by yellow colors, with some red and minor areas of green. Yellow indicates areas that are bright in both dates, because

the two different dates are displayed in red and green, and red and green makes yellow.

14. For a second time, click on *Add Layer* in the *Composer* dialog box.

15. In the *Add Layer* dialog box, change the *File Type* to *Raster Layer*.

16. Double click in the (unlabeled) file name window. In the resulting pick list, double click on **mss72_2** once again (we have already used this image for the red band.)

17. Again the new image will opaquely cover the previously displayed images.

18. In the *Composer* dialog box, click on the button for the **blue** layer.

19. The result is displayed in Figure 9.5.1.b, and shows a multitemporal false color composite, with unchanged pixels in shades of gray, and changed pixels in either green (areas where the DN values are higher in 1992) or magenta (where the DN values are lower).

Figure 9.5.1.b   Las Vegas multitemporal false color composite: 1972 as magenta, 1992 as green.

9.5.2 Digitize Change Mask

The next step is to digitize change areas with a value of 0, to mask them out from the analysis. By now you should be familiar with digitizing. However, if you feel the instructions below are too brief, please review Section 7.4.3 for more details.

Digitizing change areas on the multitemporal composite

1. The multi-temporal composite, as described above and shown in Figure 9.5.1.b, should be displayed in the *DISPLAY* window.

2. From the main icon toolbar, select the icon for *Full extent normal.*

3. Click on the icon for *Full extent maximized.*

4. Select the *Digitize* icon.

5. The *Digitize* dialog box will open. In the textbox for *Name of layer to be created*, enter **Mask**.

6. In the text box for *ID or Value* enter **0**.

7. Click on *OK*.

8. Digitize a large, single polygon that encloses the majority of the changed (i.e. pixels with magenta and green colors) pixels (Figure 9.5.2.a). The unchanged areas, left outside the polygon, should have a wide range of brightness levels (gray tones), to give the most reliable regression. Note that it is not necessary to digitize in very fine detail, because a few changed pixels will not affect the overall regression, as the sample will have many thousands of pixels.

9. Right-click to close the polygon.

10. Click on the icon *Save digitized data*.

11. Close the *DISPLAY* window.

Figure 9.5.2.a   Digitizing the changed areas. Note that the polygon outline is somewhat rough, as the selection of change pixels is very broad.

9.5.3 Rasterize the Vector Mask

The mask we have created is a vector file. In order to apply the mask, it must be rasterized. The rasterization process has two parts. First, a blank file, with a value of 1 in every pixel location, is created. This file will have the dimensions of the MSS images. In the second step, the vector file is used to over-write 0 in each pixel within the polygon just created.

Create a new file prior to rasterization

Menu location: **Data entry – INITIAL**

1. Start the INITIAL program from the main menu.

2. In the INITIAL window, confirm that the radio button has been selected for *Copy spatial parameters from another image.*

3. Also confirm that the *Output data type* has been set to *byte*.

4. Enter the *Output image* file name: **Mask**.

5. Double click in the text box next to *Image to copy parameters from*. In the resulting pick list, double click on **mss72_1**.

6. Change the *Initial value* from the default 0 to **1**.

7. Figure 9.5.3.a shows the *INITIAL* window with the processing parameters specified.

8. Click on *OK*.

9. Because the image is uniform, with every pixel having a value of 1, the image is not displayed. Therefore, once you have confirmed from the progress meter that the program has completed, close the *INITIAL* window.

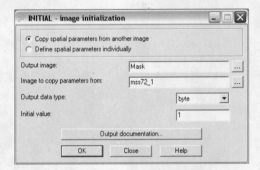

Figure 9.5.3.a   The *INITIAL* window.

In the second step, the vector file is used to over-write 0 in each pixel within the polygon just created.

Rasterize the vector file with the polygon of change areas

Menu location: **Reformat - RASTERVECTOR**

1. Start the RASTERVECTOR program from the main menu.

2. In the *RASTERVECTOR* window, select the radio button for *Polygon to Raster*.

3. Double click in the *Vector polygon file* text box, and in the resulting pick list double click on **Mask**.

4. Double click in the *Image file to be updated* text box, and in the resulting pick list, double click on **Mask**.

5. Click on *OK*.

6. The mask will be displayed automatically (Figure 9.5.3.c).

Figure 9.5.3.b   *RASTERVECTOR* window.

Figure 9.5.3.c   Rasterized mask of change areas.

You should now confirm in your rasterized mask (Figure 9.5.3.c), by checking the legend, that the central area, corresponding to the region of the city, has a value of 0, and the surrounding areas have a value of 1.

9.5.4   Regression of the Masked Imagery

In the regression analysis, we would like to find an equation that converts the 1972 DN values so that in areas did not change in the twenty year interval, the DN values will be similar to those of the 1992 image. The formula we are looking for has the form:

  1992 DN = a + b * 1972 DN

where a and b are the regression parameters. Therefore, we will specify the 1992 image as the *dependent* variable, and 1972 as the *independent* variable in the regression, even though it is actually the 1972 data that will be modified in the application of the formula for the image normalization.

Regression estimation
Menu location: **GIS analysis – Statistics - REGRESS**
1. Start the REGRESS program from the main menu.

2. In the *REGRESS* window, double click in the *Independent variable* text box. In the resulting pick list, double click on **mss72_2**.

3. Double click in the *Dependent variable* text box. In the resulting pick list, double click on **mss92_2**.

4. Double click in the *Mask name (optional)* text box. In the resulting pick list, double click on **Mask**.

5. Figure 9.5.4.a shows the *REGRESS* window, with the processing parameters specified.

6. Click on *OK*.

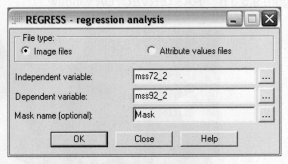

Figure 9.5.4.a   The *REGRESS* window.

The program output is a scatter plot, along with a listing of the regression parameters (Figure 9.5.4.b). Note the regression at the top left of the output window (Y = 4.989321 + 0.844283 X for the mask used in the example; your equation should be similar, but will not be precisely the same because your digitized mask will be different). Write down the equation from the regression for later use.

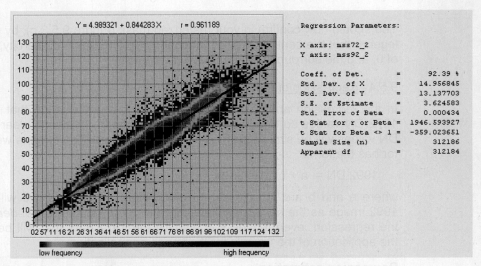

Figure 9.5.4.b   Regression of 1992 and 1972 band 2 images.

We will now repeat the regression calculation using the same dates, and mask, but changing the bands from 2, to 4 (i.e. use **mss72_4** and **mss92_4**).

Regression estimation (cont.)

7. The *REGRESS* window should still be open from the first regression.

8. In the *REGRESS* window, double click in the *Independent variable* text box. In the resulting pick list, double click on **mss72_4**.

9. Double click in the *Dependent variable* text box. In the resulting pick list, double click on **mss92_4**.

10. Confirm that the *Mask name (optional)* text box still contains the file name **Mask**.

11. Click on *OK*.

Write down this second regression equation.

9.5.5 Normalize the 1972 data using the regression equation

We have now gathered the data we need for the normalization, and are ready to apply the correction from the regression equations to the 1972 images. A convenient tool for applying the equations is the IMAGE CALCULATOR. The IMAGE CALCULATOR program was introduced in Section 6.4.2.

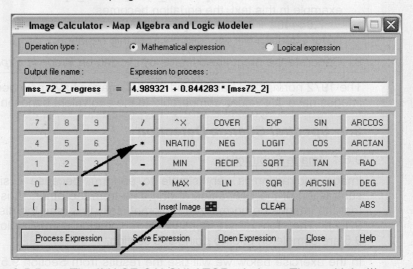

Figure 9.5.5.a   The IMAGE CALCULATOR window. The multiply (*) and *Insert Image* buttons are arrowed.

Apply normalization equation

Menu location: **Modeling – Model Deployment Tools - IMAGE CALCULATOR**

---

1. Open the IMAGE CALCULATOR program from the main menu or toolbar.

2. In the *IMAGE CALCULATOR* window, enter in the *Output file name* text box **mss_72_2_regress**.

3. Enter the equation you wrote down for the band 2 regression (i.e. the first regression), in the *Expression to process* text box.

    Use * to represent multiply.
    Instead of entering X, click on the button for I*nsert Image*. In the resulting pick list, double click on **mss72_2**. This will place the file name in

parentheses in the equation.
Thus, for example, in the example in this text, the equation becomes:
4.989321 + 0.844283 * [mss72_2]
(Note that your values of your equation will vary slightly, but should be in the same range.)

4. Figure 9.5.5.a shows the equation entered in the *IMAGE CALCULATOR* window.

5. Click on *Process Expression*.

6. The output image will be displayed automatically.

We will now repeat the development of the equation for the 1972 band 4 data.

Apply normalization equation (cont.)

7. In the *IMAGE CALCULATOR* window, change the *Output file name* text box to **mss_72_4_regress**.

8. Enter the equation you wrote down for the band 4 regression (i.e. the *second* regression), in the *Expression to process* text box. Be sure to change the file that is processed from **[mss72_2]** to **[mss72_4]**. Thus, for the data in the example in this text, the equation becomes:
7.044464 + 0.965945 * [mss72_4]
(Your equation will vary slightly from this equation.)

9. Generate the normalized image by clicking on *Process Expression*.

The 1972 normalized band 2 and band 4 images have now been created. These images have DN values comparable to the equivalent bands in the 1992 images.

9.6 *Spectral Change Detection*

9.6.1 Image Subtraction

Image subtraction is very simple to perform, because it simply requires the subtraction of the DN values of one date from the other. It is essential, though, that the images be normalized radiometrically first (see the discussion in Section 9.1.2). Therefore, it is essential that radiometric normalization exercises 9.4 or 9.5 are completed prior to doing this section.

In the exercise below we will use the results from Section 9.5, the normalization using regression. However, if you prefer to use the results from Section 9.4, the normalization using the IDRISI routine that converts DNs to radiance, simply substitute the images ***mss72_2_rad*** for ***mss_72_2_regress*** and ***mss_92_2_rad*** for ***mss92_2*** in the instructions below.

Image subtraction can be performed using the *IMAGE CALCULATOR*, or alternatively, with the dedicated change detection program, *IMAGEDIFF*. We will use the latter program, which gives you 4 choices for the type of output, as discussed in the introduction to this chapter. We will first select a type of classification in which the differenced image output is grouped into 6 classes. The classes are calculated by converting the raw differenced DN values to z-scores. Z-scores are simply a type of transformation, where the values are expressed as a distance from the mean of the change DN values, in units of the standard deviation of the distribution. Standard deviation units are often used as a way of grouping the otherwise continuous change values.

Image differencing

Menu location: GIS Analysis – Change/Time Series – IMAGEDIFF

1. Start the IMAGEDIFF program from the main IDRISI menu.

2. In the *IMAGEDIFF* window, double click in the text box for *Earlier image*. In the resulting pick list, double click on **MSS_72_2_REGRESS**.

3. Double click in the text box for the *Later image*, and in the resulting pick list, double click on **mss92_2**.

4. In the text box for *Output filename*, enter **72-92-imagediff**.

5. For the *Output optio*n, select the radio button for the *Standardized class image*.

6. Figure 9.6.1.a shows the IMAGEDIFF window with the processing parameters specified.

7. Click on *OK*.

8. IDRISI will automatically display the resulting image (Figure 9.6.1.b).

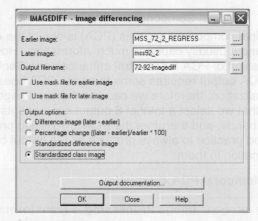

Figure 9.6.1.a   The *IMAGEDIFF* window.

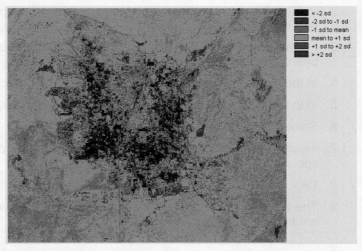

Figure 9.6.1.b   Results of image differencing using MSS band 2 (red) for 1972 and 1992.

The image differencing image (Figure 9.6.1.b) shows a very interesting and distinct pattern of land use change. To understand this pattern we need to think about how vegetation affects red reflectance. Desert soil will be brightest, especially where salts have accumulated. The chlorophyll in vegetation absorbs red radiance, and thus vegetated areas will be darker. Desert vegetation is relatively sparse, and not very green. Thus, natural desert vegetation will be darker than exposed soil, but not as dark as irrigated green vegetation, especially residential lawns and golf courses. With that background, we can now interpret the image.

The center of the city has not changed appreciably. It is therefore shown in the change classification in the pastel colors of yellow and pale green, representing respectively a small drop, or small rise, in radiance. Surrounding this unchanged core, is a "U" of change, shown in red and orange, and representing growth to the east, south and west. The new urban land cover, especially residential development with lawns, is much darker in the red band than the relatively sparsely vegetated desert. On the edge of the city is a ring of higher red radiance, shown in shades of green. These areas of higher reflectance represent new construction, and general disturbance of desert vegetation, for example by off-road vehicle traffic.

9.6.2 Principal Component Analysis

Principal component analysis (PCA) is one of the easiest analysis methods to run, and it usually captures much information. However, as we saw in the discussion of PCA for spectral enhancement, Section 6.3.3, the interpretation of the PCA output requires some thought. PCA does not require image normalization; therefore we can use the raw images. In the instructions below, note that we select a total of 8 output components. This is because we have 8 input bands, and therefore the PCA processing produces up to 8 output bands. It is good practice to always produce all the output bands, in order to evaluate the information in them.

Multitemporal PCA calculation

Menu location: **Image Processing – Transformation - PCA**

1. Start the PCA program from the main menu.

2. In the PCA window, click on the button to *Insert layer group…* In the resulting pick list, double click on ***mss72***

3. For a second time, click on the *Insert layer group…* button. In the resulting pick list, double click on ***mss92***.

4. In the *Number of components to be extracted:* text box, enter **8**.

5. In the *Prefix for output files (can include path):* text box, enter **PCA**.

6. Select the radio button for *Complete output*.

7. Figure 9.6.2.a shows the PCA window with the processing parameters specified.

8. Click on *OK*.

9. The text results are displayed in a new window, *Module Results*. The images are not displayed automatically.

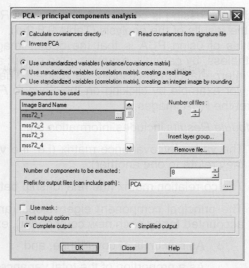

Figure 9.6.2.a   The *PCA* Window.

Table 9.6.2.a   The PCA *Module Results* output.

VAR/COVAR	mss72_1	mss72_2	mss72_3	mss72_4	mss92_1	mss92_2	mss92_3	mss92_4
mss72_1	165.28	221.90	199.75	174.17	94.82	138.59	144.11	123.94
mss72_2	221.90	316.40	282.57	245.96	128.84	197.40	205.44	176.99
mss72_3	199.75	282.57	268.40	239.72	115.38	175.90	193.42	171.59
mss72_4	174.17	245.96	239.72	222.11	101.24	154.19	175.49	159.48
mss92_1	94.82	128.84	115.38	101.24	91.29	137.83	133.59	111.34
mss92_2	138.59	197.40	175.90	154.19	137.83	223.15	214.03	179.02
mss92_3	144.11	205.44	193.42	175.49	133.59	214.03	228.25	200.06
mss92_4	123.94	176.99	171.59	159.48	111.34	179.02	200.06	183.95

COR MATRX	mss72_1	mss72_2	mss72_3	mss72_4	mss92_1	mss92_2	mss92_3	mss92_4
mss72_1	1.00000	0.97037	0.94839	0.90906	0.77193	0.72164	0.74197	0.71082
mss72_2	0.97037	1.00000	0.96964	0.92780	0.75806	0.74291	0.76446	0.73366
mss72_3	0.94839	0.96964	1.00000	0.98181	0.73712	0.71876	0.78146	0.77225
mss72_4	0.90906	0.92780	0.98181	1.00000	0.71096	0.69259	0.77941	0.78900
mss92_1	0.77193	0.75806	0.73712	0.71096	1.00000	0.96572	0.92546	0.85919
mss92_2	0.72164	0.74291	0.71876	0.69259	0.96572	1.00000	0.94837	0.88359
mss92_3	0.74197	0.76446	0.78146	0.77941	0.92546	0.94837	1.00000	0.97638
mss92_4	0.71082	0.73366	0.77225	0.78900	0.85919	0.88359	0.97638	1.00000

COMPONENT	C 1	C 2	C 3	C 4	C 5	C 6	C 7	C 8
% var.	85.67	10.34	2.53	0.62	0.49	0.13	0.12	0.09
eigenval.	1455.45	175.69	43.04	10.45	8.37	2.27	2.03	1.51
eigvec.1	0.3139	−0.2684	−0.3138	−0.3349	0.6354	0.3319	0.3157	−0.0731
eigvec.2	0.4423	−0.3627	−0.3273	−0.3676	−0.5034	−0.0835	−0.3922	−0.1276
eigvec.3	0.4104	−0.3392	0.1674	0.2419	−0.1025	−0.3908	0.4607	0.5046
eigvec.4	0.3668	−0.2875	0.4381	0.5182	0.1398	0.2971	−0.2994	−0.3535
eigvec.5	0.2221	0.2554	−0.3241	0.2316	0.4760	−0.4963	−0.4836	0.1414
eigvec.6	0.3451	0.4738	−0.4216	0.3809	−0.2832	0.4545	0.1682	0.1361
eigvec.7	0.3644	0.4266	0.1937	−0.1724	−0.0415	−0.3705	0.3440	−0.6006
eigvec.8	0.3189	0.3565	0.5041	−0.4441	0.0664	0.2274	−0.2533	0.4467

LOADING	C 1	C 2	C 3	C 4	C 5	C 6	C 7	C 8
mss72_1	0.9314	−0.2767	−0.1601	−0.0842	0.1430	0.0389	0.0350	−0.0070
mss72_2	0.9487	−0.2703	−0.1207	−0.0668	−0.0819	−0.0071	−0.0315	−0.0088
mss72_3	0.9556	−0.2744	0.0670	0.0477	−0.0181	−0.0360	0.0401	0.0378
mss72_4	0.9389	−0.2557	0.1929	0.1124	0.0271	0.0301	−0.0287	−0.0291
mss92_1	0.8868	0.3542	−0.2225	0.0784	0.1441	−0.0783	−0.0722	0.0182
mss92_2	0.8813	0.4204	−0.1852	0.0824	−0.0548	0.0459	0.0161	0.0112
mss92_3	0.9202	0.3742	0.0841	−0.0369	−0.0080	−0.0370	0.0325	−0.0488
mss92_4	0.8971	0.3484	0.2438	−0.1059	0.0142	0.0253	−0.0266	0.0404

After the processing is completed, the *Module Results* window will display a text file of the results of the analysis (Table 9.6.2.a). As mentioned above, one of the difficulties of using PCA is that the output images can be difficult to interpret. Nevertheless, by carefully examining the output as shown in the *Module Results*, some interpretation can usually be made. Therefore, these results should be saved, for example by clicking on the *Save to File* button, because they help to interpret the PCA images.

The *Module Results* includes information on:

- The variance/covariance matrix (i.e. the variability of the bands, and how they relate to one another),

- The correlation matrix (the relationship between the bands)

- The principal component eigenvalues (amount of variance explained, or accounted for by each new component), expressed in two forms:

  o As raw units of covariance, and

  o As a proportion of the total variance ("% var.") in the output.

- The eigenvectors, which give the equation to convert the input data to get the output data.

- The Loadings, which provide information on the correlation between the original bands and the new components.

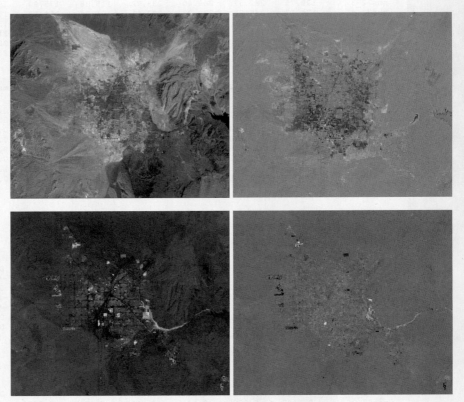

Figure 9.6.2.b   Upper left: ***pcacmp1***. Upper right: ***pcacmp2***. Lower left: ***pcacmp3***. Lower right: ***pcacmp4***.

In order to interpret the text output, it will be useful to have the PCA images displayed. Therefore, use the IDRISI Display launcher to display the 8 output files, each time using a GreyScale Palette file (Figure 9.6.2.b shows the first four PCA images). For the discussion below, you should refer to the relevant images, Table 9.6.2.a, as well as the two original false color composites of 1972 (**mss72_fcc**) and 1992 (**mss92_fcc**), to see if you can verify the interpretations suggested.

In interpreting the values for the Las Vegas change data (Table 9.6.2.a), we see that the first four components (C1, C2, C3 and C4) comprise a total of over 99% of the original variance (i.e. 85.67% + 10.34% + 2.53% +0.62%= 99.16%) This suggests that the majority of the information has been captured in these first four components. Note how the images appear to get progressively more noisy with higher numbers. For example, notice how **pcacmp1** shows the pattern of land use clearly, but **pcacmp8** is dominated by the image striping.

The eigenvectors help us understand what the output bands mean. For example, we find that the eigenvectors for C1 are all positive, and similar (0.22 to 0.44). This suggests that C1 (the image **pcacmp1**) represents an average of all the bands, of both dates. Indeed, the loadings show that C1 is highly correlated with all the input bands (the values are approximately 0.9 or greater).

C2, on the other hand, has negative eigenvectors for the bands for date 1, and positive values for the bands for date 2. This implies that C2 (the image **pcacmp2**), is a difference image of 1992-1972, and is thus somewhat similar to the results of the image differencing exercise we completed earlier.

C3 is notable for having negative values for the visible bands (original image bands 1 and 2) for the 1972 and 1992 data, but positive values for the near infrared bands (original image bands 3 and 4). Since the difference between the visible and near infrared bands is a measure of vegetation presence, this suggests C3 (**pcacmp3**) is an average of the vegetation for the two dates.

C4 is similar to C3, in that it has negative values for the visible bands for 1972, and positive values for the near infrared bands for the same year. However, C4 has the opposite pattern for the 1992 bands, thus suggesting this component is a vegetation difference image, of 1972-1992. Note that this means that new vegetation in 1992 will show as dark, not bright, in the image **pcacmp4**.

AS a final step, the PCA components can be visualized as a false color composite, using components 1, 2, and 4. (Since component 3 is an average vegetation image, it is not so useful, and therefore is not used.) Based on the discussion above, however, before using component 4, we should first reverse this image. This will make new vegetation bright in the image, instead of dark, and thus make interpretation of the false color composite easier. This reversal will make no other difference to the outcome.

Create inverse image with SCALAR
Menu location: **GIS Analysis – Mathematical operators - SCALAR**
1. Start the SCALAR program from the main IDRISI menu.
2. In the *SCALAR* window, double click in the Input image text box. In the resulting pick list, double click on **PCAcmp4**.
3. In the *Output image* text box, enter **pcacmp4a**.
4. In the *Scalar value* text box, enter **-1**.
5. Select the radio button for *Multiply*.

6. Figure 9.6.2.c shows the *SCALAR* window with the processing parameters selected.

7. Click on *OK*.

8. The image is automatically displayed.

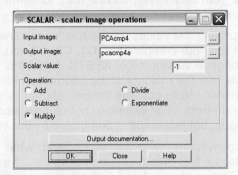

Figure 9.6.2.c   The SCALAR window.

You are now ready to create the false color composite, as described below.

Create a color composite image

Menu Location: **Display - COMPOSITE**

1. Start the COMPOSITE program using the main menu or tool bar.

2. In the *COMPOSITE* dialog box, double click in the *Blue image band* text box, and then double click on the file **pcacmp1**in the subsequent *Pick list*.

3. Double click in the *Green image band* text box, and then double click on **pcacmp2**.

4. Double click in the *Red image band* text box, and then double click on **pcacmp4a**.

5. Enter the *Output image* filename in the text box provided: **pca124fcc**.

6. Click *OK* to create and display the false color composite.

Figure 9.6.2.d   Multitemporal PCA false color composite.

In the resulting image (Figure 9.6.2.d), see if you can relate the colors to your knowledge of the original bands. For example, red should be new vegetation in 1992, and green to cyan should represent areas where the albedo (average brightness) increased. Note, however, that the image presents an interesting overview of the pattern of change in Las Vegas – with most growth occurring in a ring to the east, south and west, and comparatively little growth to the north.

9.6.3 Change Vector Analysis

Change vector analysis, like image differencing, requires radiometrically normalized data. It is therefore essential to complete sections 9.4 and 9.5 prior to working through this exercise. We will use the regression-normalized data (i.e. from Section 9.5) for this exercise. However, if you wanted to use the radiance-based data, you would use the images **mss72_2_rad**, **mss72_4_rad**, **mss92_2_rad** and **mss92_4_rad.**

Although some users of change vector analysis use spectrally transformed data as input into change vector analysis, we will use the radiometrically normalized MSS bands. Using the MSS bands will make it easier to compare the results to other methods.

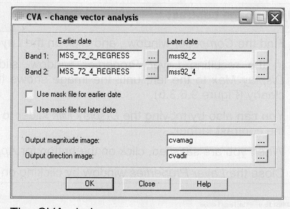

Figure 9.6.3.a   The *CVA* window.

Change vector analysis

Menu location: **GIS Analysis – Change/Time Series – CVA**

1. Start the CVA program from the main IDRISI menu.

2. In the *CVA* window, double click in the text box for the *Earlier date* and *Band 1*. In the resulting pick list, double click on **MSS_72_2_REGRESS**.

3. Double click in the text box for the *Earlier date* and *Band 2*. In the resulting pick list, double click on **MSS_72_4_REGRESS**.

4. Now chose the files for the *Later date*. Start by double clicking in the *Band 1* text box. In the resulting pick list, double click on the raw 1992 band 2 data **mss92_2**.

5. Double click in the *Later date* and *Band 2* text box. In the resulting pick list double click on **mss92_4**.

6. In the Output magnitude image text box, enter **cvamag**.

7. In the Output direction image text box, enter **cvadir**.

8. Figure 9.6.3.a shows the CVA window with the processing parameters specified.

9. Click on *OK*.

Unlike other IDRISI programs, CVA does not open the output images. Start by opening the change magnitude image.

Display image

Menu: **Display – DISPLAY LAUNCHER**

1. Start the DISPLAY LAUNCHER from the main menu or icon bar.

2. In the *DISPLAY LAUNCHER* window, double click in the text box for the file name, and then double click on the file ***cvamag***.

3. Select the radio button for the *GreyScale* palette file.

4. Click on *OK* to display the image.

After the image has opened, adjust the contrast of the image.

Adjust image contrast

1. Find the *Composer* window., and click on the *Layer properties* button.

2. In the resulting *Layer Properties* window, slide the *Contrast Setting* for *Display Max* to the left, until the image shows the patterns of change more clearly (Figure 9.6.3.b).

3. You can also try moving the *Display Min* slider to the right, in order to improve the contrast farther.

4. When you are satisfied, click on the button for *Apply*

5. Close the *Layer Properties* window by clicking on *OK*.

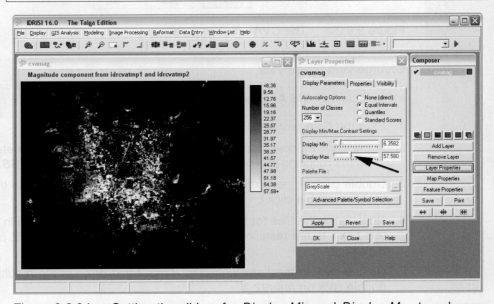

Figure 9.6.3.b   Setting the sliders for *Display Min* and *Display Max* to enhance the magnitude of the spectral change.

Figure 9.6.3.b displays the areas of change very clearly. The center of the city has not changed appreciably. On the other hand, change is concentrated across the south of the city, and to a slightly lesser extent to the east and west. Only isolated areas of change are indicated in the desert, associated with local changes such as landslides, changes in the Las Vegas Wash (the river running through Las Vegas), water levels in Lake Mead, and mining.

Now display the change direction image using the *IDRISI Default Quantitative* palette.

Display image

Menu: **Display – DISPLAY LAUNCHER**

1. Start the DISPLAY LAUNCHER from the main menu or icon bar.
2. In the *DISPLAY LAUNCHER* window, double click in the text box for the file name, and then double click on the file **cvadir**.
3. Click on *OK* to display the image (Figure 9.6.3.c).

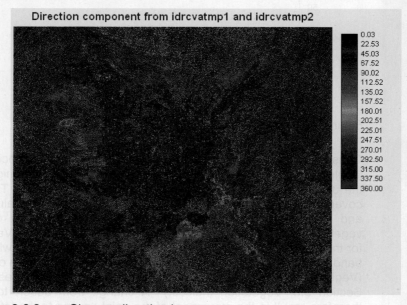

Figure 9.6.3.c   Change direction image.

Interpreting the change direction image is more difficult than the magnitude image. However, with a little background information, the meaning of this image becomes much clearer.

Use the cursor inquiry tool from the main menu to query the pixel values in this image. The DN values are in units of degrees, and can be interpreted with reference to the legend and also Figure 9.6.3.d, as will be explained in more detail below. (Note that the IDRISI help for this program appears to be incorrect in specifying that the angles are those from date 1, though the figure in the help file correctly shows the angles as being calculated from date 2.)

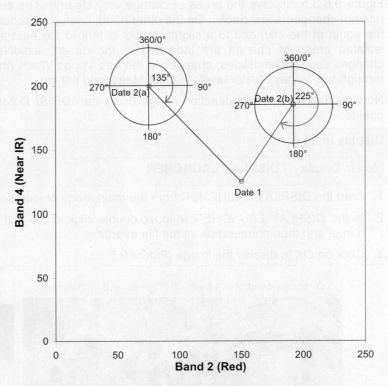

Figure 9.6.3.d   Interpreting the CVA direction angles.

Consider a pixel, which has a combination of DN values associated with the point labeled *Date 1* in Figure 9.6.3.d. Hypothetically, this point might be a pixel from the undisturbed desert, with only sparse vegetation cover. This type of ground cover is likely to have moderate to high reflectance in DN values in both the red and near infrared bands. If this pixel is subsequently converted to lush vegetation, for example one of the many golf courses in Las Vegas, the DN value for the red band will decrease due to chlorophyll absorption, whereas the infrared band will increase due to scattering off the spongy mesophyll of the grass leaves. (Vegetation is characteristically bright in the near infra-red, as was discussed in Section 5.3, Vegetation Indices.) A change from desert to green grass will therefore result in the movement of the point up and to the left in the graph (see the point labeled Date 2(a) in Figure 9.6.3.d). This direction of movement, *measured from the second point's location*, is an angle of 135°. With reference to the legend of the change direction image for Las Vegas (Figure 9.6.3.c), we see that change of approximately 135° is represented in shades of green.

It is important to realize that CVA separates change magnitude from direction. Changes associated with the greening of previously built suburbs will also have the same change direction as new vegetation due to the construction of a new golf course in what was previously desert. However, the greening of a suburb will, at least over the short term, have a much smaller magnitude of change compared to the new golf course. Thus, not all the green in change direction image represents change between land cover classes, but instead may represent subtle changes within a relatively consistent land cover class.

An alternative change scenario to the one just described is presented by the pixel labeled *Date 2(b)* in Figure 9.6.3.d. This pixel could represent a desert area that is disturbed, for example, due to construction activities or even recreational off-road vehicle use. In this circumstance, the loss of the sparse vegetation and erosion of surface material will result in both red and near-infrared DN values increasing. This direction of change is associated with a 225° change, and is shown in the change direction image legend as an orange color. It is clear from Figure 9.6.3.c that this degradation of land cover is extensive on the periphery of Las Vegas.

9.7 Post Classification Change Detection

Post-classification change detection is the GIS overlay operation of two previously classified images. Therefore, the major part of applying post-classification change detection is classification.

Chapter 7 describes classification in detail, and the section on supervised classification (7.3) should be completed prior to doing this section. Therefore, the instructions for classification will be rather brief in this section. If it is some time since you completed the classification section, or you find the instructions below to brief, you may wish to refresh your memory by rereading through that material.

Note: The classification of land use in Las Vegas is a challenge, especially because the geology of the area is so varied, and some of the geological classes are spectrally similar to the urban land use classes, especially that of commercial activities. Readers wishing to skip over the classifications, and directly apply the GIS overlay operation may go directly to Section 9.7.9, and use the classifications provided with this chapter's data.

9.7.1 Preparatory

You should have already copied the data from the CD, as described in Section 9.2. In addition, as described in Section 9.3, you should have established the **Chap9** project file within the *IDRISI EXPLORER*.

For this section, we will use the original raw data, and not the normalized images created in the previous sections.

Display the two false color composites created in Section 9.3, as described below.

Initial display of images
Menu: **Display – DISPLAY LAUNCHER**
1. Start the DISPLAY LAUNCHER from the main menu or icon bar. 2. In the *DISPLAY LAUNCHER* window, double click in the text box for the file name, and then double click on the file **ms72_fcc**. 3. Click on *OK* to display the image. 4. Start the DISPLAY LAUNCHER again. 5. In the *DISPLAY LAUNCHER* window, double click in the text box for the file name, and then double click on the file **ms92_fcc**. 6. Click on *OK* to display the image.

9.7.2 Develop a List of Spectral Classes

The first step is to develop the list of spectral classes. Examine the 1972 false color composite (**mss72_fcc**). Five informational classes can be identified, as listed in Table 9.7.2.a. The Desert class is very variable, and consists of at least

8 or 10 different spectral classes. We will therefore need to collect training signatures for each of the various spectral desert classes. We will leave this to last in the digitizing order.

Table 9.7.2.a   Supervised classification classes for Las Vegas.

Class Number	Name	Color in false color composite	Texture
1	Water	Black	Smooth
2	Vegetation	Bright red	Moderate
3	Commercial / Industrial / Transportation	Blue to gray; black	Rough
4	Residential	Dark red to magenta	Rough
5	Desert	Highly variable: brown, black, gray, white	Moderate

9.7.3 Digitize Training Polygons for the 1972 Image

Our overall aim is to classify each of the two images using maximum likelihood classification in separate classifications. This means that we will need to collect a set of class signatures for each image independently.

Figure 9.7.3.a   False color composite of 1972 MSS data with training polygons overlaid. Note the more than 10 training polygons (each comprising a separate spectral class in the classification, and thus having a unique associated number) for the Desert class.

After you have developed the list of spectral classes, digitize the polygons over the 1972 image. Figure 9.7.3.a shows a recommended number and extent of the polygons required. The instructions below describe the procedures for digitizing the polygons for the training areas. Those who feel the instructions are too brief might review Section 7.4.3.

Digitizing training polygons
Menu location: Main tool bar icons only (Note that the icons are grayed out if an image is not yet displayed.)

1. The false color image ***ms72_fcc*** should already be displayed in a Viewer.
2. Click on the *Full extent normal* icon from the main tool bar, to return the image to the default zoom if you have zoomed in on part of the image.
3. *Full extent maximized* icon from the main tool bar, to enlarge the image display.
4. Click on the *Zoom window* icon. Draw a zoom box around the lake on the right side of the image (this is a corner of Lake Mead, created by the Hoover Dam, on the Colorado River.)
5. Click on the *Digitize* icon. A dialog box labeled *DIGITIZE* will open.
6. Enter the file name **Water** in the text box labeled *Name of layer to be created*. Leave all other values at their defaults.
7. Click on *OK* to close the *DIGITIZE* window.
8. Move the cursor over the image, and the cursor will become a *Digitize* icon, instead of the normal arrow.
9. Digitize the first vertex of the water polygon by pressing the *left* mouse button. Continue clicking in the image to specify the outer boundaries of the polygon you wish to digitize.   <u>Note</u>: Try to avoid the small islands in the lake.
10. Close the polygon by pressing the *right* mouse button. Note that the program automatically closes the polygon by duplicating the first point; so you do not need to attempt to close the polygon by digitizing the first point again.
11. Save the polygon file by clicking on the *Save digitized data icon*.
12. A *Save prompt* dialog box will open. Click on *Yes*.
13. Click on the *Full extent normal* icon from the main tool bar, to return the image to the default zoom.
14. Click on the *Full extent maximized* icon from the main tool bar.
15. Click on the *Zoom window* icon. Draw a zoom box around the bright red vegetation in the irrigated fields to the right (east) of the city.
16. Now start digitizing the polygon for vegetation by clicking on the *Digitize* icon.
17. The *DIGITIZE* dialog box will open again.
18. Select the radio button for *Create a new layer for the features to be digitized*.
19. Click *OK*.
20. Another dialog box labeled *DIGITIZE* will open.
21. Enter the file name **Vegetation** in the text box labeled *Name of layer to be created*. Leave all other values at their defaults.
22. Click on *OK* to close the *DIGITIZE* window.

23. Digitize the vegetation polygon with left mouse clicks. Close the polygon with a right mouse click. <u>Note</u>: Digitize the bright red region only.

24. Save the polygon file by clicking on the *Save digitized data icon*.

25. A *Save prompt* dialog box will open. Click on *Yes*.

26. Repeat the sequence of restoring, maximizing and zooming, (steps 13-15 above), only this time zoom in on the dark downtown region, representing the commercial core of the city. Name the file **commercial**.

27. Add to the commercial class by digitizing a second polygon, this time over the airport runway, south of the city. (The runway is a good example of the transportation part of this class.) Follow steps 13-15 to zoom in on in the runway.

28. Click on the Digitize icon.

29. This time, when the *DIGITIZE* dialog box opens, accept the default radio button for *Add features to the currently active vector layer.*

30. Click *OK*.

31. Another *DIGITIZE* dialog box will open.

32. The ID for the polygon will be incremented automatically. Be sure to set it back to 1, as both commercial polygons should be digitized as part of the same class.

33. Digitize the polygon.

34. Save the polygon file by clicking on the *Save digitized data icon*.

35. A *Save prompt* dialog box will open. Click on *Yes*.

36. Now digitize the residential class. Follow steps 13-15 to zoom in on a dark red area of the more mature suburbs.

37. Click on the *Digitize* icon.

38. The *DIGITIZE* dialog box will open again.

39. Select the radio button for *Create a new layer for the features to be digitized*.

40. Click *OK*.

41. In the text box labeled *Name of layer to be created*, enter **Residential**.

42. Click on *OK*.

43. Digitize the residential polygon.

44. Save the polygon file by clicking on the *Save digitized data icon*.

45. A *Save prompt* dialog box will open. Click on *Yes*.

So far we have created the polygons for all the training areas, except the desert. Because the desert is so complex, we will now digitize multiple spectral classes for this area. These will be classified separately, and then only after the classification will they be grouped to a single desert class. Figure 9.7.3.a gives the approximate distribution of training areas. Be sure to include the very bright playas and very dark rocks, too.

Digitizing training polygons (cont.)

46. Click on the *Full extent normal* icon from the main tool bar, to return the image to the default zoom.

47. Click on the *Full extent maximized* icon from the main tool bar, to enlarge the image display.

48. Click on the *Zoom window* icon. Draw a zoom box around the first desert area.

49. Click on the *Digitize* icon.

50. A dialog box labeled *DIGITIZE* will open.

51. Select the radio button for *Create a new layer for the features to be digitized*.

52. Click *OK*.

53. Another dialog box labeled *DIGITIZE* will open.

54. Enter the file name **Desert1** in the text box labeled *Name of layer to be created*. Leave all other values at their defaults.

55. Click on *OK* to close the *DIGITIZE* window.

56. Digitize the first desert polygon.

57. Save the polygon file by clicking on the *Save digitized data icon*.

58. A *Save prompt* dialog box will open. Click on *Yes*.

59. Digitize additional desert polygons, by following steps 48 to 57 as many times as necessary. Each time give the file a new name, e.g. **Desert2, Desert3,** etc.

60. Once you have completed all 5 desert classes, close the displayed image. IDRISI will prompt you to save any unsaved polygons.

9.7.4 Create Signatures with MAKESIG

We are now ready to run the MAKESIG program to generate the signature files. (See also Section 7.4.4).

Create signature files using MAKESIG

Menu location: **Image Processing - Signature development – MAKESIG**

1. Start the MAKESIG program from the main menu.

2. In the *MAKESIG* dialog box, click on the Pick list button (…) to the right of the text box of *Vector file defining training sites.*

3. In the Pick list window, double click on the **Water** file.

4. In the *MAKESIG* dialog box, click on the button *Enter signature filenames*.

5. The *Enter signature filenames* dialog box will open. In the blank cell to the right of 1, type **Water**.

6. Uncheck the box labeled *Create signature group file*.

7. Click on *OK* to close the *Enter signature filenames* dialog box.

8. In the *MAKESIG* dialog box, click on the button for *Insert layer group*.

9. From the *Pick list,* double click on ***ms_72***.

10. The *MAKESIG* dialog box should now show the four bands of the MSS data.

11. Click *OK* to create the signature file.

12. Now create the next signature file, for vegetation. Start by double clicking in the *MAKESIG* dialog box text box for *Vector file defining training sites* .

13. In the resulting pick list, double click on **Vegetation**.

14. In the *MAKESIG* dialog box, click on the button *Enter signature filenames*.

15. The *Enter signature filenames* dialog box will open. In the blank cell to the right of 1, type **Vegetation**.

16. Click on *OK* to close the *Enter signature filenames* dialog box.

17. In the MAKESIG dialog box, click *OK* to create the signature file.

18. Repeat steps 12-17 for each of the remaining vector files: *commercial, residential, desert1, desert2, desert3, desert4, and desert5.* Remember each time to click on the Enter signature filenames button, and change the right cell to the appropriate file name.

Now create a signature group file with the combined list of signatures. In Section 7.4.5, we used the IDRISI EXPLORER. In this section we will use the IDRISI COLLECTION EDITOR.

Create signature group file with the COLLECTION EDITOR

Menu location: **File – COLLECTION EDITOR**

1. Open the COLLECTION EDITOR from the main menu.

2. In the *COLLECTION EDITOR* window, use the menu for *File – New*.

3. In the resulting *New file…* window, click on the pull-down menu next to the text box for *Files of type*. Select *Signature group files (*.sgf)*.

4. In the *File name* text box, type **mss72**.

5. Click on *Open*.

6. The *COLLECTION EDITOR* window will now show the list of potential signatures in the left column. The right column, currently blank, is where signatures will be entered (Figure 9.7.4.a).

7. In the left column click on **Water**.

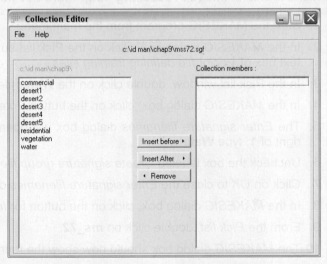

Figure 9.7.4.a   The *COLLECTION EDITOR* window after specifying the new signature group file name.

8. Click on the button *Insert after >*

9. The Water signature should now be listed in the right column.

10. Repeat steps 7 and 8, to insert, in the following order, ***vegetation, commercial, residential, desert1, desert2, desert3, desert4,*** and ***desert5*** (Figure 9.7.4.b).

11. In the *COLLECTION EDITOR* window, use the menu to select *File – Save*.

12. Close the *COLLECTION EDITOR* window. (It is important to close the window, even though we will use the program again later.)

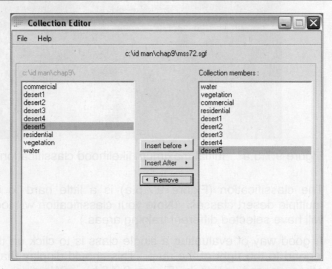

Figure 9.7.4.b   The COLLECTION EDITOR window with signatures specified in order.

9.7.5 Classify the 1972 Image

Classify the 1972 MSS raster group file using maximum likelihood program, as described below.

Classify an image with MAXLIKE
Menu location: **Image processing - Hard classifiers – MAXLIKE**

1. Start the MAXLIKE program from the menu.

2. In the *MAXLIKE* dialog box, click on the *Insert signature group* button.

3. In the *Pick List*, double click on the ***MSS72*** signature group file.

4. In the MAXLIKE dialog box, specify the *Output file name* as **Max72a**.

5. Click on *OK* to run the classification.

6. The classification is displayed automatically (Figure 9.7.5.a).

7. Close the *MAXLIKE* dialog box, even though we will use this program again later.

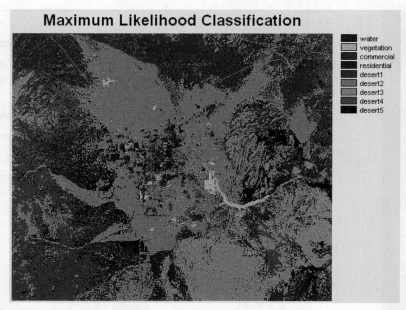

Figure 9.7.5.a   Initial maximum likelihood classification

The classification (Figure 9.7.5.a) is a little hard to interpret because of the multiple desert classes. (Note your classification will look different, because you will have selected different training areas.)

A good way of evaluating a single class is to click on the class color chip in the legend to the right of the map. This should display that class in red, and all the other classes in black (Figure 9.7.5.b). (Warning: we have noticed some anomalous behavior where this option does not always work correctly.)

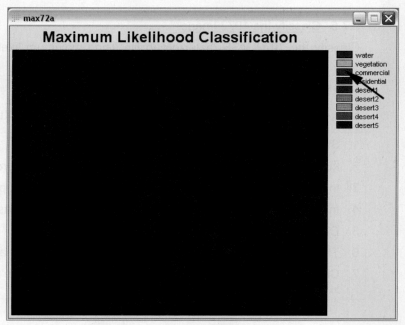

Figure 9.7.5.b   Map display when cursor (not shown) is clicked on the *Commercial* class color chip (see arrow).

Figure 9.7.5.b indicates that large areas of the desert are being confused with the commercial class. Therefore, we need to collect additional desert training areas, focused on the areas where *the confusion is most common*.

9.7.6   Add Additional Desert Spectra to the Classification

To collect the addition spectra we need to do the following: display the false composite, digitize additional desert training areas (in the regions of common errors), run MAKESIG on these areas, add these additional spectra to the signature group file, and run the classification again. These steps are described briefly below.

9.7.6.1 Display the False Color Image

Initial display of images
Menu: **Display – DISPLAY LAUNCHER**

1. Start the DISPLAY LAUNCHER from the main menu or icon bar.
2. In the *DISPLAY LAUNCHER* window, double click in the text box for the file name, and then double click on the file *ms72_fcc*.
3. Click on *OK* to display the image.

9.7.6.2 Digitize Additional Desert Training Areas

Carefully examine the areas where desert is incorrectly classified as commercial. Identify about 5 such areas.

Digitize additional training areas

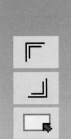

1. The false color image ***ms72_fcc*** should already be displayed in a Viewer.
2. Click on the *Full extent normal* icon from the main tool bar, to return the image display to the default zoom.
3. Click on the *Full extent maximized* icon from the main tool bar, to enlarge the image display.
4. Click on the *Zoom window* icon. Draw a zoom box around the first new desert location.
5. Click on the *Digitize* icon. A dialog box labeled *DIGITIZE* will open.
6. Enter the file name **Desert6** in the text box labeled *Name of layer to be created* (adjust the name of this class if necessary, so that it is the next number in your list of desert classes.)
7. Click on *OK* to close the *DIGITIZE* window.
8. Digitize the desert polygon with left mouse clicks. End the polygon with a right mouse click.
9. Save the polygon file by clicking on the *Save digitized data icon*.
10. A *Save prompt* dialog box will open. Click on *Yes*.
11. Click on the *Full extent normal* icon from the main tool bar, to return the image display to the default zoom.
12. Click on the *Full extent maximized* icon to return the display of the image to the entire image.
13. Click on the *Zoom window* icon.

14. Draw a zoom box around the next desert polygon.

15. Click on the *Digitize* icon.

16. The *DIGITIZE* dialog box will open again.

17. Select the radio button for *Create a new layer for the features to be digitized*.

18. Click *OK*.

19. Another dialog box labeled *DIGITIZE* will open.

20. Enter the file name **Desert7** in the text box labeled *Name of layer to be created*.

21. Click on *OK* to close the *DIGITIZE* window.

22. Digitize the next polygon.

23. Save the polygon file by clicking on the *Save digitized data icon*.

24. A *Save prompt* dialog box will open. Click on *Yes*.

25. Repeat steps 11-24 to create 5 more desert polygons.

26. When you are done digitizing, close the DISPLAY. You will be prompted to save any unsaved polygons.

9.7.6.3 Run MAKESIG on the New Signatures

Create additional signature files using MAKESIG

Menu location: **Image Processing - Signature development – MAKESIG**

1. Start the MAKESIG program from the main menu.

2. In the *MAKESIG* dialog box, click on the Pick list button (…) to the right of the text box of *Vector file defining training sites.*

3. In the Pick list window, double click on the **desert6** file.

4. In the *MAKESIG* dialog box, click on the button *Enter signature filenames*.

5. The *Enter signature filenames* dialog box will open. In the blank cell to the right of 1, type **desert6**.

6. Uncheck the box labeled *Create signature group file*.

7. Click on *OK* to close the *Enter signature filenames* dialog box.

8. In the *MAKESIG* dialog box, click on the button for *Insert layer group*.

9. From the *Pick list,* double click on **ms_72**.

10. Click *OK* to create the signature file.

11. Now create the next signature file, for *Desert7*. Start by double clicking in the *MAKESIG* dialog box text box for *Vector file defining training sites*.

12. In the resulting pick list, double click on **desert7**.

13. In the *MAKESIG* dialog box, click on the button *Enter signature filenames*.

14. The *Enter signature filenames* dialog box will open. In the blank cell to the right of 1, type **desert7**.

15. Click on *OK* to close the *Enter signature filenames* dialog box.

16. In the MAKESIG dialog box, click *OK* to create the signature file.

17. Repeat steps 12-17 for each of the remaining vector files: **desert8, desert9, desert10.** Remember each time to click on the Enter signature filenames button, and change the right cell to the appropriate file name.

9.7.6.4 Add Signatures to the Signature Group File

Add signatures to a signature group file with the COLLECTION EDITOR

Menu location: **File – COLLECTION EDITOR**

1. Open the COLLECTION EDITOR from the main menu.

2. In the *COLLECTION EDITOR* window, use the menu for *File – Open.*

3. In the resulting *Open file…* window, click on the pull-down menu next to the text box for *Files of type.* Select *Signature group files (*.sgf).*

4. Double click in the *File name* text box, and in the resulting pick list, select **mss72**.

5. Click on *Open.*

6. The *COLLECTION EDITOR* window will now show the list of potential signatures in the left column, and the list of current signatures in the right column.

7. Click on the last signature in the right column (e.g. **desert5**).

8. In the left column click on **desert6**.

9. Click on the button *Insert after >*.

10. The desert6 signature should now be listed at the bottom of the right column.

11. Repeat steps 8 and 9, to insert, in the following order the remaining desert signatures: **desert7, desert8, desert9**, and **desert10**.

12. Figure 9.7.6.4.a shows the *COLLECTION EDITOR* window with the additional signature files specified.

13. In the *COLLECTION EDITOR* window, use the menu to select *File – Save.*

14. Close the *COLLECTION EDITOR* window.

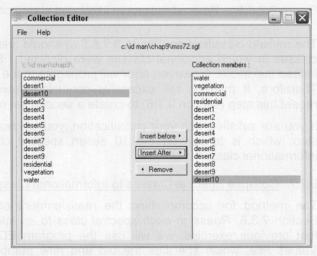

Figure 9.7.6.4.a The *COLLECTION EDITOR* window with additional desert signatures.

9.7.6.5 Reclassify the Image with Maximum Likelihood

Classify an image with MAXLIKE
Menu location: **Image processing - Hard classifiers – MAXLIKE**
1. Start the MAXLIKE program from the menu.

1. Start the MAXLIKE program from the menu.

2. In the *MAXLIKE* dialog box, click on the *Insert signature group* button.

3. In the *Pick List*, double click on the **MSS72** signature group file.

4. In the MAXLIKE dialog box, specify the *Output image* as **Max72b**.

5. Click on *OK* to run the classification.

6. The classification is displayed automatically (Figure 9.7.6.5.a).

7. Close the *MAXLIKE* dialog box.

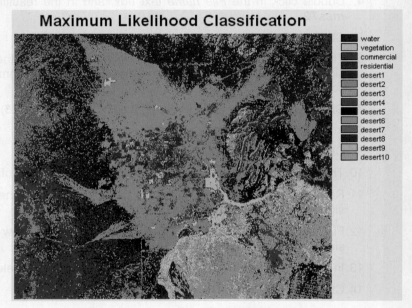

Figure 9.7.6.5.a Revised maximum likelihood classification.

The revised classification (Figure 9.7.6.5.a) should show an improvement for the classes in which additional classes were digitized. Some error is acceptable, indeed inevitable. However, error will propagate to the change detection product. Therefore, if there is still excessive confusion between classes, you should repeat this step (section 9.7.6) to create a second set of additional classes.

If you are satisfied with your classification, you are ready to proceed to the next step, which is to convert the 10 desert spectral classes to a single desert informational class.

9.7.7   Collapse Spectral Classes to Informational Classes

The method for accomplishing the reassignment of classes is described in Section 7.3.6, *Reassign each spectral class to an informational class.* As with that previous exercise, we will use the program EDIT to create an *Attribute Values File*, which specifies the old and new numbers for each class. The *Attribute Values File* is then one of the inputs for the program *ASSIGN*, which creates a new file with the final informational classes generated by combining the spectral classes.

In this case, the Water, Vegetation, Commercial and Residential classes will not change. Only the multiple Desert classes will be collapsed into one class. Therefore, spectral classes 1-5 will stay the same, and the desert classes (10, or the number you have chosen) will all be assigned to the new class 5.

Enter the recode values table with EDIT

Menu location: **Data Entry – EDIT**.

---

1. Open the program EDIT from the main menu or the main icon bar.

2. The *IDRISI TEXT EDITOR* window will open.

3. In the blank window enter the spectral class number, leave a space then enter the associated informational class number, with each spectral class on a new line. Thus each line has just two numbers: the old and new DN value for that class. Start with spectral class 1 and end with the last spectral class number. See Figure 9.7.7.a for an example of how the completed list might look.

4. Use the *IDRISI TEXT EDITOR* menu to save the file: **File – Save As.**

5. A *SAVE AS* dialog box will open. In the Save as type text field, click on the pull-down list, and select *Attribute Values File*.

6. Enter the file name **reclass72**.

7. Click *SAVE*.

8. A *Values File Information* dialog box will open. Take the default *Integer* option, and click on *OK*.

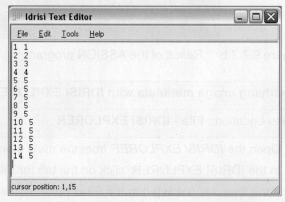

Figure 9.7.7.a   The *IDRISI TEXT EDITOR* window with the assignment values specified.

The next step is to use the *Attribute Values* file you have just created to generate a new image, with DN values recoded according to the scheme specified in the text file.

Create a new image with informational class numbers using ASSIGN

Menu location: **Data Entry – ASSIGN**

---

1. Use the IDRISI main menu to start the ASSIGN program.

2. In the *ASIGN* window, double click in the *Feature definition image* text box. In the resulting pick list, double click on the image you wish to reclass: **max72b**.

3. In the *Output image* text box type: **max72final**.

4. Double click in the text box next to *Attribute values file*. In the resulting pick list double click on **reclass72**.

5. Enter an Output title, such as: **1972 Classification**.

6. Click on *OK*.

The ASSIGN program will automatically display the resulting image (Figure 9.7.7.b). This new file will have just numbers for classes. We therefore need to add class names using the IDRISI EXPLORER.

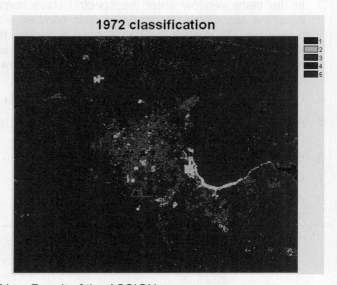

1972 classification

Figure 9.7.7.b   Result of the ASSIGN program.

Modifying image metadata with IDRISI EXPLORER

Menu Location: **File - IDRISI EXPLORER**

1. Open the *IDRISI EXPLORER* from the main menu or the main toolbar.

2. In the IDRISI EXPLORER, click on the tab for *Files*.

3. If the files are not listed in the *Files* pane, double click on the directory name to display the files.

4. If the *Metadata* pane is not shown below the *Files* pane, right click on **max72final.rst**. In the pop-up menu, select *Metadata*.

5. If the Metadata pane is already shown, click on **max72final.rst**.

6. In the *Metadata* pane, scroll down to *Categories*.

7. Double click in the blank cell next to *Categories*.

8. The *CATEGORIES* window will open.

9. Click four times on the *Add Line* icon on the right of the *CATEGORIES* window, so that five blank lines are shown.

10. In the first blank line, under *Code*, enter **1**.

11. In the next cell, under Category, enter **Water**.

12. In the subsequent blank line, enter **2** and **Vegetation**, and in the following lines **3** and **Commercial**, **4** and **Residential** and **5** and **Desert**.

13. Figure 9.7.7.c shows the CATEGORIES window with the classes specified.

14. Click on *OK*.

15. In the bottom left corner of the *Metadata* pane of the *IDRISI EXPLORER*, click on the *File save* icon.

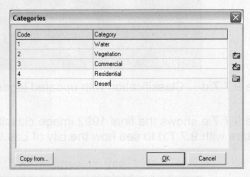

Figure 9.7.7.c   The *CATEGORIES* window.

Now redisplay the max72final image using the DISPLAY LAUNCHER, as described below.

Display image

Menu: **Display – DISPLAY LAUNCHER**

1. Start the DISPLAY LAUNCHER from the main menu or icon bar.

2. In the *DISPLAY LAUNCHER* window, double click in the text box for the file name, and then double click on the file ***max72final***.

3. Click on *OK* to display the image.

9.7.8 <u>Classification of the 1992 Image</u>

Once you have completed the classification for the 1972 data, you should repeat the classification exercise, except this time using the 1992 MSS data (***mss92_fcc***). You will need to collect a new set of signatures. It is essential, however, that you should end up with the same specific informational classes, which associated with the same DN values. For example, since 1 represents Water for the 1972 data, 1 should also represent Water for the 1992 data.

Note that IDRISI places each signature in its own file, as well as linking them through the group file. Therefore, for the 1992 signatures, it is very important that you specify a name that differs from those of the 1972 signatures. One way to ensure all the signature names are different is to add the numerals 92 in front of each name, thus Water becomes 92Water.

The final image, after running the ASSIGN program, should be called ***max92final***.

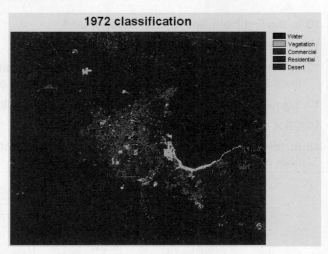

Figure 9.7.7.d   Classification with updated legend.

Figure 9.7.7.e shows the final 1992 image classification, with an updated legend. Compare with 9.7.7.d to see how the city of Las Vegas has grown.

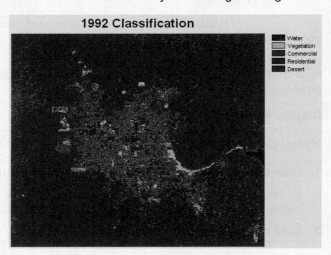

Figure 9.7.7.e   Classification of the 1992 MSS image of Las Vegas.

9.7.9   Overlay of Two Independent Classifications using CROSSTAB

After you have classified the 1992 MSS image, you are ready for the final step, which is the overlay of the two separate classifications, to obtain a single change map.

Note: If you have skipped the previous classification steps, Section 9.7.1 through 9.7.8, and wish to use the classifications provided with the data for this exercise, simply use the following files in the CROSSTAB program: *max72final_cd* and *max92final_cd* instead of *max72final* and *max92final*.

Overlay operation with CROSSTAB
Menu location: **GIS Analysis – Database Query – CROSSTAB**
1. Open the CROSSTAB program from the main IDRISI menu.

2. In the *CROSSTAB* window, double click in the text box next to *First image (column)*. In the resulting pick list, double click on ***max72final***.

3. Double click in the text box next to *Second image (row)*. In the resulting pick list, double click on ***max92final***.

4. In the region marked *Output type*, select the radio button for *Both cross-classification and tabulation*.

5. In the Output file name text box, enter **72-92-Crosstab**.

6. Figure 9.7.9.a shows the *CROSSTAB* window, with parameters specified.

7. Click on *OK*.

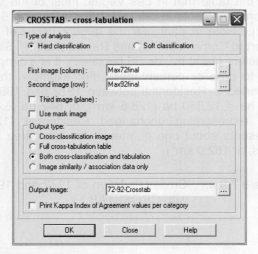

Figure 9.7.9.a   *CROSSTAB* window.

The output of the CROSSTAB program is a post-classification change map (Figure 9.7.9.b) and a table (Table 9.7.9.a). (Note, since your classifications will be different, unless you are using the classifications provided on the CD, the change map and table will be slightly different, however the overall patterns should be the same.)

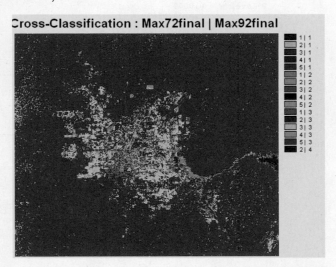

Figure 9.7.9.b   Crosstabulation of the 1972 and 1992 classifications.

The change map has a separate category for each possible transition. Thus the legend is indicated as a series of pairs of numbers, each pair with a separating vertical bar. Thus, the first legend category, **1|1** represents the combination (or change transition) of class 1 in 1972 and class 1 in 1992 (i.e. pixels that remained as Water in both years.) This class is dominated by the small area of Lake Mead in the right side of the image, displayed in red. Likewise, **1|2** represents the transition from Water in 1972 to Vegetation in 1992.

Since each classification had 5 classes, there are 5*5 = 25 possible transitions. However, only a small number of transitions dominate the map, as can be observed by just a few dominant colors in the image. This dominance of just a few classes is confirmed in the table of transitions (Table 9.7.9.a). It is notable from the table that in Las Vegas, most of the largest change classes (i.e. off-diagonal elements in the table) are in column 5 (i.e. pixels that were Desert in 1972). Note in particular the large number of pixels that have changed from Desert to Commercial (3) and Residential (4). Since each pixel represents 60 by 60 meters (3600 m^2, or .36 hectares), it is a simple matter to convert the change data to area or percentages. For example, the area of the Desert that was converted to Residential between 1972 and 1992 is 35,695 pixels, or 35,695 x 0.36 ha = 12,850 ha (128.5 km^2), or 642 ha (6.4 km^2) per year. Note that the area representing unchanged Residential (12,582 pixels, or 45.29 km^2), represents about one quarter of the total area in Residential by 1992 (50,552 pixels, or 182.0 km^2)

Table 9.7.9.a.   Cross-tabulation of 1972 and 1992 classifications as calculated with CROSSTAB.

```
Cross-tabulation of Max72final (columns) against Max92final (rows)

              1          2          3          4          5      Total
         -------------------------------------------------------------
    1 |      1578         44        318         28        297 |    2265
    2 |         3       3650         38       1167       4266 |    9124
    3 |        13        116       3327        430      14230 |   18116
    4 |         0       1865        410      12582      35695 |   50552
    5 |         4       1268       5087       1997     609557 |  617913
         -------------------------------------------------------------
Total |      1598       6943       9180      16204     664045 |  697970


        Chi Square =    804105.18750
               df =          16
          P-Level =      0.0000
        Cramer's V =        0.5367


        Proportional Crosstabulation

              1          2          3          4          5      Total
         -------------------------------------------------------------
    1 |    0.0023     0.0001     0.0005     0.0000     0.0004 |  0.0032
    2 |    0.0000     0.0052     0.0001     0.0017     0.0061 |  0.0131
    3 |    0.0000     0.0002     0.0048     0.0006     0.0204 |  0.0260
    4 |    0.0000     0.0027     0.0006     0.0180     0.0511 |  0.0724
    5 |    0.0000     0.0018     0.0073     0.0029     0.8733 |  0.8853
         -------------------------------------------------------------
Total |    0.0023     0.0099     0.0132     0.0232     0.9514 |  1.0000


        Overall Kappa         0.3804
```

Afterword

Congratulations on completing this manual! Now that you have completed the exercises we have provided, we encourage you to explore the rich functionality of IDRISI on your own. It is worth emphasizing that this manual has covered only a small proportion of the nearly 300 modules in IDRISI. The emphasis on only a core set of modules was necessary because it would take many manuals similar to this volume to cover the entire range of programs in IDRISI. With the background you have gained, and access to IDRISI's excellent help and tutorial documentation, you are now ready to venture on your own through the remaining modules. A wide range of powerful tools awaits your exploration.

Finally, if you have any suggestions for improvement of this manual, or have found errors, we would be most grateful if you would let us know through the website: http://idrisimanual.blogspot.com/. Thank you.

References

Chavez, P.S., 1996. Image-Based Atmospheric Corrections – Revisited and Improved. *Photogrammetric Engineering and Remote Sensing*: 62(9): 1025-1036.

Clark, R. N., G. A. Swayze, R. Wise, K. E. Livo, T. M. Hoefen, R. F. Kokaly, and S. J. Sutley, 2003. USGS Digital Spectral Library splib05a. USGS Open File Report 03-395.

Dozier, J., 1989. Spectral signature of alpine snow cover from the Landsat Thematic Mapper. *Remote Sensing of Environment* 28: 9-22.

Eastman, 2009. IDRISI Taiga: Guide to GIS and Image Processing. Clark Labs, Worcester, MA, 342p. (Provided as PDF document with the Taiga software in the \IDRISI Taiga\Documentation directory as *Taiga Manual.pdf*)

Gillespie, A. R., A. Kahle and R. E. Walker, 1986. Color enhancement of highly correlated images. I. Decorrelation and HSI contrast stretches. *Remote Sensing of Environment* 20: 209 - 235.

Jensen, J. R., 2005. Introductory Digital Image Processing: A Remote Sensing Perspective, Third Edition. Prentice Hall, Upper Saddle River, NJ, 526 p.

Lauer, D.T., S.A. Morain, and V.V. Salomonson, 1997. The Landsat program: Its origins, evolution, and impacts. *Photogrammetric Engineering & Remote Sensing* 63: 831-838.

Lillesand, T. W., R. W. Kiefer, and J. W. Chipman, 2004. Remote Sensing and Image Interpretation, Fifth Edition. John Wiley and Sons, New York, 763pp.

Maune, D. F. (Ed.), 2001. Digital elevation Model Technologies and Applications: The DEM Users Manual. The American Society of Photogrammetry and Remote Sensing, Bethesda, MD, 359p.

Mika, A. M., 1997. Three decades of Landsat instruments. *Photogrammetric Engineering and Remote Sensing* 63 : 839-852.

Nellis, M. D., T. A. Warner, R. Landenberger, J. McGraw, J. S. Kite and F. Wang, 2000. The Chestnut Ridge Anticline: The first major ridge of the Appalachian Mountains. *Geocarto International* 15 (4): 73-78.

Rowan, L. C., Wetlaufer, P. H., Goetz, A. F. H., Billingsley, F. C., and Stewart, J. H., 1974. Discrimination of rock types and detection of hydrothermally altered areas in south-central Nevada by use of computer-enhanced ERTS images: U.S.G.S. Prof. Paper 883, 35 p.

Sabins, F. F., 1997. Remote Sensing. W. H. Freeman and Company, New York, 494p.

Snyder, J. P., 1987. Map Projections - A Working Manual. United States Geological Survey Professional Paper 1395, US Government Printing Office, Washington, DC, 383 pp. Also available at: http://pubs.er.usgs.gov/usgspubs/pp/pp1395

USGS, 2006. *SLC-off products*: Background. http://landsat.usgs.gov/data_products/slc_off_data_products/slc_off_background.php (Last date accessed: September 2, 2006)

Warner, T., A., 2005. Hyperspherical Direction Cosine Change Vector Analysis. *International Journal of Remote Sensing* 26(6): 1201-1215.

Warner, T. A., and D. Campagna, 2004. IDRISI Kilimanjaro Review. *Photogrammetric Engineering and Remote Sensing* 70 (6): 669-673, 684.

Warner, T. A., M. D. Nellis and G. Foody (eds), 2009a. The Handbook of Remote Sensing. SAGE, London, UK.

Warner, T. A., A. Almutairi, and J. Y. Lee, 2009b. Remote sensing of land cover change. Chapter 33 in T. A. Warner, M. D. Nellis and G. Foody (eds), The Handbook of Remote Sensing. SAGE, London, UK.

Wikipedia, 2005. Muhammad al-Idrisi. http://en.wikipedia.org/wiki/Al-Idrisi (Last date accessed: January 5, 2006.

Appendix

Sources of Free Data

There is a surprisingly large number of websites with free or relatively inexpensive imagery available. Often these images are directly available on-line.

EROS, at the **United States Geological Survey** maintains a number of free data sets of the United States, including the entire Landsat MSS, TM, and ETM+ archives:

http://edc.usgs.gov/products/satellite.html

An excellent supplementary source of free remote sensing data with global coverage is the **Global Land Cover Facility** at the **University of Maryland**. Their holdings include Landsat (MSS, TM and ETM+), as well as MODIS, ASTER and SRTM.

http://glcf.umiacs.umd.edu

Another good source of imagery of the United States is **AmericaView**. Individual AmericaView states that are members of the AmericaView consortium maintain their own websites. Each state in the consortium has its own slightly different collection of types of imagery.

http://www.americaview.org/ (follow link to *Data holdings*).

Sources of Data for Sale

Although their data are not free, **Landsat.org** has a very good collection of data that they provide for a relatively small fee.

http://www.landsat.org/

Most major commercial and national space agencies have data for sale.
Below we present a partial list:

SPOT Image   www.spot.com
Digital Globe   www.digitalglobe.com
GeoEye   www.geoeye.com

Many organizations that collect data sell their data through local agents. For example, The Geocarto International Center, publishers of this manual, also act as resellers for a wide variety of satellite imaging companies
http://www.geocarto.com/

Index